REGULATION A+ AND OTHER ALTERNATIVES TO A TRADITIONAL IPO

Since 1996, Bloomberg Press has published books for financial professionals on investing, economics, and policy affecting investors. Titles are written by leading practitioners and authorities, and have been translated into more than 20 languages.

The Bloomberg Financial Series provides both core reference knowledge and actionable information for financial professionals. The books are written by experts familiar with the work flows, challenges, and demands of investment professionals who trade the markets, manage money, and analyze investments in their capacity of growing and protecting wealth, hedging risk, and generating revenue.

For a list of available titles, please visit our website at www.wiley.com/go/bloombergpress.

REGULATION A+ AND OTHER ALTERNATIVES TO A TRADITIONAL IPO

Financing Your Growth Business Following the JOBS Act

David N. Feldman

WILEY

For general information on our other products and services or for technical support, please contact our Customer Care Department within the United States at (800) 762-2974, outside the United States at (317) 572-3993, or fax (317) 572-4002.

Wiley publishes in a variety of print and electronic formats and by print-on-demand. Some material included with standard print versions of this book may not be included in e-books or in print-on-demand. If this book refers to media such as a CD or DVD that is not included in the version you purchased, you may download this material at http://booksupport.wiley.com. For more information about Wiley products, visit www.wiley.com.

Library of Congress Cataloging-in-Publication Data:

Names: Feldman, David N., 1960- author.
Title: Regulation A+ and other alternatives to a traditional IPO : financing
   your growth business following the Jobs Act / By David N. Feldman.
Description: Hoboken, New Jersey : John Wiley & Sons, 2018. | Includes index.
   | Identifiers: LCCN 2017049244 (print) | LCCN 2017051461 (ebook) | ISBN
   9781119416197 (pdf) | ISBN 9781119416128 (epub) | ISBN 9781119416159
   (cloth)
Subjects: LCSH: United States. Jumpstart Our Business Startups Act. | Small
   business—Finance—Law and legislation—United States. | New business
   enterprises—Finance—Law and legislation—United States. | Going public
   (Securities)—Law and legislation—United States.
Classification: LCC KF1659 (ebook) | LCC KF1659 .F743 2018 (print) | DDC
   346.73/0652—dc23
LC record available at https://lccn.loc.gov/2017049244

Cover Design: Wiley
Cover Image: © simon2579/iStockphoto

Printed in the United States of America.

10 9 8 7 6 5 4 3 2 1

MIX
Paper from
responsible sources
FSC® C132124

To my amazing family—actual, immediate, and extended. Your support means more than you can ever know and I love you all. Andrew, you are everything. Carol and Mom, I can never thank you enough. Victoria, love you and thanks for being my BFF.

Contents

Preface

It all started with my blurting out a suggestion in 2010 at the annual Securities and Exchange Commission (SEC) small business conference where recommendations are developed. Small companies were struggling to raise capital following the 2008 market crash. Reverse mergers with shell companies, utilized as a workable if clunky way for smaller companies to go public during the 2000s, were moving out of favor thanks to a number of high-profile alleged frauds. In addition, the SEC was imposing new restrictions on post–reverse merger companies' ability to uplist to national exchanges.

I had always said we would not need reverse mergers if initial public offerings (IPOs) were easier to do. SEC Regulation A, around since the 1930s but almost never used because of certain significant disadvantages, could be improved, said I. Increase the amount that can be raised from $5 million and otherwise make it better, and maybe call it Regulation A+.

The rest, as they say, is history, along with more history yet to be made. The formal recommendations from that conference included the term *Regulation A+* and it just stuck from then on as the unofficial moniker for what has developed since (though the SEC also uses the term). In early 2012, Congress picked up the recommendation and chose to include Reg A improvements in the Jumpstart Our Business Startups (JOBS) Act of 2012. The SEC then took three years to write the required rules to implement the exciting changes, and in June 2015, final rules took effect. A lawsuit by two states brought at that time slowed the adoption of new Reg A+ until the case was dismissed in July 2016.

Since then, there have been approximately 70 (through September 30, 2017) completed public offerings raising over $600 million dollars for smaller companies and creating many, many jobs. The groundswell of excitement over this very attractive new method to raise money in a cheaper, faster, more streamlined process is growing almost daily at the time of this writing. That excitement reached a crescendo in summer and fall of 2017 when the first seven Reg A+ deals to list on national exchanges were completed, and the queue of future deals appears healthy indeed.

Some Wall Street players have resisted utilizing Reg A+ thus far, either because they do not yet understand it, or because they fear explaining it to investors may be too complicated. As more deals are completed, that issue continues to abate. The hope is that this book will further speed the process of education for dealmakers, entrepreneurs, and others who advise them.

Some readers may be aware that I published the text *Reverse Mergers* in 2006 to explain the legitimate and transparent way to go public through a shell merger as well as other alternatives to a traditional IPO. This led to a second edition of that book in 2009. In 2013, I also published *The Entrepreneur's Growth Startup Handbook,* focusing on the seven things most likely to go wrong while building a business and how to treat and prevent them as you go. Yes, I was also practicing law full time through all these efforts!

My intent with this book is twofold. First, we seek to focus in depth on Regulation A+ as the new leading alternative to a traditional IPO. Second, we hope to provide an update on and introduction to reverse mergers, self-filings, and the other IPO alternatives, which were the focus of the prior books. There have been some important regulatory changes since the 2009 second edition with regard to a number of these alternatives, so even those who have perused the previous books should benefit from the updated report. Here is a brief overview of the book.

Chapters 2–7 focus on Reg A+. Before that, however, in Chapter 1, we ask the simple question, "Why go public?" There are advantages and disadvantages to doing so, and it is not the right choice for every company. It is important, however, to dispel some preconceived notions about which businesses can benefit the most from a publicly traded stock. The idea that only very mature, very profitable companies deserve an IPO is outdated. That said, a careful analysis of why a company wants to be public and whether it can benefit from it and bear the costs of doing so needs to be undertaken.

With Chapter 2 we commence the Reg A+ discussion. That chapter covers the history of Regulation A as well as a review of small-company IPOs going back to the 1990s. It is still not clear why these IPOs suddenly ceased around 2000 despite numerous studies seeking to explain it. Other alternatives such as reverse mergers took up some of the slack, but smaller companies struggled to raise capital in the otherwise roaring early to mid-2000s. This chapter sets the stage for the emergence of new Reg A+.

Chapter 3 introduces us to the JOBS Act and how it came about, starting with the discussion at the 2010 SEC small business conference. We outline Reg A as it existed just prior to the JOBS Act. We also include a brief review of the remainder of the JOBS Act, which is having tremendous positive impact on our capital markets, in particular the new "IPO on-ramp." Then we review the relatively brief JOBS Act Title IV language on Regulation A+.

The deftly crafted SEC rules developed under Title IV are covered in detail in Chapter 4. We start by discussing the initial proposed rules the SEC released in late 2013. It is important to understand what changed between the proposed and final rules as these were issues very important to the dealmaking community. Eligibility, the offering statement, ongoing reporting, and testing the waters are the focus of the rules.

After a discussion of the very active public comment period that followed release of the initial proposed rules, we then turn to the final rules, which became effective in June 2015. One major change in the final rules was to allow companies completing a Reg A+ offering to immediately become full SEC reporting companies and trade on national exchanges. That provision has paved the way for the seven companies that have already done so and many others being planned. Chapter 4 finishes up with a brief discussion of the unsuccessful lawsuit by Massachusetts and Montana seeking to invalidate the new rules.

Chapter 5 delves deeper into the mechanics and process of preparing a Reg A+ public offering, as well as complying with the new process of "light" reporting for those not choosing to become full SEC reporting companies. We review the scaled disclosure permitted and note the items the SEC has chosen to eliminate in Reg A+ offerings that are required in traditional Form S-1 IPOs.

Next we cover the light reporting process following the IPO and new forms developed in the Reg A+ rules. The bottom line: Less disclosure is required than in a full SEC reporting company. The key material disclosure items remain, however, to protect investors. Compliance costs for light reporting issuers certainly will be lower than in the past. The chapter concludes with a detailed review of testing the waters and issues to be addressed in a campaign to develop indications of interest prior to SEC approval of the IPO.

An overview of the early experience with Reg A+ is the topic of Chapter 6. Subtitled, "Wall Street Partners with Main Street," we cover the four main types of offerings we are currently seeing in these first few years after the SEC rules became effective. Following this is a discussion of the types of companies and industries that might find Reg A+ most attractive.

In Chapter 7 we conclude the Reg A+ content with a review of ideas for improving Reg A+, with the hope to take something very good and make it even better. Ideas such as allowing full SEC reporting companies the opportunity to use Reg A+ and preempting stock resales from state regulation are covered. A few items already have been addressed by the SEC and Congress is looking at others.

Chapters 8–13 cover a number of other alternatives to a traditional IPO, with an introduction to and update on reverse mergers in Chapters 8 through 10. This is a bit condensed from the seven chapters in the 2009 second edition of *Reverse Mergers*, mainly because the market for shell mergers has been substantially reduced since that time. That said, despite changes in regulations and other challenges, a number of these transactions continue to be completed for a variety of reasons that we cover.

Chapter 8 provides a basic introduction to reverse mergers, updated to the more complex regulatory world of today as against 2009. A number of shady players have been jailed or sued by the SEC. New regulations make it tougher for post–reverse merger companies to uplist their stock trading to a national exchange. In this chapter we compare and contrast reverse mergers with IPOs, including Reg A+ IPOs. Depending on the circumstances, a reverse merger could still have certain advantages over an IPO.

We then turn to the history of regulation of reverse mergers starting with the seminal Rule 419, and where things stand today. The importance of due diligence in these transactions next is reviewed to conclude this chapter.

In Chapter 9, we discuss how the reverse merger market sadly unraveled starting in around 2010 for a variety of reasons. The first is the bursting of the bubble of Chinese companies completing U.S. reverse mergers, as a result of a number of alleged frauds. We then review the controversial "seasoning rules" that the SEC imposed following these allegations, which put a near-fatal stab in the market for these transactions. Following their adoption, certain types of transactions were able to continue while others were immediately unworkable.

The chapter then turns to a review of a series of strong civil and criminal actions against a number of players in the reverse merger space starting in 2014. While it is tough to watch well-known attorneys and others arrested, these actions help those of us seeking to complete legitimate transactions to more clearly advise clients of the risks of being involved with questionable shells or players.

Chapter 10 focuses on the future of reverse mergers. As already noted, there remain certain advantages to certain companies in certain situations. For example, mergers with legitimate public operating businesses that are not "shell companies" can be followed by an immediate uplisting since the seasoning rules do not apply. We also cover the future supply and cost of shells, which may be challenging.

In Chapter 11 we introduce the exciting world of special-purpose acquisition companies (SPACs). These are shell companies that complete an IPO raising tens or even hundreds of millions of dollars to be used in an eventual acquisition of a private company. SPACs are active in some periods and dormant in others, but currently there is a strong and steady flow of new SPACs entering the market, led in part by attractive changes in the typical deal structure.

Chapter 12 covers another interesting option for taking a company public—a self-filing. Also known as a direct listing, it allows a company to get its stock trading at a time when it does not need to raise money. It can also be combined with other fundraising, such as a private offering of securities. Self-filings received some recent attention when music purveyor Spotify, flush with billions in recently raised capital, announced it might consider this method of going public.

We first review a self-filing through a so-called "resale registration" on Form S-1. The chapter concludes by explaining a self-filing through a Form 10 Securities Exchange Act registration.

A group of other interesting IPO alternatives is introduced in Chapter 13. We first cover SEC Rule 504 under Regulation D. The SEC recently increased the amount one can raise with this previously not much utilized technique to $5 million, attracting new interest. Conducting a solely intrastate offering is another approach we review next. Finally, with Regulation S a U.S. company can raise money offshore in a very attractive manner.

As with my reverse merger books, we conclude in Chapter 14 by hearing from some of the experts in the space about where Reg A+ and these other techniques may be headed in the years to come. They have some interesting and not always the same views on the future of IPO alternatives.

Acknowledgments

It is Labor Day 2017 and, at long last, having commenced the process in wintry February, I have completed the first draft of the book. I have many to thank for this, my fourth book, for Reg A+, and for the success I have been fortunate to have had in my more than 30 years of professional life.

First to the Wiley publishing team, led as always by Bill Falloon and Stephen Isaacs. Your support and encouragement are greatly appreciated. You took a chance on Reg A+ well before it was clearly the exciting new trend it has become and I thank you for it.

My family means everything. My mom, sister, brother-in-law, and nieces all have truly been there for me in so many ways. And, of course, my 15-year-old son, Andrew, amazes me constantly with his incredible acting, singing, musical, and academic talent and, more importantly, by having become the fine and respected young man he is. I am super-proud of you and love you very much! Also sending lots of love to my very talented and caring daughter, Sammi. Missing my Dad, whom we lost in 2001, and Mom's longtime boyfriend, who left us in 2016. I know you are up there watching!

My "Reg A+ friends" are also important. Mark Elenowitz, Lou Taubman, Dave Bukzin, journalist Teri Buhl, Dan McClory and Myomo CEO Paul Gudonis, thanks for being part of this movement with me. To Karen Weidemann, the SEC staffer who contributed substantially to the Reg A+ rules, well done! Thanks also to Sebastian Gomez Abero, head of the SEC Small Business Policy office, and the encyclopedic Jenny Riegel of his team, for your strong support of and assistance to those working hard to make Reg A+ successful.

I remain appreciative of mentors who continue to be there for me, including my uncle, Len Rivkin, and fellow super-lawyer Dave Mazure. To my relatively new colleagues at the incredible AmLaw 100 Duane Morris LLP, thanks for your talent, hard work, and strong ethics. A special nod to Nanette Heide for bringing me into the firm; former Chair John Soroko; new Chair Matt Taylor; Corporate Practice Group head Brian Kerwin; Darrick Mix, the head of our Capital Markets Group; Michael Grohman, who runs our New York City office; marketing gurus Mark Messing and Ellen Auwarter; awesome corporate partners Richard Silfen, Dean Colucci, Jim Seery, and Michael Schwamm; and my amazing legal assistant and bureaucracy navigator, Nancy Menna. Thanks also to super-talented New York/Newark corporate associates (by their office location) Phil Goldstein, Kristen Lin, Neeraj Kumar, Lily Gao, Miguel de Leon Perez, Leigh Krafchek, and Kelly Dabek.

I am very grateful to Elena Karabatos, Lisa Schoenfeld, David Smith, Kenny Lindenbaum, Rick Wien, Jen Rosen Nosenchuk, and my college roomie and Paul Weiss partner, Eric Goodison, for your wonderful personal help during some pretty challenging periods over the decades. Thank you, thank you, thank you to my great friends, Victoria Feuer, my "nieces," Lauren Feuer and Akina Nolan (and yes, you, too, Nicole Lvov), Shannon Harvey,

Dick Auletta, Lucy Goetz, Keith Lippert, Gabrielle Guttman, the late Gregg Feinstein (RIP my friend), Michelle Vallejo, Jen Lee, Faquiry Diaz and Amelia Balonek, Drs. Jay and Nina Rechtweg, Veronica Zanca, Maria Solorzano, Heather Schwartz, theater pal Steph Cartin, Larry Langs, Lisa Reitman-Dobi, BJ Ostrover Levy, the Katies—Shea and Schloss, Dale Weill, Dannah Chaifetz, law firm buddies Evan Michailidis, Justin D'Elia, Christi Campbell, Patricia Heer, and Brian Siff, and many others for adding so much meaning to my life. I am very lucky, honored, and humbled to have such wonderful people around me, especially during the last five years.

I have been on the board of YRF Darca (www.yrfdarca.org) for *28 years*! This incredible charity runs public high schools in disadvantaged areas of Israel under contract with the government. Thanks to fund-raising they offer much larger budgets, resulting in smaller classes, better-paid teachers, and incredible technology. Thanks to Mark Rowan, Sam Katz, and Paul Schnell for so many years of leadership of this awesome cause.

Finally, thanks to my longtime readers, who keep reminding me that my books are not just doorstops. To my business contacts, clients, and referral sources, it has been my pleasure building my network by making friends with you all. I am blessed truly to love what I do, and it is in large part because of the wonderful people I encounter along the way. I am just getting started!

REGULATION A+ AND OTHER ALTERNATIVES TO A TRADITIONAL IPO

CHAPTER 1

Why Go Public?

Before deciding how to go public, a company must decide *whether* to go public. As I often tell my clients, if you can benefit from being public, and can bear the costs of becoming so, you should seriously consider it, regardless of your company's stage of development.

Advantages of Being Public

In general, there are five major advantages to being public: easier access to capital, greater liquidity, ability to grow through acquisitions or strategic partnerships, ability to use stock options to attract and retain senior executives, and increased shareholder confidence in management.

Access to Capital

It is easier for public companies to raise money than it is for private companies. Regardless of the merits of any specific private company, public companies have five characteristics that make them more attractive to investors than private companies.

First, by law most public companies must disclose their financial results (good or bad) and other material developments to the SEC and the public regularly and in great detail. Disclosure requirements build investor confidence because it is harder for a public company to hide problems than it is for a private one to do so.

The second major benefit to investors is that there are more opportunities for a public company to create liquidity for their investment. This increases a public company's access to capital. Those who invest in private companies always worry about the "exit strategy" and look for companies that wish to be sold or to go public eventually. If a company is already public, it significantly enhances the investor's ability to exit.

The fact that one can trade a public company's stock creates liquidity because an investor can sell the stock in the public markets. Typically, public company investors obtain the ability to sell their shares publicly within three to five months after their investment. In an IPO, of course, investors usually can sell their shares immediately. At worst, they must wait six months after investing in a company (if it has not been a shell company for the past six months), or at most one year following most reverse mergers or if a company is not SEC reporting. This is significantly faster than the three to five years, or more, that a venture capitalist generally expects to wait for an investment to pay off.

The third major benefit to a company that completes a financing as a public company rather than a private one is that it is not bound by the restrictions and covenants that private equity or venture capital investors customarily require. Venture capitalists view themselves as management's partners, and require veto power on many different aspects of decision making in a company.

In general, once a company is public, investors stop demanding these powers. Thus, even if a private company is able to attract private equity investors, it still may want to consider going public, because IPO and private investment in public equity (PIPE) investors or others who finance public companies generally put fewer restrictions on the company's activities, decision making, and so on.

The fourth advantage of seeking financing after going public is valuation. The markets judge shares in a public company to be worth roughly twice as much as shares of similarly situated private companies. When a financing takes place as part of the going-public event itself, the value of the company before the investment (known as the "pre-money value") is almost always materially higher than the value a private equity investor would place on the same company. This makes perfect sense when one considers that investors place a premium on liquidity.

Even though it is easier for public companies to raise money than private ones, this is not a sufficient reason for going public, as many companies who go public solely to obtain one round of financing learn to their dismay. Companies that follow this path frequently regret the decision; many in fact end up going private again. Companies that make the most out of being public also make use of some or all of the following benefits.

Liquidity

Liquidity gives all investors the opportunity to enhance their exit strategy by being able to turn their investments into cash. New investors are not the only ones who want to be able to exit. Sometimes one of the main reasons for bringing a private company public is so company founders, former investors, and senior executives holding stock positions can take money out of the business without selling the company outright or losing practical control. There are as many reasons owners might want cash as there are owners.

The challenge in this situation is to avoid a great wave of share sales by company insiders. There are two reasons for this. First, if too many insiders sell out, those who built the company in the past will lose the incentives that would encourage them to continue building the company in the future. Second, Wall Street notices when insiders are selling out. Generally, a wave of insider sales discourages outsiders from investing in a company. Therefore, a company should consult its advisors and design an appropriate, rewarding, but measured selling plan.

For example, a former client took his company public through a reverse merger. Shortly thereafter, the company founder actively began to sell his stock. He sold nearly $5 million worth of stock before the price began to drop precipitously. This caused prospective investors to lose interest in the company. Today the company is out of business and in bankruptcy. This is also the type of situation that leads to SEC investigations of investors' activities.

Another client took a more circumspect approach, with great success. He restricted when, in what amount, and how often insiders could sell their shares. He meticulously consulted with legal counsel before each such insider sale to determine whether there was a risk of insider trading. Today, the company is growing, its stock price is rising steadily, and the founders have been able to sell enough stock, slowly and deliberately, to begin to realize their exit strategies.

Growth Through Acquisitions or Strategic Partnerships

The second most popular reason for going public (after the need to raise capital) is to pursue a strategy of growth through acquisition, joint venture, or strategic partnership. As noted earlier, investors are more willing to provide financing to a public company, even when the purpose of the financing is to fund acquisitions. In addition, a public company often can use stock as currency or "scrip" in the package of consideration to be provided to a company it is acquiring or collaborating with. Indeed, sometimes the only consideration given is stock.

In general, the value of the stock provided exceeds the agreed-upon value of the transaction because there is some risk the stock will drop in value down the road. In other words, if a company is to be acquired for $20 million, including $10 million in cash, a seller may demand the balance to be equal to $12 million or $13 million in stock to offset the risk of stock price volatility. Public buyers generally are willing to be flexible in this regard, as purchasing with stock circumvents the need to raise cash for the purchase. It also allows a company to retain its cash for other purposes such as reserves or capital investments.

Stock Options for Executives

Many companies have difficulty attracting talented senior management. Public companies have an advantage over private ones in the competition for top people because they can offer stock options and other equity incentives—the "brass ring" of affiliation with a public company—as part of the compensation package. Frequently, compensation for top executives at public companies seems exorbitantly high. However, the fine print often reveals that the vast bulk of a multimillion-dollar compensation package comes not in the form of wages, but in the form of stock or stock options. (Stock options aren't just for high-ranking executives. Many stories have been written about the millionaire secretaries at Microsoft, Facebook, eBay, Google, and other companies.)

Private companies also have the option of setting up stock option plans; however, the problem, as with all investments involving private companies, is liquidity. Private company executives know that they cannot make money from owning stock unless there is some form of liquidity event. The company must go public, be sold, or initiate a major dividend distribution to turn shares into cash. Stock options in a public company are much more versatile and, therefore, more valuable.

Options are attractive to those who lead public companies because they align management's incentives with company performance as judged by the market. Option holders are highly motivated to build the company's success so that its stock price will go up. The vesting process, whereby options become available based on an executive's time with the company, encourages a long-term commitment. I know many senior executives who stay with a company longer than planned simply to ensure that their options vest.

Confidence in Management

Because of SEC disclosure requirements, shareholders of public companies feel more confident that the actions of management and the operation of the company will be transparent. The SEC requires reporting companies to reveal financial results regularly (providing explanations of period-to-period changes), including executive compensation, related-party transactions, material contracts, liquidity, capital resources, and the like. Public companies create this stream of information as required by SEC rules, and the result is to help shareholders feel knowledgeable about the company's operations and challenges. The scaled disclosure permitted by some companies after completing a Reg A+ IPO, as we will discuss, does not materially reduce the quality or quantity of the information available to investors.

On the other hand, state laws generally limit the type and quantity of information that a shareholder of a private company may obtain. Rarely can a shareholder legally obtain a financial statement and a list of shareholders more than once a year. Some states require a shareholder to show cause or even bring a court proceeding before obtaining this or other information. Investors in private companies typically negotiate broader and more frequent information delivery, but still find extracting pertinent information to be a constant challenge.

That being said, it must be remembered that even public company filings can be misleading or fraudulent. The lessons of Enron, WorldCom, and others are not terribly distant and will linger. Nonetheless, private companies still have greater incentives to play games than do public ones. After all, the public company that plays fast and loose with disclosure requirements faces a greater risk of SEC investigation, criminal prosecution, and class action lawsuits.

It is not unusual for a senior executive of a public company to ask my firm to figure out how *not* to disclose something, which is almost always something bad. Even when disclosure is not mandatory, when the decision is on or even near the borderline, we usually take the view that disclosure is recommended. (We don't recommend it in every case. For example, the departure of a CEO's longtime personal assistant generally would not need to be disclosed. However, the departure of a director certainly would.)

Disadvantages of Being Public

There are five well-recognized disadvantages of being public: pressure to please Wall Street by emphasizing short-term results; mandatory public disclosure of company information, which makes "warts" hard to hide; vulnerability to fraud (even after Sarbanes-Oxley); higher annual expenses, because of the costs of fulfilling SEC reporting and auditing requirements; and vulnerability to lawsuits.

Emphasis on Short-Term Results

If a public company is lucky enough to have its stock covered by Wall Street analysts, the pressure to please "the Street" is intense and constant. Every quarter, the question on analysts' minds is whether the company will meet or beat expectations in the market. There is a healthy aspect to this because management must keep its eye on stated goals. The negative, of course, is that short-term results become more important than the long-term goals every company must pursue in order to build shareholder value.

A public company must concentrate both on making wise decisions and on how those decisions will be perceived by analysts. This can cause problems. Say a company with a strong cash position decides to spend a portion on long-term capital expenditures. Some Wall Streeters will see the long-term benefit—but some will simply see the erosion of cash reserves. Another example: If the underwriters in an initial public offering (IPO) did not insist that the company shed an early-stage or R&D opportunity and that opportunity continues to drain cash, Wall Street may not respond kindly. Additionally, investments in systems, real estate, or overhead in anticipation of future business may be negatively received.

Conflicts also arise when companies "do the right thing." When I ran my own law firms, I made financial decisions based on my business philosophy of doing right by my vendors, my clients, and my staff. This may mean, for example, keeping problem employees on if I feel they are working diligently to correct their deficiencies. It may mean a larger raise for an employee who is going through tough times, or experiencing unusual personal circumstances. Or it may mean cutting a client's fee, even when he does not request it, if I feel that we may have spent too much time on something. If my firm were public, I would feel more pressure to base my decisions on the smartest financial strategy, regardless of whether I was doing the right thing.

Some recently have proposed changing the quarterly reporting standard for U.S. public companies. The leader of one of the most profitable corporate law firms in the United States suggested several years ago that reporting twice a year would allow companies to think and plan on a more strategic and long-term basis. Former Vice President Al Gore has expressed similar sentiments. In addition, the European Union eliminated mandatory quarterly reporting for listed companies in 2013.

Quarterly reporting was not always the rule in the United States. Through the 1950s the SEC required only annual reports. They then went to twice a year. It was not until 1970 that quarterly reporting was mandated. As we will see, under the new Regulation A+ rules, a post-IPO company trading its stock in the over-the-counter markets can choose a "light" reporting option where filings are made twice a year instead of quarterly.

Public Disclosure

Earlier I described some of the advantages of the public disclosure of financial results, executive compensation, and the like. However, public disclosure is not always beneficial. All of a company's significant problems have to be revealed without delay. If its financial statements are being restated, or the company loses a major customer, or an executive has strong personal or family ties to a major vendor, or a board member resigns, the public will find out immediately.

Disclosure requirements also make it more difficult to keep important information away from competitors. I had a public client, since sold, whose business primarily involved obtaining military contracts. SEC rules require that major new contracts must be filed and disclosed. Unfortunately, one contract included a copy of the company's original bid, which was very specific and detailed regarding pricing and other terms.

The company challenged the filing requirements on the grounds that the original bid was confidential. Unfortunately, the SEC ruled that the contract must be disclosed, confidential bid and all—and the company's competitors were easily able to obtain this information on the SEC's website. Granted, the information was also obtainable with a Freedom of Information Act (FOIA) request (which was the reason the SEC deemed it not confidential). However, the process of obtaining information through FOIA is more cumbersome, and our client's competitors generally do not seek information in that manner.

The other side of public disclosure is that good news travels fast. When positive things are happening at a company, press releases and SEC filings help promote the company's success.

Fraud and Greed (Even After Sarbanes-Oxley)

Congress passed the sweeping Sarbanes-Oxley Act of 2002 (SOX) in reaction to the scandals at Enron, WorldCom, and other corporations. SOX instituted the most wide-ranging changes in securities laws since 1934.

Yet fraud and greed are still alive and well in corporate America. In some ways, public companies have more incentives to engage in deceptive practices than private companies do. This is because, as we described earlier, public companies are under so much pressure to meet or exceed Wall Street's expectations for their performance. Here are some of the tricks companies still use.

Unscrupulous management may engage in "Enronomics," which wordspy.com defined as "a fiscal policy or business strategy that relies on dubious accounting practices, overly optimistic economic forecasts, and unsustainably high levels of spending."

Then there is the euphemistic term, *earnings management*, which works like this: A product has been ordered and produced and is sitting on the shipping dock of the company-owned warehouse. On March 31, a customer informs the company that a truck is on the way to pick up the product within a couple of days. Is this a sale under accrual-based accounting rules on March 31? Absolutely not. A sale does not occur until the customer's truck arrives and picks up the product; however, some companies will record this as a sale anyway. That's earnings management: improving sales in the current quarter. Earnings management is a risky business. I had at least one public client whose earnings management, in the form of questionable inventory auditing techniques, caused it ultimately to lose its key lender and therefore its nearly $100 million business, leading to bankruptcy.

Companies also "manage" expenses. In this scenario, a bill arrives on March 31 for work done by a consultant. The CEO places the bill in his bottom drawer until the next day. Is this an expense on an accrual basis? Absolutely. Do some companies pretend not to incur this expense until the next day? Absolutely. This, too, is earnings management, because it reduces expenses in the current quarter.

Other tricks include complex off-balance-sheet transactions and multitiered corporate structures designed to hide underperforming assets or the involvement of a questionable player. In the late 2000s, as we will discuss, several dozen Chinese companies that had gone public in the United States through reverse mergers were accused of fraud and other securities law violations. Alleged tricks included bribing local bank branch employees to create phony bank statements and filing different financial statements with the SEC than those filed with the Chinese tax authorities.

It's Expensive!

A company that is considering going public needs to prepare for significant additional costs—both hard and soft—in connection with this change in status. Even the smallest private company could see annual expenses rise anywhere from $500,000 to $1 million when it goes public. For some companies, these additional expenses are the difference between positive and negative net income.

Additional costs include:

- Retaining attorneys to deal with the SEC
- Instituting internal financial controls that comply with SOX Section 404
- Hiring auditors to perform the annual audit and review each quarterly financial statement
- Adding additional company staff, in particular finance and shareholder relations staff, to deal with additional requirements
- Engaging a public relations and investor relations firm
- Paying travel and entertainment costs in connection with Wall Street activities

As we will see, one of the goals of the new Reg A+ rules is to help smaller companies reduce these offering and compliance costs. Between speedier SEC review of the IPO disclosure and the light reporting option following the IPO, companies can access public capital markets in a more cost-efficient manner. Some Reg A issuers, as we will see in Reg A Tier 1 offerings, can choose to be non-reporting companies even while their stock is able to trade.

Public Companies Attract Lawsuits

Twitter, Google, Instagram, Wells Fargo, PayPal, Hyundai, and Halliburton are just some of the companies that settled class action lawsuits in 2017. Not all were securities related, but there is no question that public companies face a greater risk of lawsuits, in particular from shareholders and in particular when a stock price takes a dive.

In 2016, according to NERA Economic Consulting, 300 securities class action lawsuits were filed, a one-third increase over the prior year. The average settlement: $72 million. A majority of the cases were against finance industry companies. About a quarter of the filings were related to alleged misdeeds connected to merger transactions.

The law firms that bring these cases on behalf of plaintiffs generally do so on a contingency basis and seek to earn millions. In some of these law firms, attorneys take turns sitting in front of a Bloomberg stock quote machine, watching to see if any particular stock takes a precipitous drop. When that occurs, the firm files a lawsuit, even if there are no facts whatsoever to suggest any wrongdoing. In many of these cases, companies settle quickly to avoid the negative publicity and the costs of defending even a frivolous suit.

In the United States, the threat of such a case is enough to send a stock price reeling. Most of the time, such cases eventually are dropped. Occasionally one is successful, and the lawyers get to defend the purported "rights of shareholders." I have received several notices that I was part of various classes in these cases. When, for example, a major alleged case of overbilling involving my cell phone provider reached settlement, each of us received a $10 phone card as our settlement. The lawyers received a $2.5 million fee.

Unfortunately, most cases are no more than legalized extortion. It is no surprise that the partners of one major plaintiff's firm became subjects of a criminal investigation, and the firm and several of its partners were indicted for alleged illegal payments to so-called lead plaintiffs in dozens of cases in the late 2000s.

A class action bill signed into law in early 2005 has helped reduce the number of truly egregious cases. In the meantime, however, there is no question that private companies considering going public sometimes choose not to do so primarily because of the concern over potential litigation.

Weighing the Pros and Cons

Each company must evaluate the pros and cons in light of its specific circumstances. Let's look at how one potential client did the math. This company, which is in the industrial equipment business, had generated about $25 million in revenues annually for each of the past five years. It expected to stay at this revenue level for the foreseeable future. From this revenue, the company derived earnings of about $2 million, all of which went to the founder, who was enjoying his success and working hard. The company wished to purchase a large warehouse as well as a significant piece of equipment. However, the conservative elderly founder abhorred debt and did not want to make the purchases with a mortgage or equipment financing.

His CFO suggested he meet with a hedge fund investor, who seemed willing to provide $15 million in equity financing for the purchases, if the company was willing to go public. The investor would provide everything necessary to get the job done—what amounted to a turnkey solution. The result would be a much stronger balance sheet, the elimination of certain warehousing and other outsourcing costs, no debt, and a fair equity position for the investor. It sounded logical.

I advised the potential client that he should think very seriously before going forward with the transaction, and ultimately the client decided not to. On one hand, going public would neatly provide the capital he wanted to pursue his business goals. On the other, raising this single round of capital was his only reason for going public. He did not want to make acquisitions, did not need stock options, and had no plans for future financings. Critically, he had no plans to pursue a growth strategy—something investors practically demand from public companies.

If he went ahead, he would incur the extra costs of being public, possibly eliminating a meaningful portion of the company's earnings (offset only in part by cost savings from the new warehouse and equipment). In addition, he would expose his company to the risks of lawsuits and scrutiny of quarterly results, and the burden of hiring additional financial staff. In sum, after this one round of financing, the company would see no other benefit from being public but would bear all of its costs and burdens.

Ultimately, the company found a private investor, who did not require the company to go public, to put up money to buy the building and equipment. The structure of the transaction allowed the company to buy out the investor at a future date. This occurred five years later, providing a healthy return to the investor and giving the company the continued benefit of using the assets it had acquired.

And so . . .

Going public is not for every business. At least a third of the companies that come to me and are ready to go public ultimately realize it is not in their best long-term interest. The manager for a recently deceased mega–rock star had come to me a few years ago with a plan to take a company public that had the star's financial backing and was involved in the Internet space.

When I told the manager that the star's 12% ownership in the company would have to be disclosed, he called me the next day and said that the star had abandoned the going-public plan. These disclosure issues often become the reason companies choose to remain private.

Going public can be, however, a valuable and lucrative path to growth for many emerging companies. As we will cover, recent legislation and SEC rulemakings have expanded the number of arrows in the quiver of companies seeking to grow and raise capital by going public.

Some companies choose the traditional initial public offering (IPO) approach, and many guides and texts can help them through that process. As indicated in the introduction, we are here to cover a very exciting new tool to complete a streamlined, cost-efficient, and speedy IPO through Regulation A+, as well as a number of other alternatives to traditional IPOs such as reverse mergers and self-filings. Let's get started!

CHAPTER 2

Pre-2012: The History of Regulation A and the Death of Small-Company IPOs

Regulation A—Not Too Popular Before 2012

Before learning about the details of Regulation A and the new Regulation A+, it is helpful to understand where we stood in 2012 before the passage of the Jumpstart Our Business Startups (JOBS) Act of 2012. That law updated this and other rules relating to the ability of smaller companies to access capital for growth.

As we will outline ahead, Regulation A offers a method for companies to complete a public offering that generally raises less money and involves a more streamlined process than in a traditional IPO. In 2012, however, very few companies were utilizing Regulation A. The SEC noted this in its commentary to its proposal for new rules regarding Regulation A under the JOBS Act. There they acknowledged that, in the year 2012, only eight Regulation A offerings seeking to raise a total of $34 million were approved, or, the term of art we will learn, *qualified*, by the SEC.

At the time, as will be discussed, the most a company could raise under Reg A was $5 million. The SEC compared these numbers to private securities offerings under SEC Regulation D in the same year seeking to raise no more than $5 million to see which was utilized more. That comparison is laid out following this brief overview of Regulation D.

Reg D, which enjoys continuing strong popularity, operates as a safe harbor under the Securities Act of 1933. In that seminal Depression-era statute, the Congress declared that public offerings of securities were to be scrutinized separately, ultimately setting up the registration process that requires SEC review and approval of almost all public offerings of securities, with substantial disclosure and in many cases post-offering reporting obligations.

Implied in the law was that *non*-public offerings (often called private offerings or private placements) generally would not require SEC scrutiny. However, the Securities Act did not define "public offering," which would have helped issuers determine whether they needed SEC review and detailed disclosure. Between 1933 and 1982, courts grappled with determining which offering was public and which was not.

The courts mostly did agree, in analysis under what is now known as Section 4(a)(2) of the Securities Act, on the factors to be reviewed in determining whether a company is conducting a public offering. These factors included the amount to be raised, the number of offerees, their sophistication, their access to company information, and what portion of their net worth was being invested.

Courts were, however, unable to agree on how to weight the various factors. About all we knew for sure was that if the only person you talk to about investing in your company is Bill Gates and you are asking him for $10,000, it was not a public offering. It was also clear that if you make an offer to 10,000 uneducated grandmas and grandpas, each of whom was investing their last $100,000, you had a public offering. Everything in between frankly was uncertain.

Thus, in 1982 the SEC decided to pass Regulation D, a safe harbor making clear to companies that if they comply with the rules in Reg D, their offering would not be deemed a public offering. The most popular rule within Reg D (we will discuss recent changes to Reg D Rule 504 later), known as Rule 506(b), focuses on two things: which investors are *accredited* and what information is provided to them.

In general, accredited individuals have either an income of $200,000 (or $300,000 with their spouse) or a $1 million net worth not counting their primary residence. These numbers have not changed in the rules since 1982 (although the exclusion of your primary residence in the net worth calculation was added more recently), but as of this writing the SEC is conducting an examination as to whether to change or update these standards.

Reg D allows companies to offer stock with no dollar limit in a private placement to any number of accredited investors with *no specific information* required to be given to them. You can have up to 35 unaccrediteds but then detailed disclosure information has to be provided to them. This great flexibility has made Reg D 506(b) very popular.

The rule does prohibit any "advertising or general solicitation" of the offering. Later we will review Reg D 506(c), adopted as part of the JOBS Act, which allows private offerings to accredited investors only, but *with* advertising and online promotion permitted so long the company takes "reasonable steps" to verify their accredited status. The rule also prohibits the participation of "bad actors" in Reg D deals. These are individuals generally with securities-related legal issues in their relatively recent past.

So in comparing Reg D offerings in 2012 versus Regulation A deals, how many Reg D offerings did the SEC count against the eight Reg A deals? Nearly *8,000* Reg D deals seeking less than $5 million each and looking to raise a total of *$7 billion* were filed in 2012. Quite the contrast from the eight Reg A deals seeking a mere $34 million that year.

In addition, frankly, there were a few questionable players in the small group of Reg A dealmakers around the time of the JOBS Act. This added to the unattractiveness of Reg A to many—a perception, somewhat born of reality, that the space was populated with unsavory types. "How great is this?" these shady actors would say. Raise money from unsuspecting small investors with very little disclosure and no reporting obligations after the IPO and you can trade the stock without revealing down the road who owns your stock or even too many details about financial performance.

As we will discuss later, most believe the low offering threshold and burdensome state review and approval of Reg A IPOs under pre-JOBS Act rules dissuaded companies from utilizing it in the years leading up to 2015 when the SEC approved new Reg A rules. But the negative perceptions did not help, either.

Reg A Through the Years

Now that we understand the world as it existed in 2012, let us return to the beginning. In 1936, the fairly new SEC issued what unconfirmed lore claims was its first regulation—Regulation A (hence the name, goes the story). The rule allows smaller issuers to raise smaller amounts of money in a public offering with lower disclosure and reporting obligations than larger companies. The nation was battling the Great Depression and anything to make it easier to raise money, especially for the engine of job growth, small business, was attractive.

Before the Securities Act was passed in 1933, the states generally governed securities regulation. The stock market crash of 1929 finally led Congress to take over, or at least supplement, that state regulation with federal oversight of the stock exchanges and securities markets.

Congress followed in 1934 with the passage of the Securities Exchange Act, which governs broker-dealers, helped establish the uniform disclosure system now known as Regulation S-K, and organized the SEC. Not many know that the first chairman of the SEC, from 1933 to 1935, was Joseph P. Kennedy, father of future President John F.

Joe Kennedy later became Ambassador to Britain and famously got out of the stock market a very wealthy man before the 1929 crash. He was, however, alleged to be a bootlegger during Prohibition, an insider trader before the Securities Act, and was known to many as a bit of scoundrel. Many believe then-President Franklin Roosevelt thought it a good idea to "put the fox in charge of the henhouse."

Before Reg A was adopted, it was, as described on the SEC's website, "a collection of individual rules issued by the Federal Trade Commission during the period of 1933–1936. Each such rule exempted particular classes of securities from registration under the Securities Act."

Now remember as noted above that Section 4(a)(2) of the Securities Act regulates initial public offerings and requires the shares that are proposed to be publicly offered to be registered with the SEC. The need to file a registration statement and obtain SEC approval of the IPO disclosure is the basic requirement. Reg A operates as an *exemption* from that requirement to register; thus it is both a public offering and an unregistered one.

The result is essentially the same; however, with Reg A you can offer shares to the public and after you do the shares are freely tradeable. Reg D is an exemption from registration that is a *private* unregistered offering where shares are not tradeable (except in limited circumstances under Reg D Rule 504 raising $5 million or less as we will discuss).

In the original 1936 rule, Regulation A's annual offering limit was $100,000. According to www.dollartimes.com, $100,000 in 1936 had the same buying power as $1,749,507 in 2017. That is still low even by today's standards. After World War II, the SEC increased the maximum limit to $300,000. They raised it again in 1970 to $500,000, then $1.5 million in 1978, and finally to $5 million back in 1992. That $5 million is worth $8,753,879 today, an amount still well below what would attract many legitimate investment banks and dealmakers.

Before 2012, though, as we will outline in the next chapter, "old" Reg A allowed you the option to conduct a public offering with relatively limited disclosure, even in a Q&A format if you preferred. You also did not have to take on long-term SEC reporting obligations, even if your stock was trading after your Reg A public offering. There was, therefore, some theoretical attraction to use the technique to obtain a trading stock with pretty low upfront and ongoing compliance cost, even though the offering limit also was low.

The dollar limit, however, was not the only problem. Like most public offerings through the years, Reg A deals also had to be reviewed and approved by each state in which you wanted to offer the stock to the public. In larger "big-company" IPOs, however, that process was managed with a large and very expensive legal team. In addition, the states seemed to provide more deference to the SEC and did not seem to be as skeptical of the larger companies seeking public offerings. The delays and substantial cost of state "blue sky" reviews to smaller companies seeking a Reg A public offering simply were overwhelming.

Why was it such a problem dealing with the states? The various state securities regulators *presumably* are well intentioned and seek a reasonable balance between encouraging capital formation and protecting investors. In reality, however, the state regulators have been, and to some extent still are, in your author's humble opinion, all over the lot in terms of their skills, responsiveness, experience, and at times even intelligence. Remember these are generally low-paid local government workers. Of course some are diligent, smart, responsive, and reasonable. Many, however, unfortunately are not.

The federal agency employees at the SEC's Division of Corporation Finance oversee review of public filings. While they are tough at times, they generally are smart and accessible and rarely unpredictable. Most SEC examiners of public offerings are attorneys or accountants and are well trained. Many end up leaving the SEC for lucrative private law and accounting firm positions.

Before 1996, every single IPO, even the large ones planning to list on national exchanges, had to go through this full state blue sky review. This was a mega-task. Large law firms had dozens of blue sky lawyers doing nothing but dealing with these local regulators on public offerings.

In 1996, the Congress passed the National Securities Markets Improvement Act (lovingly known as NSMIA and pronounced "niss-mee-uh"). NSMIA created the concept of "covered securities" that would be preempted from state blue sky review. How can Congress just do this?

The good old U.S. Constitution: Article VI's Supremacy Clause basically says federal law trumps (you should excuse the expression) state law when they conflict and that the feds can take over regulating something from the states. Of course the Tenth Amendment to the Constitution says the feds only have those rights given to them in the Constitution and the rest belong to the states. The feds do, however, get to control interstate commerce. So if a public offering is happening across state lines, guess who wins? (Note that states are free to regulate offerings happening solely within their states, called "intrastate" offerings.)

So NSMIA said it's too much of a burden for large companies doing IPOs onto national exchanges to also go through the states, especially since many of these large IPOs were being sold in all 50 states. The SEC review of their offerings, plus the protections of the exchanges, were deemed sufficient.

In addition, in most cases these larger deals included major law and accounting firms, adding to the comfort level. The only real exception: mutual funds going public still have to go through state review. Great for companies, not so great for the blue sky lawyers. They had to all reinvent themselves, and most did. A small shout-out to decades-old friend Joe Krassy, the true dean of the blue sky lawyers both pre- and post-NSMIA, who recently retired. Joe responded to NSMIA by becoming the part-time blue sky lawyer for a handful of major law firms. Joe, we will miss your practical approach to this arcane area of law.

But what did NSMIA not do? It did not include securities sold in IPOs onto the lower over-the-counter trading platforms in the definition of covered securities. So if you want to do an IPO but not list on Nasdaq, NYSE, or similar national exchanges, and prefer to trade in the over-the-counter markets, as of 1996 you still have to go through full state review—hence one of the major negatives (along with the $5 million limit) of old Reg A if you planned, as almost all did at the time primarily due to the small offering limit, not to list on a national exchange.

So it was indeed a big deal that the JOBS Act, as we will see, increased the Reg A limit from $5 million to $50 million *and* preempted blue sky review of Reg A IPOs planning to trade in the over-the-counter markets. It seems equally impressive to me that something designed in the 1930s, when radio and talking movies were new, to help the country survive one of the, if not the most calamitous time in our country's economic history, has survived to be molded into a modern, Internet-savvy technique that has attracted hundreds of companies since the rules became effective in June 2015.

Why did Congress decide to do this? Patience, dear reader, the chapters ahead will explore.

Why Small Companies Struggled to Go Public Before the JOBS Act

There was another problem in 2012. There was no shortage of emerging companies interested and seeing benefit in having a publicly trading stock. Small-company IPOs, however, which had been dominant in the go-go Internet years of the 1990s, had virtually disappeared starting in the late 1990s. In addition, "reverse mergers," in which private companies went public by merging with an existing public vehicle, often deemed a shell, also were facing significant challenges. Let's discuss each.

Death of Small IPOs

There has been a tremendous amount of time and money devoted to analyzing why smaller company IPOs virtually disappeared at the end of the Internet boom. A recent article published in the *Harvard Business Law Review* (*HBLR*) (Paul Rose and Steven Davidoff Solomon, "Where Have All the IPOs Gone? The Hard Life of the Small IPO," 6 *Harv. Bus. L. Rev.* 83 (2016), http://scholarship.law.berkeley.edu/facpubs/2601) provides the startling facts. Here is the blunt opening to the article: "The small company initial public offering (IPO) is dead. In 1997, there were 168 exchange-listed IPOs for companies with an initial market capitalization of less than $75 million. In 2012, there were seven such IPOs, the same number as in 2003."

Rose and Solomon conducted a thorough analysis to conclude that, despite the existence of a number of theories, no one really knows for sure what caused the small-company IPO market to dry up. That also means it may be tough to figure out what will retrigger the deal flow. They appear to side a bit with those who believe that investors simply got tired of investing in small companies that had a lower likelihood of success than IPOs of larger companies. It is not exactly clear what caused that to happen around the time of the end of the Internet bubble. Here is a review of the potential causes cited by the article.

Sarbanes-Oxley

First, they say, many believe the Sarbanes-Oxley (SOX) Act of 2002, implemented after the massive Enron, Tyco, and WorldCom scandals, is the culprit. SOX was the subject of rapid Congressional adoption with virtually no hearings, and in particular no discussion of the potential impact on smaller public companies, even though its goal was to prevent the next multibillion-dollar fraud.

There is indeed no question that SOX added burdens to public companies, especially smaller ones. The most significant: (1) requiring public companies to have an outside auditor attest to the adequacy of the company's internal financial controls and (2) requiring CEOs and CFOs to personally certify to this adequacy in every public company periodic report.

When SOX was adopted, I informed the CEO of a public client of mine that this was now his responsibility. He took out a pen, wrote something down, and slid it across the table to me. I looked at the note, which said, "I resign." He didn't, but we got the point. Since then the rules have been relaxed so that so-called "smaller reporting companies" (generally below $75 million in market capitalization) do not have to hire an outside auditor to assess financial controls, but management still has to certify that they have done the assessment and opine as to the adequacy thereof. The JOBS Act codified this and expanded it, providing that "emerging growth companies," which are companies going public with as much as $1.07 billion in revenues, also are exempt from the outside auditor attestation.

The *HBLR* article points out that smaller company audit bills initially more than doubled after SOX, but after 2008 came back to earth and now are around 25 percent higher than pre-SOX. The law certainly caused a ruckus of frustration, and was used by foreign stock exchanges as leverage to convince companies to stay out of U.S. trading. Over time, however, that concern has been proven to have been significantly overhyped.

Market Ecosystem Theory

The next alleged culprit, according to Rose and Solomon, of the death of small company IPOs: the so-called "market ecosystem" theory. This posits that the adoption by the SEC in 2000 of Regulation FD and the 2002 massive Global Research Analyst Settlement (GRAS) are partially to blame. This theory suggests that market analysts' incentives to follow smaller stocks were significantly reduced by these changes.

Another part of this theory says that 1997 changes in the so-called "order handling rules" (OHRs) and reductions in tick-size spreads around 2001 contributed as well. Here is a review of these various potential villains.

Regulation FD, which one would think always should have been the law, says a public company cannot selectively disclose material nonpublic information. In other words, the old small conference calls with a few select stock analysts who get a jump on the overall market were over. The major exception is you can disclose things to people who sign a nondisclosure agreement. It seems rather obvious that this did take away certain benefits from the analysts.

The GRAS was a huge coup for then-not-yet-disgraced New York Governor Eliot Spitzer. Things were just too cozy between the major Wall Street houses' investment banking and analyst arms. The bankers want to sell a deal and the analysts are looking for objective research, which do not necessarily always jibe. There was some evidence that the analysts were being pressured by the bankers to produce, shall we say, not-so-objective research, and that this practice was rather pervasive throughout the industry.

The settlement required the separation of the analyst and investment banking functions, taking away analyst compensation for equity research. It also prohibited the analysts from attending investor roadshows promoting deals. The *HBLR* article points out that analyst coverage, on average, tends to increase a public company's stock price by about 5 percent. So less of it would clearly not be good. As we will see, to some extent the JOBS Act sought to reverse this.

Moving on, without getting too much into a super-complicated set of rules, the OHRs required much more disclosure of price quotes than before, which many believe negatively affected the economics of market makers, who secure trading in public stocks, and made their involvement in smaller public companies less attractive.

Then, there is the tick-size problem. In 2009, Grant Thornton published a wide-ranging study asserting that the main cause of small company IPOs disappearing was the reduction in spreads between "bid" and "ask" prices in 2001. (See the study at David Weild and Edward Kim, "Capital Market Series: Market Structure Is Causing the IPO Crisis," Grant Thornton LLP 9 (2009), http://www.grantthornton.com/staticfiles/GTCorn!Public%20companies%20and %20capital%20markets/FilesllP0%20crisis%20-%20 Sep%202009%20-%20FINAL.pdf.)

Market participants, especially in electronic markets such as Nasdaq, were able to share pieces of this price spread with those who helped bring buyers and sellers together. This was how now-infamous Bernard Madoff allegedly made his first legitimate fortune when he was also chairman of the Nasdaq. Some say that the change in the tick-size spreads dried up his income, leading to his more nefarious Ponzi scheme that stole billions from many, including his close childhood friends. We may never know, however, as old Bernie is not talking from his jail cell. More on the Madoff scandal and its impact on the SEC is to come.

Once the bid–ask spreads went to one penny, after having been as high as 25 cents, there is no question many were driven out of the market. The idea of decimalization of the spread was to put more money in investors' pockets as opposed to pulling out the money in the spreads to hand out like candy. The result, however, certainly was not positive for the small-company IPO market.

As of this writing and since October 2016, the SEC has been conducting a two-year pilot tick-size study. The purpose of the study is to see if it would be worthwhile to move back to larger spreads. They are sampling about 1,400 small capitalization stocks (with less than $3 billion in market capitalization) with a five-cent tick-size spread.

Their hope is the study will show less volatility and increased liquidity in the selected stocks. If so, they might consider expanding the study, increasing tick sizes across the board, or possibly giving companies the right to determine their own tick spreads. What the study shows: The SEC realizes that decimalization, while it had understandable aims, may have had some unintended negative consequences.

A last part of this theory suggests that the move to online brokerage accounts made IPOs tougher. Without the usual salesforce at a brokerage firm pushing stocks, it was tougher to find investors interested in participating in IPOs. The Grant Thornton study suggests this caused many brokers to move to jobs in asset management, taking them away from the day-to-day selling process of IPOs and helping kill the Internet IPO craze.

Economic Scope Theory

The last major explanation for the small-company IPO problem is laid out in yet another fairly recent paper on the subject (Xiaohui Gao, Jay R. Ritter, and Zhongyan Zhu, "Where Have All the IPOs Gone?," 48 *J. Fin. Quantitative Analysis*, 1663, 1688 (2013)). This one is a little depressing as it suggests that there are bigger, more fundamental changes in the markets that simply reward larger businesses more than the small ones, that the only way for businesses to succeed is to be large, to grow by acquisition, and eventually be sold themselves rather than go public. Under this theory, as our world gets smaller and technology faster and more complex, being larger is simply a necessity.

So what caused the death of small IPOs before almost anyone had heard of a thing called Facebook? No one knows for sure. Is that important? It can be, if part of the purpose of this book is to help answer the question or whether it is a good idea for small companies to be public, and if so, what the best way is to get there. We may never know for sure, and it is important for any company considering the public route to keep these factors in mind.

Death of Reverse Mergers?

The end of IPOs might not have been the worst thing ever, but there was another problem small businesses faced in 2012. We will delve into reverse mergers much more starting in Chapter 8. For the purposes of the discussion here, however, it is important to note that as IPOs disappeared, in many cases reverse mergers rose to take their place and help small companies go public, albeit in a nontraditional manner. In a reverse merger, a private company goes public by merging with an already-existing public entity that in many cases has no operations and is deemed and in many cases actually called a "shell" company.

As we will discuss in greater detail later, in the late 1990s and into the 2000s, shell mergers slowly increased in popularity. The technique mostly shook off its previously shady reputation developed in the 1980s, which resulted from some bad players being in the space at the time. The death of small IPOs only accelerated the need to find legitimate methods for small companies to go public to access capital and grow.

There were several hundred reverse mergers completed annually through most of the 2000s, many with contemporaneous financings and follow-on public offerings. Venture-backed companies mostly stayed away, with the exception being companies in the life sciences industry. Biotechs embraced the technique vigorously, especially after some major successes like Cougar Biotechnology, which was sold to Johnson & Johnson for about $1 billion just a few years after its reverse merger in 2006.

In addition, in the second half of the 2000s, hundreds of Chinese companies went public in the United States through reverse mergers. This added dramatically to the deal flow, and investment banks and deal participants had a field day. Sadly, around 2010, in part resulting from research published by some short sellers betting on stocks to go down, several dozen of these companies ended up accused of fraud.

Lawsuits and SEC investigations of these alleged Chinese frauds ensued. Some cases were dismissed, others settled. A few ended up with actual legal determinations of fault and fraud. Fingers were pointed at advisors to these companies. It goes without saying that all the stocks of these Chinese companies, even those not accused of anything and showing strong earnings, suffered tremendously.

Some of these "innocent" Chinese companies simply gave up and went private. Some remained public and their stocks have mostly rebounded. But it was a mess for sure. Not helping the matter was the 2008–2009 Wall Street and economic meltdown. It was not a good time for small and microcap players.

Let us briefly review what frauds the Chinese companies were accused of, which we will cover in greater depth in Chapter 9. Again we say *alleged* and in most cases not proven. Here, however, are a few examples. In several cases, the companies were accused of colluding with local bank branch employees to phony-up bank statements. Opening and closing balances could not be changed, but they would insert much more in and out in between, to allow companies to show more revenues (and expenses)—allegedly. Result: Smart auditors now realize they ask for bank statements only from the bank's *headquarters*. In other alleged frauds, one day the CEO, and all the company's assets, allegedly disappeared and neither can be located.

In another series of alleged frauds, the company's tax returns filed with the Chinese tax authorities showed financial results that were significantly different from the audited financial statements filed with the SEC in the United States. This actually happened in a number of cases. Most of these cases, however, were thrown out. The plaintiffs first had to prove that the results were actually different, since they were prepared with different accounting principles. Assuming they could do that, they had to be able to prove that the U.S.-filed accounting information was in fact the wrong set of financials, as opposed to the ones filed with the Chinese tax authorities. Plaintiffs' attorneys mostly realized this was going to be extremely difficult to do.

After this, and I believe because of the Chinese alleged (and some actual) frauds, the SEC took action that mostly shut the door on how many reverse mergers were completed. As we will describe later, in 2011, it "encouraged" the major stock exchanges to request, and the SEC approved, new regulations known as the "seasoning rules."

An extremely popular method of reverse merger involved two steps. First a private company would merge with a so-called Form 10 shell (again, more on this later) and complete a private financing, say of around $5 million. Now as a public reporting but nontraded company, they would immediately file for a public offering of $15–20 million and immediately start trading on Nasdaq or the NYSE American (then known as the American Stock Exchange).

At least one of my clients at the time, who had created dozens of these Form 10 shells and operated a broker-dealer, completed many, many deals this way. The seasoning rules, unfortunately, now require that after a merger with a shell company, the merged company must trade on the over-the-counter markets (as opposed to national exchanges such as Nasdaq) for at least one full fiscal year before even applying to uplist to the national exchange. Only a public offering of at least $40 million lets you bypass this speedbump under the new rules. Most small companies are not big enough to justify this type of raise.

We will get into some of the (in my view significantly flawed) reasoning for these new rules later. We will also discuss how some players have tried to get around these restrictions by merging with public entities that are not technically shell companies. Unfortunately, in the last several years a number of players, including previously prominent attorneys, have been sued by the SEC, criminally charged, or jailed for misdeeds in creating bogus public vehicles pretending to be operating businesses to avoid the shell designation.

Reverse mergers are not quite dead. Clients of mine completed one in December 2016 and another in March 2017. The biotech world still likes the shells'. To be frank, however, as we will see, Regulation A+ IPOs offer much more to companies that would have considered a reverse merger, especially after implementation of the seasoning rules made reverse mergers more problematic.

Reg A versus Private Offering Under Regulation D

This seems as good a place as any to compare a Regulation A IPO to a private offering under Regulation D, since many of the comparisons apply both before and after the JOBS Act improvements. There are really six major differences between the two.

Reg D Is Faster

Both before and after the JOBS Act changes, Reg A IPOs still have to be filed with and approved by the SEC. Reg D offerings do not. You can complete a private offering under Reg D as quickly as you can prepare subscription and disclosure documents and get investors to sign them. Then within 15 days after closing you complete a simple filing of something called Form D with the SEC and any state in which you complete the offering.

If there is a need for speed, Reg D may be a better choice. In fact, many companies working on Reg A IPOs complete an interim "bridge" financing under Reg D first. Many companies, however, do not have an urgent need for capital. They have raised prior funds or have profits to fund operations.

We are also very pleased that, as will be discussed, the SEC has instructed its examiners to provide a very limited and expedited review of Reg A filings. This has dramatically reduced the average time that issuers are spending in SEC review of Reg A submissions, reducing the difference in time to completion as against Reg D.

Reg D Is Cheaper

With Reg D, if you accept only accredited investors, there are no specific information delivery requirements as long as there is nothing misleading or fraudulent going on. If you have some unaccredited investors (Rule 506(b) allows up to 35), in most cases you must provide them a full disclosure document, often referred to as a Private Placement Memorandum (PPM). The cost of preparing that PPM, however, is still meaningfully less than a full Reg A IPO. This is another reason that some companies choose a Reg D deal followed by a Reg A IPO.

If you choose a Reg D 506(c) offering as now permitted under the JOBS Act (see Chapter 13), you can advertise or publicly solicit investors as noted earlier. In those transactions, costs might be higher if a company engages a marketing or investor relations firm to develop a social media or crowdfunding campaign for the offering.

Reg D Can Raise More than $50 Million

Reg D Rule 506 offerings have no dollar limit. Some larger companies find a benefit in being able to raise significant funds this way. Even post-JOBS Act, as we will outline, Reg A IPOs are limited to $50 million per 12-month period, although the SEC has the authority to raise that amount and as of this writing a bill is moving through Congress to raise the limit to $75 million. Most companies contemplating a Reg A offering, however, do not need to raise more than $50 million.

Reg D Rule 504 offerings allow a company to raise up to $5 million from an unlimited number of accredited and unaccredited investors with no specific information delivery requirements. This expands the pool of potential investors but obviously limits the amount that can be raised compared to Reg A.

Reg D Rule 506 Limits Investor Status

Reg D Rule 506 limits who can invest. In 506(b), an unlimited number of accredited investors and up to 35 unaccredited investors can participate with no advertising. With 506(c), advertising is permitted so long as your offering is limited to accrediteds. Reg A offerings can include an unlimited number of investors regardless of accredited status.

The one limitation, as we will see in Chapter 4, is that an issuer in a Reg A offering that plans to trade its stock in the over-the-counter markets must limit the amount that each unaccredited investor purchases based on their income or net worth. Those limits do not apply to a Reg A deal where the plan is to trade the stock on a national exchange.

Reg A Offers Liquidity

Possibly the most significant advantage of Reg A over Reg D is that shares issued in the Reg A offering are immediately tradeable. Only in certain Reg D 504 offerings (limited to $5 million) is trading possible, and even then generally only on the least desirable trading platforms. It is typically much easier to raise money from investors when they know there is a current path to near-term liquidity of their investment. A company also may be able to sell stock at a higher per-share price when investors know they will have an option to sell their stock publicly soon thereafter.

It appears likely, though not yet clear as of this writing (in fall 2017), that most companies conducting Reg A IPOs will choose to trade their stock over-the-counter. The platforms operated by OTC Markets Group include the OTCQX, the OTCQB, and OTC Pink, in reducing order of stature. Most Reg A deals this writer is aware of plan to trade on QX or QB, and not national exchanges such as Nasdaq or the NYSE.

In many cases they simply will not be able to satisfy the listing standards of the larger exchanges. As previously noted, however, trading of the first group of Reg A IPOs on the larger national exchanges such as Nasdaq and NYSE began in June 2017.

In general, the volume of trading and liquidity is better on the exchanges than in the over-the-counter markets. The exchanges, however, have many more requirements with respect to corporate governance, board independence, shareholder approval of certain actions, and the like. Many companies whose management is new to being public find a benefit to ease into public status where the compliance obligations are a bit less in the over-the-counter markets.

Reg A Offers Unlimited Testing of the Waters to All Investors

As we will discuss, Reg D Rule 506(c), created under the JOBS Act, does allow a private offering with advertising, general solicitation, and "testing the waters." That rule, however, only allows accredited investors to invest in these deals, and in many cases they must obtain a certification from a third party as to their accredited status or the company must otherwise take "reasonable steps" to verify the investor's accredited status. In Reg A+, advertising and testing the waters can take place before or after SEC filing of your proposed disclosure (on what we will learn is called an offering statement) seeking interest from *any* investor, whether or not accredited.

As a result of this change, a brave new world of social media and online marketing of Reg A+ deals has developed. In some cases it represents the only source of potential funding; in other cases it is combined with proceeds raised by investment banks or funds brought to the table from a company's own crowd of fans, followers, and customers (much more on this later).

And so . . .

The world in 2012 before the JOBS Act was not too interested in Reg A. The low dollar limit and state blue sky review pretty much killed any attraction Reg A may otherwise have had as a public offering with testing the waters. Reg D was (and remains) tremendously popular but retains restrictions. How the two will play together will be an interesting development to watch.

As we get ready to talk next about how Reg A+ developed under the JOBS Act, understanding why the small-company IPO market dried up around 2000 remains mostly a mystery despite the best efforts of some very smart researchers. Whether updated Reg A+ will solve the challenges that are still unclear is, well, unclear. What is clear is that there are a number of experienced Wall Street players getting very excited about, and helping dozens of companies reap, the benefits of a Reg A+ IPO for smaller companies, so let's go there now.

CHAPTER 3

The JOBS Act and Its Genesis

"Old" Regulation A

Before 2012, as mentioned, Reg A was not utilized very much. Here are some of the highlights of how Reg A worked before the JOBS Act.

Limited Offering Amount and Mandatory Blue Sky

One of the big problems of Reg A was that only $5 million could be raised. As mentioned, this cap had been increased steadily from its original $100,000 limit in 1936, and some companies might have liked to raise $5 million. Most investment banking firms interested in IPOs, however, did not see sufficient potential commissions in raising such a small amount.

The other big problem, as mentioned: Every deal had to go through full state blue sky review, unless the company was considering a listing on a national exchange. Both the rules themselves, and the limited amount to be raised, made it all but impossible for a Reg A issuer before 2012 to consider a national listing.

As we have discussed, the blue sky review was time-consuming, expensive, and unpredictable. This significantly enhanced the cost for IPOs in a situation where the amount to be raised was capped at a low level.

Simplified Disclosure and Reporting

One perceived advantage of old Reg A was that issuers had the option of using a simple Q&A format to provide disclosure. In addition, issuers were "non-reporting" following their IPO. The stock could trade, but they would not become subject to the SEC reporting requirements. This meant lower compliance costs, but also greater difficulty in attracting support for the trading of their stock, obtaining analyst coverage, and the like. It also meant trading was limited to the over-the-counter markets.

Old Reg A also did not require audited financial statements to be included in the offering statement. Again, this reduced the cost of the offering, but turned away a number of investors who felt less confident about the reliability of financial information.

Testing the Waters

Old Reg A permitted an issuer to gauge investor interest before filing its offering statement with the SEC. The theory was that this permitted companies to get a sense of whether they are being realistic about their potential for raising money, and of investors' views on valuation and offering terms. This was, and remains, a very attractive feature of Reg A.

As we will see, the final SEC rules under the JOBS Act go further and allow issuers to continue testing the waters *after* filing their offering statement with the SEC, combined with strict but manageable rules about how the campaigns can be conducted.

U.S. and Canadian Companies Only

Old Reg A could be used only by companies that are incorporated in and whose principal place of business is in the United States or Canada. As we will see and discuss in further detail, the SEC retained that restriction in the new JOBS Act rules. While there has been conjecture about why they did not change this limitation in the new rules, which we will cover, it has never been clear why this restriction was originally included in 1936. It may be that the old Reg A, enacted during the Great Depression, was focused on helping American companies, but then one wonders why Canada also was included.

I have made a semi-diligent search for any explanation published at the time to explain the reason for this limitation. A special evening reviewing the SEC's annual report for 1936 was particularly squint-inducing, soporific, and not particularly insightful. Not to offend my very good friends and clients in the Great White North, but it appears the origin of this restriction shall remain a mystery.

Nomenclature

It is helpful to cover a few of the key terms used uniquely in both old and new Reg A. We will add some more that appear in the new SEC rules later, but let us get these out of the way.

- "Offering Statement"—similar to a registration statement in a traditional IPO, this is filed on SEC Form 1-A and includes Part I with basic information about the offering and the company, Part II, which comprises the Offering Circular, and exhibits. This is the main SEC filing for a Reg A deal.
- "Offering Circular"—similar to a prospectus in a traditional IPO, has disclosure concerning the issuer's business, ownership, and financial condition. Old Reg A permitted either a narrative or Q&A format; new Reg A eliminates Q&A. Each investor must receive or have access to an Offering Circular.
- "Qualification"—similar to "going effective" in a traditional public offering, the official approval by the SEC of the Reg A public offering, allowing the issuer to raise funds.
- "Testing the Waters"—the process of enticing and determining investor interest before (old Reg A) or before and after (new Reg A) filing the Offering Circular.

Let us now explore how the JOBS Act and revisions to "old" Reg A developed.

Feldman First Proposes "Reg A+" at SEC Conference

History of the SEC Small Business Conference

The SEC has been statutorily required to hold an annual conference on small business finance since 1982. Dubbed the Government-Business Forum on Small Business Capital Formation, it is mandated under the Small Business Investment Incentive Act of 1980.

The GBFSBCF (not the greatest acronym—we can just call it "the Conference") is typically held each November at the SEC's big auditorium in the basement of their office building in Washington. In November 2017, however, it was held in Austin, Texas, the first time it took place outside the Beltway. It is also webcast live and the webcast is archived and available. In recent years it has become typical for some, if not all, of the SEC Commissioners to attend and give welcoming remarks about how important small business is, how it is the engine of growth, and that encouraging capital formation is key. The Democratic members also typically add that we have to remember that there is also fraud in small business and enforcement remains important.

It is rare that anything the Commissioners say at the Conference becomes news. I believe the webcasting and archiving are what draw them to attend and repeat customary supportive platitudes. They tend to discuss small business achievements at the SEC that almost always were imposed upon them by law. In the November 2017 Conference, for example, new Trump-appointed SEC Chair Jay Clayton spoke. His remarks focused on helping what he called "Mr. and Ms. 401(k)" obtain opportunities to invest in growth companies. He acknowledged that a "one size fits all regulatory structure does not fit all" as he talked about the benefits of scaled disclosure for smaller issuers. He acknowledged there is room for improvement in the regulations to remove some of the "speed bumps" in the path to capital formation. He also hinted at expanding which companies can benefit from reduced disclosure as "smaller reporting companies."

The SEC's Office of Small Business Policy historically has run the Conference. Their hardworking staff has been spending quite a bit of time each year planning it. The daylong event typically starts with a panel or two (your author was honored to speak on a panel in November 2016 about Regulation A+). Then there are several breakout groups. The purpose of the breakouts is to develop recommendations to the SEC. Once the recommendations are decided, the participants rank which they consider the most important. Then the SEC publishes the results with the recommendations ranked. The ranking of the 2016 Conference recommendations was released in late March 2017.

Until recently, there was no particular limit on the number of recommendations, but the SEC published only the top 25. In the last few years, however, the SEC has limited each of the three breakout groups to five recommendations each. There were folks coming to the Conference with their one pet issue and pushing it year after year with very little support from others. By imposing a limit, the SEC believes each breakout group will include only suggestions the group as a whole reaches consensus on.

In December 2016, the lame-duck Congress passed and outgoing President Obama signed into law the SEC Small Business Advocate Act of 2016. The law mandates the creation of a new quasi-independent position at the SEC called the Advocate for Small Business Capital Formation. The law also created a permanent new SEC advisory committee known as the Small Business Capital Formation Advisory Committee. The Advocate is charged, among other things, with organizing the Conference going forward. As of this writing, the SEC is considering applications to fill the Advocate position under Chairman Clayton.

In February 2016, the U.S. House of Representatives passed the Small Business Capital Formation Enhancement Act, but it had not been approved by the Senate as of fall 2017. The bill focuses on the Conference and provides that, after each set of recommendations is made, the SEC must "promptly issue a public statement . . . assessing the finding or recommendation of the forum; and disclosing the action, if any, the Commission intends to take with respect to the finding or recommendation." It would be great if this was passed, but it seems unlikely.

The Conference and the recommendations are important because, sometimes, the SEC looks at them and takes action. This happened under SEC Chair Cox in 2007 and 2008. Congress also looks at the list. The various already existing advisory committees the SEC has had focusing on small and emerging companies also looked at the Conference recommendations in fashioning their agenda.

There are, of course, years where the recommendations seem to gather dust on a shelf and be ignored. Truthfully, the SEC over the last 10 to 15 years has done very little on its own initiative to help reduce smaller companies' regulatory burden. The ideas the Conference participants consider important, however, tend to be repeated year after year. This increases the chance they will be noticed at some point.

The breakout participants at the Conference try not to simply create a wish list. They generally seek to develop recommendations that seem doable and do not appear to create concerns for investor protection. Your author was honored to moderate the breakout on smaller reporting companies in November 2016.

The Conference usually ends with a gathering of all the breakout groups to announce their recommendations; then the group and SEC staffers retire to a local restaurant for drinks and banter. The opportunity for practitioners in the field to spend time with the regulators is helpful and important, and those who participate only through the webcast lose this valuable opportunity to hobnob with senior staffers who help fashion the SEC's small business agenda.

The Seminal 2010 Conference

In November 2010, I was present as always at the annual Conference. I have been and still am somewhat well known in reverse mergers, having written two texts on the subject. Much more about this in later chapters since, as mentioned, reverse mergers still are utilized by some private companies seeking a publicly traded stock. In a reverse merger with a "shell company," the process is efficient and cost-effective, but has been controversial over the years.

As discussed in the previous chapter, small-company IPOs dried up around 2000, but there was no shortage of companies seeking to go public. Thus, reverse mergers grew in popularity, and a group of us sought to steer companies to do so legitimately and cleanly. This continued through the 2000s until the industry faced the challenges to Chinese companies brought by short sellers as discussed.

It was pretty clear reverse mergers were headed for trouble, and the "seasoning" rules ensued as described. As noted in the Preface, I had always said that we would not need reverse mergers if smaller company IPOs were easier to do. The reverse mergers were (and are) somewhat awkward, have a bit of a shady history, and are clearly disfavored by the SEC. Reverse mergers often were referred to somewhat derogatorily as "backdoor" listings because you can take your company public through a reverse merger with no regulatory involvement or filings prior to closing.

I came to the 2010 Conference, therefore, armed with an idea. I had heard of a few people trying to use the then-version of Regulation A for small IPOs. It seemed they struggled with the dollar limit and blue sky review, but were undaunted. I started to think about that and wondered, "What if we can make that better?" I particularly wanted to see the dollar limit go up.

The idea was in my head but not necessarily the exact method of presenting it. So I sort of blurted out, "What if we improve Regulation A, call it, I don't know, Regulation A+, and allow companies to raise more money and become full reporting companies?" The ultimate official recommendation, which the moderator transcribed, was this: "Add an alternative to Regulation A (call it Regulation A+), pursuant to which an issuer can raise more than $5 million (up to a maximum of $30 million) . . . ." It ended up being ranked by participants as #5 out of 25 recommendations at the 2010 Conference.

Who knew Congress would ultimately take it up to $50 million when we only asked for $30 million! My blurted-out term, *Reg A+*, thanks to its inclusion in the formal recommendation, went into the regular parlance of practitioners after the recommendation was released and then picked up by Congress. Many from the SEC chair on down refer to the amended Reg A as Reg A+ in speeches and in some formal issued guidance, but it is not an official term used in the actual Reg A+ SEC rules.

So, yes, I coined the term. The current head of the SEC's Office of Small Business Policy, Sebastian Gomez Abero, confirmed this in publicly introducing me at the November 2016 Conference, although he said that I, "possibly along with others," coined the term (okay, good enough).

My clients who are aware of this have taken to embarrassing me about it. One calls me the "Godfather of Reg A+." He even greets me that way, "Glad to have you on the call, Godfather." I was happy because I wanted to get rid of another moniker a client offered, calling me the "Grandfather" of the new rules. (As they say online, lol.)

One last semiserious thing about the term *Reg A+*. We should agree on how it applies. Some have used the term to apply to all of Reg A as it now stands post-JOBS Act. Others have used it to apply only to so-called Tier 2 offerings (more about this later), since Tier 1 deals are basically like the "old" Reg A and only Tier 2 offerings are state blue sky preempted. I think it makes sense to use Reg A+ to refer to Tier 2 deals. That was the "plus" that I was referring to when I first used the term. Tier 1 is just Reg A as it was. Hopefully that approach will be adopted by my fellow practitioners.

Development and Enactment of the JOBS Act

The final report of the 2010 Conference containing the Reg A+ recommendation was released in June 2011. Just six months later, in December 2011, the JOBS Act first was introduced in the Republican-controlled Congress. A few months later, it passed the Senate 73–26 and in the House a whopping 390–23. It was, after all, a big Congressional election year, and supporting small business seemed like a no-brainer for incumbents on both sides of the aisle. Plus, who wanted to be against a bill with the acronym "JOBS"?

The JOBS Act ultimately was signed into law by Pres. Obama on April 5, 2012, in a splashy Rose Garden signing ceremony. Apparently referring to Reg A, he said,

> [F]or start-ups and small businesses, this bill is a potential game changer. Right now, you can only turn to a limited group of investors—including banks and wealthy individuals—to get funding. Laws that are nearly eight decades old make it impossible for others to invest. But a lot has changed in 80 years, and it's time our laws did as well. Because of this bill, start-ups and small business will now have access to a big, new pool of potential investors—namely, the American people. For the first time, ordinary Americans will be able to go online and invest in entrepreneurs that they believe in.

Making the Reg A+ Sausage

As the bill was being developed before introduction, I worked with the House Financial Services Committee staff on what ultimately became Title IV, which ordered the SEC to implement amendments to Regulation A. The House version of Title IV was not changed at all when the Senate took up the bill, and it was retained in the final JOBS Act. That is not true of Title III, to the great disappointment of crowdfunding advocates, as we will discuss later.

When I talked with Congressional staff members, I made two things clear. First, the maximum amount that could be raised had to be increased substantially. Second, blue sky state law review of Reg A offerings had to be preempted. Without both of these changes, I argued, Congress should not even bother with Reg A reform. With them, a revolution of successful small-cap public offerings could ensue.

Reading between the lines, it appeared that Congress was hoping Title IV would help eliminate the controversial reverse merger backdoor listings. They also realized that the duplicative levels of both state and federal review remained a significant barrier to small-company capital formation. They further seemed to understand the prior IPO underwriting culture that saved initial offering shares for special and favored customers of investment banks, leaving out the average investor. (Well, maybe I am giving Congress too much credit—who knows?)

States Were Not Pleased

I believe Congress also knew this was not going to go over well with the individual states, even with the then-anticipated large bipartisan support of the JOBS Act. The North American Securities Administrators Association (NASAA, another unfortunate acronym sometimes causing it to be mistaken for the space agency) is a lobbying and advocacy group that represents all the states' securities regulators.

It did take quite an effort for the Congress to pass the JOBS Act, with its state review preemption in Title IV, over their very strenuous objections. NASAA's lobby is usually a pretty powerful one. Congress, however, was hearing from many different quarters that the state review of filings was a significant impediment to capital formation, which leads to job creation.

NASAA argued that it could implement a "coordinated review" process with filings in multiple states. They would appoint a single state regulator to represent a group of states and companies would deal with just one review. They could never ensure, however, that every state would participate, and many of those that tried to be part of the early efforts with this were, shall we say, disappointed.

When the SEC finally wrote their JOBS Act Title IV rules, making clear that Tier 2 deals would not require state review, they acknowledged the states' desire to seek to streamline their review process. The SEC's response in the final full release was, essentially, we appreciate the effort but there is no real proof that it can work. If you come back to us later to show us otherwise, they said, we would be happy to revisit the question.

As we will discuss in Chapter 4, this did not go over well. The state securities regulators already had been beaten down dramatically by NSMIA back in 1996, preempting public offerings on national exchanges. Very popular Reg D Rule 506 deals also are preempted from state review, though states require notice filings and take fees for each filing.

In May 2015, as we will discuss, the States of Massachusetts and Montana brought a lawsuit in response to the new Reg A rules implemented by the SEC and that broadly applied the state preemption in Title IV. In the case, the states tried to argue the SEC exceeded their statutory authority and were acting in an arbitrary and capricious manner in creating the rules, and that the rules should be declared invalid.

Spoiler alert: The case, filed in the D.C. Circuit Court of Appeals, was dismissed, but it took until July 2016 for that to happen. More on this later. Fun fact about losing plaintiff Massachusetts: Back in 1980 when Steve Jobs took Apple Computer public, Massachusetts deemed the IPO "too risky" for their residents and barred the IPO from being offered there. Radio Shack had more sales of personal computers at that point, so Massachusetts was concerned.

As Congress contemplated all these issues, a big bet they made was on how the SEC would actually write the rules to implement the Act. As we will cover later, the SEC was given very broad discretion in Title IV to write the rules mostly as they saw fit. If the SEC did not truly support Reg A+, they could write rules to make it unattractive for companies to utilize. Or, they could do what they did, which we will cover in the next chapter.

Other Key Elements of the JOBS Act

It is useful to provide a brief summary of other important aspects of the JOBS Act. Title IV actually got very little attention in the press coverage of the new law, which focused more on the changes in the rules governing IPOs of "emerging growth companies" and Title III crowdfunding.

Title I: The IPO "On-Ramp" and Emerging Growth Companies

Title I is indeed significant. It created a new category of issuers called "emerging growth companies" (EGCs). To qualify, you cannot already have completed an SEC registration of shares. Most already public companies therefore were not able to utilize the benefits of being an EGC. An EGC was defined as a company with less than $1 billion in gross revenues (due to inflation this was raised in 2017 to $1,070,000,000). You stay an EGC until the earlier of five years from your IPO or when you hit the limit in revenues, among a few other conditions.

I was rather stunned that Congress went this high. A billion-dollar company is *emerging?* I guess in the world of Walmart with $485 billion in revenues that makes sense. Still, most practitioners would have been thrilled if they went up to $250 million. This new definition, therefore, garnered attention from even the biggest players.

There are a number of good things about being an EGC under Title I when conducting an IPO. First, you can disclose only two years of audited financial statements. Companies that are not "smaller reporting companies" (SRCs), typically with a market value up to $75 million, otherwise have to provide three years. Second, as mentioned earlier, you are exempt from the SOX rule that an outside auditor has to attest to the adequacy of your financial controls (SRCs are exempt from this as well).

EGCs, in Title I, also were provided the opportunity to test the waters in a limited way in their IPO with institutional investors. As we know, in Reg A+ that capability is expanded to test the waters with anyone. Previously, however, the "quiet period" rules prevented this in traditional IPOs.

For the first time, Title I permits EGCs to confidentially submit their IPO registration and go through multiple rounds of SEC review before having to come out of "stealth mode," as it has come to be known. They must come out of stealth at least 15 days before the company's first roadshow. Remember, these are new rules for traditional IPOs; the Reg A+ rules are a little different as we will see.

JOBS Act Title I also allows broker-dealers to issue research reports about an IPO by an EGC, even if the broker is participating in the underwriting. This was not previously permitted, and is still prohibited with non-EGCs. In another meaningful development, as alluded to earlier, an investment bank working on an EGC's IPO can have their banker arrange meetings with their analyst, and the analyst now is permitted to attend roadshow meetings. This Chinese wall was deemed important to maintain the analyst's independence, but also was an impediment to marketing deals.

There were a handful of other goodies provided to EGCs, most of which are already available to SRCs, such as an exemption from the "say on pay" rules about compensation. Overall I believe Title I did help and is helping ease the burden on smaller companies' efforts to go public, in particular the confidential filing capability.

The combined features of Title I are known as the IPO "on-ramp" because they allow companies to work their way up to fuller large-company disclosure obligations. The concept actually came from an October 2011 U.S. Treasury Department report called "Rebuilding the IPO On-Ramp." It suggested using scaled regulation and its recommendations are replicated almost exactly in Title I.

Title II: Advertising in Private Offerings Under Regulation D 506(c)

One of my first reactions in reading the JOBS Act was to tell friends that I thought the big sleeper provision that would ultimately have a big impact would be Title II. As we have discussed, Reg D already is a very popular exemption used to raise money in a private transaction. The problem with Reg D Rule 506, however, was the fact that advertising and general solicitation were prohibited. The rule also required a preexisting substantive relationship between the investor and the company or its investment banking firm, which helped the company develop a reasonable belief that that investor was accredited.

In a world where virtually every single human is connected to the World Wide Web, it seemed anachronistic to continue to prohibit online and other general solicitation in private offerings. Congress also was concerned, however, about protecting less sophisticated investors in publicly marketed private offerings under Reg D.

If advertising is permitted, the challenge would be how to deal with the preexisting relationship issue. The Congress crafted a new rule, Rule 506(c), and codified it in Title II of the JOBS Act. It permits advertising and general solicitation in Rule 506 deals so long as you limit the offering to only accredited investors. Remember, in prior 506 deals, now known as Rule 506(b) deals, you could have up to 35 unaccredited investors if certain information was provided to them. In 506(c), if you want to advertise, it is accrediteds only.

Rule 506(c) requires "reasonable steps" to verify an investor's accredited status. The SEC mostly leaves the method of achieving this to a company. Their rules adopted under Title III provide some guidance, saying that an attorney, accountant, or broker-dealer can issue a letter confirming accredited status. This is the method almost all those using 506(c) thus far have used, but the SEC has encouraged practitioners to look for other legitimate "principles based" approaches to taking reasonable steps.

Remember, individuals are accredited based on either income or net worth. Income is pretty easy to verify; just show me your tax returns and I can issue a letter based on that. Showing that someone's net worth, not excluding their primary residence, is above $1 million is more tricky. The SEC guidance says it is sufficient to use a brokerage or bank statement on the asset side, and a traditional credit check on the liability side. To button it up, you then get a letter from the investor saying they have no debt other than what is on the credit report. Then you can issue a letter based on that.

With this, you can take out an ad in a newspaper, run radio or TV ads, and take out Facebook and Google ads and the like to promote a private offering. Website portals have been established as a place where multiple deals can be promoted and investors vetted.

Reg D 506(c) has not caught on in any substantial way as of this writing. Most believe that investors simply do not want to go through the hassle of arranging for a third party to verify their status. Services have developed to get a group of investors' letters done, but that has not yet brought a large number of dealmakers to this technique.

As a technical matter, the SEC treats 506(c) offerings as "public offerings." In this book, however, we are focusing on Reg A+ and other alternatives to a traditional public offering where trading commences as well, which is not the case with 506(c).

Title III: "Statutory" Crowdfunding

There already are and certainly will be more books on JOBS Act Title III, the only part of the law actually called crowdfunding. Many believe Titles II and IV also are forms of crowdfunding. In fact I was pleased to contribute a chapter to *Crowdfunding*, published in 2014 by my publisher, John Wiley & Sons.

I will not delve into a detailed discussion of Title III other than to say it allows an unlimited number of accredited and non-accredited investors in a private deal to raise up to $1 million (raised in 2017 to $1,070,000 due to inflation). The House-approved version had capped the amount at $2 million. The only things the Senate changed in the JOBS Act from the House version were in Title III, including lowering the maximum to $1 million. This was very disappointing for the crowdfunding advocates. Some dubbed the crowdfunding folks "the cool kids" at the Conferences leading up to final adoption of the SEC rules under Title III.

The law and rules under Title III require detailed disclosure and in many cases audited financial statements for these small deals. Services have developed to help early-stage companies "build their own disclosure" and incur minimal legal fees. As an advocate for startups, for whom Title III primarily was intended, I hope processes will develop that make statutory crowdfunding popular.

Title V: Flexibility to Remain Private

Prior to the JOBS Act, any company with more than 500 shareholders and $10 million in assets was required to become a full SEC reporting company and "go public." The JOBS Act changed the shareholder numbers to 2,000 shareholders or over 500 unaccredited investors.

Many companies that wanted to stay private or wait to go public until they achieved certain milestones had been frustrated by the prior holder limit. They usually hit the number because of stock issued to employees and insiders as compensation. Title V, therefore, also doesn't count toward the 2,000 number any employees receiving stock as compensation under certain plans. This is part of why we now see more so-called "unicorns," private companies with over $1 billion in value, remaining private longer.

Reg A+ Title IV Language

Now we can turn back to the main topic of this book. Title IV of the JOBS Act is called "Small Company Capital Formation." It has several sections but actually is a rather concise part of the JOBS Act. As noted, the bill mostly authorizes and directs the SEC to implement changes. It did not specify any time period for them to get that done, even though other provisions of the Act came with time limits for the SEC to act.

In the past, prior laws authorizing changes in Regulation A had taken up to 10 years for the SEC to implement. We were a bit worried about that when this bill was passed with no time limit for Reg A. As we will cover in the next chapter, however, the rules were finalized and implemented in June 2015, a little over three years after the signing of the JOBS Act—not ideal, but not bad overall.

Basic Provisions

Here is what Title IV provides. Section 401 amends the Securities Act to give the SEC the authority to exempt from SEC registration under Regulation A public offerings of freely tradeable "unrestricted" securities in an amount up to $50 million in a 12-month period. The SEC can permit issuers to "solicit interest" (now known as testing the waters under the ultimate SEC rules) before filing an offering statement with the SEC, on such terms as the SEC thinks appropriate.

Section 401 also makes clear that the SEC can require audited financial statements be filed with the Reg A offering statement. As noted, this was optional before the JOBS Act. The section then gives the SEC broad authority to require issuers to prepare and seek approval of an offering statement with various disclosures as it determines. The SEC also was authorized to disqualify "bad actors" from using Reg A, and to require such post-offering periodic and current reporting about the issuer's operations and financial condition as the SEC determines.

I am particularly fond of Section 401 for another reason. Congress gave the SEC authority, in their discretion, to increase the maximum that can be raised in Reg A offerings to an amount above $50 million. They went even further in the Act as well. The language is worth quoting:

> Not later than 2 years after the date of enactment . . . and every 2 years thereafter, the Commission shall review the offering amount limitation . . . and shall increase such amount as the Commission determines appropriate. If the Commission determines not to increase such amount, it shall report to the Committee on Financial Services of the House of Representatives and the Committee on Banking, Housing, and Urban Affairs of the Senate on its reasons for not increasing the amount.

This means the SEC has to look at increasing the maximum every two years and provide reasons to Congress if they do not increase. In 2014, two years after implementation of the JOBS Act, they submitted a report saying they had not yet even implemented rules under Title IV; therefore, it was not logical to consider increasing the amount. SEC staffers have not, as of this writing, clarified what, if any, report was issued in 2016. We do know, of course, that they did not increase the amount in 2016. I believe the staff feels it is just too early to tell if increasing the amount is appropriate.

If a number of larger Reg A+ deals getting close to the $50 million limit are successfully completed, I believe there will be pressure on the SEC to increase the amount. Does this matter? If Reg A+ provides a speedier, cheaper, simpler IPO where the crowd can participate and the SEC is reviewing disclosure, why not expand it to larger amounts? More and more companies might consider going public if larger amounts could be raised.

(As we will see, several companies, particularly in the real estate industry, already have completed $50 million Reg A+ public offerings. The Financial CHOICE Act, passed by the House of Representatives on party lines, would mandate an increase in the Reg A+ limit to $75 million.)

Covered Securities and "Qualified Purchaser"

Section 401 of Title IV also includes a provision making clear that Reg A securities will, under certain circumstances, be deemed covered securities under NSMIA, that key provision meaning the offering is preempted from state blue sky review. The state preemption is triggered only if the securities are offered or sold on a national securities exchange (such as Nasdaq or the New York Stock Exchange), or if they are offered and sold to "qualified purchasers."

Some Reg A deals, therefore, if not sold on an exchange or to qualified purchasers, would not have the benefit of blue sky preemption, one of the key selling points of new Reg A+. The definition of *qualified purchaser*, therefore, would seem to be rather important for IPOs planning to trade on the over-the-counter markets.

It may have been a good idea for Congress to make clear who should be qualified, but frankly I am not sure they would have had a clear enough understanding of how to make the determination. In the end, therefore, it probably was intelligent that Section 401 says that the definition of qualified purchaser will be "determined by the Commission."

To be honest, when I first read this language in the final bill I was somewhat disappointed. When one looks at the definition of qualified purchaser used in other contexts in securities regulation, it did not look good. In the Investment Company Act, a qualified purchaser is well above accredited status. In another context, in a proposed SEC rule never finalized, qualified purchaser was to be defined the same as an accredited investor.

Did this mean new Reg A+ deals, to have their blue sky preemption on over-the-counter public offerings, would have to be limited to accredited investors or an even higher standard? I was hoping that maybe, given all the disclosure being provided in these deals, the SEC might adopt a *light* accredited investor standard. I thought they might, for example, say that a qualified purchaser is someone with $100,000 income or $500,000 net worth instead of the $200,000 income and $1 million net worth current accredited standard.

Practitioners were somewhat concerned, but when the JOBS Act was signed, many of us in the trenches were very busy taking in all the other dramatic changes in the bill that are described above. Reg A just was not the focus of initial attention. *Second spoiler alert:* Because of the various investor protections in the final SEC rules, the definition of qualified purchaser was declared by the SEC in the final rules to be *any* investor in a Reg A+ (i.e., Tier 2) offering. Keep that in mind as we analyze the Massachusetts/Montana lawsuit in the next chapter.

Study on the Impact of State Blue Sky Laws

Title IV did include one provision with a deadline. Section 402 of Title IV required the U.S. Government Accountability Office (GAO) to conduct a study on the impact of blue sky laws on Reg A offerings. The report was required to be issued within three months after the JOBS Act's implementation. Why do a study *after* passing the law? It appears to have been intended to help create a guide to the SEC as they fashioned new rules under Title IV.

Right on time, the 30-page GAO study was released and delivered to applicable Congressional committees in July 2012. The GAO actually went a bit further than the limited mandate of the JOBS Act. The report is entitled "Factors That May Affect Trends in Regulation A Offerings," and did not limit itself just to the blue sky question.

The report starts by noting that the number of qualified Reg A offerings had dropped from 57 in 1997 to just one in 2011. So clearly there was a problem. As to the reasons, the GAO essentially admitted it could only do so much to determine the causes given the three-month deadline. They spoke to some securities attorneys (your humble author was not one of them nor have I heard from any of my fellow securities attorneys saying they were contacted), NASAA, and some small business advocates to make their observations.

It did seem there was strong belief that the burden, cost, and delay of state review was a real problem. The report also suggested that Reg D seemed to be a more attractive alternative than a Reg A offering for many. The GAO further noted that it was unclear if increasing the amount that can be raised above $5 million would make a significant difference in the attractiveness of Reg A.

It does not appear that the GAO study did much to change anyone's opinion on the causes of the decline in the use of Reg A, especially given its limited research and short time frame.

And so . . .

Just about every American kid, every Saturday morning from 1973 to 1985 (i.e., pretty much before cable TV), between their favorite cartoon shows, watched a fun series of animated educational musical shorts called *Schoolhouse Rock!*. Each short included a catchy tune designed painlessly to teach children about basic math, science, and history. Kids used the tunes to memorize the preamble to the Constitution, their times tables, and grammar. There was even an off-Broadway show designed for nostalgic Gen Xers that premiered in 1993, called *Schoolhouse Rock Live!*. It was based on the more well-known songs like "Conjunction Junction," "Unpack Your Adjectives," and "Interplanet Janet."

Whenever I think of the process that led to the JOBS Act's passage, representing one of my first first-hand experiences in the lawmaking process, I think of the great *Schoolhouse Rock!* song "I'm Just a Bill." The song covers how a federal law develops. I was hoping to include some of the lyrics but my publisher informs me that might be some sort of copyright violation.

The JOBS Act actually happened quickly. I made the Reg A+ suggestion in November 2010. The bill was introduced, by combining a series of other bills that had been floating around, about a year later and passed with overwhelming support about four months after that. What we learned: When elections are coming, legislation can move pretty fast. Of course, as mentioned earlier, it took another three-plus years to get the rules implemented. Now, however, we are here.

The Conference is worth our effort to attend and congeal a set of cogent and practical recommendations. It is good that the regulators and legislators do indeed look at the results of those efforts as they consider how to improve the regulatory environment for smaller companies.

The final JOBS Act has good stuff. As I blogged on the law's fifth anniversary in April 2017,

> From the new IPO on-ramp for emerging growth companies, confidential filings, new Regulation D 506(c) allowing publicly marketed private offerings, Title III crowdfunding getting going, and Title IV Regulation A+ already responsible for nearly $300 million in new capital raised and just getting started, JOBS is truly achieving its purpose. To make capital easier to access, while protecting investors, and letting companies grow and create valuable new jobs.

Now we turn to the meat of how the SEC brilliantly implemented Title IV and how deals actually are getting done.

CHAPTER 4

The SEC's Rules Under Title IV Regulation A+; Court Challenge

It took a little more than a year and a half. Commentators had spent some time wondering what rules would be proposed by the SEC under Title IV, though frankly the blogosphere was much more active speculating about Title III crowdfunding and digesting the new IPO on-ramp. Would Reg A+ really have legs? Would the SEC instead propose a draconian set of rules that would be unattractive to issuers?

Thankfully, for most dealmakers the wait was worth it. On December 18, 2013, the SEC offered up a holiday present to the small- and microcap world in the form of its proposal to implement Title IV of the JOBS Act. As with all new rule proposals, it had to be presented to the public and open to comment before the SEC could implement final rules.

Lovingly known as Release No. 33-9497, not too many were planning to make the proposed rules their Christmas reading material. That is because the proposing release was a mere 384 pages! The brainchild of many on the SEC staff, my understanding is that the super-talented Karen Weidemann was the primary driver of the innovative and disruptive approach to small-cap regulation represented by this audacious proposal. Karen, an attorney who was with the SEC Office of Small Business Policy, moved on to a position with the Public Company Accounting Oversight Board and did not have the chance to help oversee the final birth of her proposal when the permanent rules were approved in March 2015.

We did all read it, eventually. The reaction of most: To paraphrase the Good Book, it was good. In fact my own initial reaction was, "Wow." Then when I read the proposal again I realized there were some thoughts for improving it that, in some cases, did make it into the final rules (more about that later). Most importantly, however, it was immediately clear that the SEC wanted to set up its Regulation A+ rules to be attractive to companies without sacrificing investor protection. I think it is important to understand the process by which the proposal developed into the final rules, so let us first review the proposal, then the final rules, and cover what was improved between them.

SEC's Reg A+ Rule Proposal

The main topics covered in the proposed and final rules are eligibility, the offering statement, ongoing reporting, and testing the waters. We also will cover a few other topics addressed, including "bad actor" disqualification. I always laugh when I print these long SEC releases because the printout includes the many pages of the release devoted to how the release complies with the Paperwork Reduction Act. Let us review the main topics and a few spoiler alerts.

Eligibility

As previously mentioned, the proposal and final rules create two tiers of Reg A offerings. In the proposal, Tier 1 was limited to $5 million and Tier 2 was limited to any amount, above or below $5 million, up to $50 million. *Spoiler:* The final rules increased the Tier 1 limit to $20 million.

The proposal also allowed "selling security-holders" to publicly resell their equity in an amount up to 15 percent of the applicable limit (i.e., $1.5 million in the proposal for Tier 1 and $15 million for Tier 2). This resale capability also is permitted in registered public offerings. So-called private investment in public equity (PIPE) transactions, which are private placements combined with an immediate SEC filing of a "resale" registration statement to make the shares freely tradeable, presumably would benefit from this capability. *Spoiler alert:* The final rules, in addition to raising the Tier 1 limit to $20 million, allow up to $6 million sold by selling security-holders in Tier 1.

The proposal further limited what any investor can invest in a Tier 2 offering to no more than 10 percent of the greater of their net worth or income. *Spoiler:* This was changed to apply only to non-accredited investors in the final rules, so there is no limit on what accredited investors can invest. The idea of this provision was to ensure that no one investor would take on too much risk.

It is interesting to wonder why the SEC did not include this limitation in its definition of *qualified purchaser* in the rules as against simply adding it as a requirement for the Reg A exemption. Their failure to do so was part of the basis of the state lawsuit that we will discuss. Further clarification: The 10 percent limit on non-accredited investors does not apply to Tier 2 public offerings seeking to list on national exchanges.

The Offering Statement

Electronic Filings

Before 2012, believe it or not, Reg A was one of the last paper-only filings with the SEC. The JOBS Act Reg A proposal, therefore, modernized that and required electronic filing of the offering statement on the SEC's EDGAR (Electronic Data Gathering and Retrieval) system. Since 1996, the SEC has permitted or required electronic filings. Prior to that time, everything was filed on paper.

Your author is sadly ancient enough to remember that "before" time. If you wanted to get your hands on someone's SEC filing, you sent a researcher to stand at the copy machine at the SEC's reference room in Washington and copy it. Trying to learn about how different companies in an industry handled their disclosure required further research and further copying.

This sometimes took days and was fairly expensive. If you were making a filing, it either went the night before by overnight mail or courier, or someone would get on a train or plane to D.C. to file the paper on time.

The arrival of EDGAR and electronic filing was rather miraculous for us securities practitioners. We now have until 5:30 on the day of filing to "push the button" and file electronically. Not that we like last-minute filings, but it gives issuers a little more time to get them ready. Much more importantly, with the click of a mouse we now have instant access in a searchable database to *every SEC filing*. That was, and is, truly amazing and taken too much for granted these days.

EDGAR's arrival also created a cottage industry of service providers who assist you in completing the filings. That is needed because the regulations passed by the SEC to implement EDGAR are huge, and there are detailed requirements as to formatting, presentation of tables, and the like. Large law firms initially tried to provide the service to clients for a fee, and found that they lost money trying. Thus the financial printing firms, and ultimately standalone EDGAR providers, filled the niche. Nowadays the service is somewhat commoditized, with flat fee arrangements for filings and annual service available, especially for smaller issuers.

Confidential Submissions

Another important part of the Reg A proposal, to jibe with the IPO on-ramp provisions for registered public offerings, permitted non-public confidential submission of offering statements for SEC review. It permits you to remain in stealth mode for as long as you like, but you must come out of stealth no later than 21 calendar days before SEC qualification (remember that means final approval of your disclosure).

As discussed earlier, many companies are taking advantage of confidential submissions both in registered offerings and in Reg A deals. They want to make sure the SEC is not going to give their company or their offering a particularly hard time. Others are still unsure if they want to go ahead with an IPO, and can decide to pull the deal with no one being the wiser. Yet others worry about the IPO window opening and closing and might pull a deal if the IPO market slows, again without any public disclosure of their financial and other information.

There are a few things to discuss about this. First, tying public disclosure to qualification in Reg A is different from the Title I requirement, in a registered public offering, to come out of stealth 15 days before your first *roadshow*. For those unaware, a roadshow is a series of presentations to analysts, fund managers, and investors who might be interested in the IPO. In particular in IPOs utilizing underwriting firms to raise money, these presentations, often in different cities (hence "road"), are common. The JOBS Act actually pegged this at 21 days before the first roadshow for registered offerings, but a later statute shortened it to require emergence from stealth at least 15 days before the first roadshow.

Twitter's was one of the first IPOs to utilize confidential submission in its IPO. In September 2013, the company announced, appropriately in a tweet, "We've confidentially submitted an S-1 to the SEC for a planned public offering." It seemed ironic to *announce* a *confidential* filing. It allowed the buzz to begin, however, about a possible deal without their having initially to disclose their financial information. Twitter qualified as an emerging growth company under Title I because its revenues at the time were under $1 billion. In 2016, Twitter's revenues were $2.53 billion.

There has been a small amount of pushback from some analysts and investors about confidential submissions, at least in registered IPOs. Critics feel it is important to have a good amount of time before an IPO to study the company's information and disclosure well before roadshows begin. In any event, we are not sure why the SEC decided to fix the Reg A public disclosure to qualification instead of roadshow. It is possible they believed that there was a much lower likelihood of roadshows taking place in Reg A deals since they would be smaller by definition. Unfortunately, the statute that reduced the time period for registered offerings to 15 days did not do the same for Reg A offerings, which, as we recall, operates as an exemption from registration.

There is a second problem with tying public disclosure to qualification: *Companies do not control when qualification is.* How do you determine when you are 21 days before the SEC will give their final approval to your offering? You cannot. As we will discuss, the SEC reviews of Reg A offering statements have been extremely limited. The SEC has reported that as of early 2017 these filings were averaging just 74 days with the SEC before qualification.

Our experience with this has been to take as much of an educated guess as possible. Our general approach has been to ask the client this question: When would you *want* to be qualified? If the answer is within a likely realm of possibility of achieving qualification, we tie disclosure to that. Worst case is we come out of stealth less than 21 days before the SEC is ready to qualify, and the qualification date has to be delayed until the 21st day.

The reality is that if you are planning a broad testing-the-waters campaign before qualification to build indications of interest, you should have some time out of stealth before qualification to do so. Most companies with this plan start their public filings as soon as it is clear that the SEC's initial comments are light. Some wait until a filing with year-end numbers is to be included if the timing permits.

SEC Must Formally Qualify

Speaking of qualification, the proposal made another change to Reg A. Previously, a Reg A offering statement became automatically qualified if the SEC provided no comments within 20 days. The proposal eliminated the automatic qualification and required that the SEC formally qualify every Reg A offering. Not that big of a deal for companies, but the SEC could add that to the list of additional investor protections in the new Reg A rules.

Audited Financials and Aging

As permitted in the JOBS Act, the proposal mandated two years of audited financial statements in every Tier 2 offering statement. A full SEC reporting company's audit must be completed pursuant to standards of the Public Company Accounting Oversight Board (PCAOB, also referred to as "peekaboo"). The Reg A proposal eased this slightly for companies not seeking to become full reporting.

These companies may conduct an audit in accordance with either the auditing standards of the American Institute of Certified Public Accountants (AICPA) (referred to as U.S. Generally Accepted Auditing Standards or GAAS) or PCAOB standards. Reporting companies' auditors also have to be registered with the PCAOB. That is not required for Reg A issuers planning to trade over-the-counter and not seeking to become full reporting.

In addition, in a significant gift to companies, Reg A issuers can become qualified and close their public offering with financial information that can be *as much as nine months old.*

In registered offerings, financial information goes stale in 135 days (i.e., 4.5 months). This means, for example, your September quarterly information in a registered offering goes stale in mid-February, thus requiring your year-end audit to be done by then if December is your fiscal year-end.

Confirming a brief reference in the final rules, in late 2017 the SEC clarified in interpretive guidance that (1) any company, even those seeking a national exchange listing, may rely on the right to include more aged financial statements and (2) those companies do not instantly become in violation of securities law for not having current financial information immediately following completion of their public offering. A company planning to become full reporting and trade on a national exchange is given 45 days following their closing to file any quarterly filing on Form 10-Q that would have been otherwise due and 90 days to file any annual filing on Form 10-K.

As an example, a company completed their Reg A+ IPO onto Nasdaq in late August 2017 with no financial information from 2017 included. Under the new SEC guidance, that company then had 45 days to submit their Forms 10-Q for the first two quarters of 2017. In a registered offering, that same company would have had to include those first two quarters of information in its IPO prospectus.

Level of Disclosure

The proposal also eliminated the old Q&A approach to providing disclosure as previously discussed. Narrative disclosure is now required in Reg A. The proposal permitted disclosure to be the same as the first part of a registration statement for a registered offering, on Form S-1. A company also had the right, however, to scale its disclosure a bit, though frankly not in a significant way.

Spoiler: In the final rules, if you want to be a full SEC reporting company, you have to do essentially full S-1 level disclosure. That is required for any company seeking to list its stock on a national exchange such as Nasdaq or NYSE. If you seek to list on the over-the-counter markets, the reduced disclosure, which we will review, is an option.

Post-Offering Disclosure: The Dawn of Light Reporting

The development in the Title IV rules of what we are now calling the "light reporting" option for Reg A issuers planning for their stock to trade in the over-the-counter markets is indeed bold. Implementing something like this would not really have been conceivable even 10 years ago under former SEC leadership, which was very leery of small public companies.

First, with respect to post-offering disclosure, the SEC treated Tier 1 offerings much like old Reg A. Namely, Tier 1 issuers have no ongoing periodic reporting obligations following their offering. As you may recall, however, Tier 1 offerings do not have the benefit of the state blue sky preemption, making them less attractive in most situations. For smaller offerings, however, especially if they are limited to a few states, where there is a desire to minimize post-offering compliance costs, a Tier 1 offering can make sense.

In the proposal with respect to Tier 2, however, the SEC does require post-offering reporting. They proposed, however, the right to meaningfully reduce a company's reporting obligations post-IPO. If you choose light reporting, you file a semiannual and annual report, a limited amount of important interim developments between reports, and that is it. The names and timing of filing of these new forms are listed in what follows. This is as opposed to the quarterly filings and other filing obligations required if you are a full SEC reporting company.

A light reporting company also is not subject to the proxy rules. If you choose to hold a shareholders' meeting, a simple one-page notice to shareholders of the meeting under state law is sufficient, as opposed to the detailed proxy statements, reviewed by the SEC, that are required for full reporting companies.

Light reporting companies also are exempt from Securities Exchange Act Section 16. That requires officers, directors, and 10 percent owners of full reporting companies to report their initial ownership of stock, and then any changes in those holdings within two business days. The rule also includes the "short swing profit" restriction. That prohibits these insiders from buying and then selling, or selling and then buying the stock within six months and earning a profit. If they do, the profit is disgorged back to the company.

I was somewhat surprised by this exemption. To offer these companies the ability to allow their insiders to hide their ownership except for a once-a-year disclosure on their annual report, and to trade in and out of the stock as well, seems to create some risk of fraud and insider trading. It is possible they thought, in comparison to non-reporting companies, this is still better since the twice-a-year reports provide more information than companies that do not report at all.

The proposal also permits a company to leave the light reporting system at the end of the fiscal year in which their offering is qualified by filing an "exit report," as long as the Reg A offering has ended and the company has fewer than 300 shareholders "of record." The concept might be a bit misleading, because the term *of record* does *not* include investors holding stock in what is known as "street name," in other words, people who hold stock electronically as opposed to holding an actual stock certificate. The SEC has maintained this somewhat archaic method of counting for a number of rules despite the advent of electronic trading, and they continue to use it for this purpose.

Therefore, to exit light reporting you just need 300 holders who have an actual physical stock certificate. In addition to those investors, each broker-dealer who acts as custodian for shares held by shareholders owning their shares in street name counts as one additional holder. If you have, therefore, 200 stock certificates issued and 25 brokerage firms that hold shares in your company for 10,000 of their customers electronically, your company has 225 holders of record.

Here is a good place to learn the names of some of the new forms:

- *Form 1-Z*—the exit report to leave the light reporting system. This form is also used by Tier 1 issuers to report how many shares they sold within 30 days of completing their Reg A offering.
- *Form 1-K*—the new annual report to be filed by Tier 2 light reporting issuers within 120 days of the end of the fiscal year (full SEC reporting companies file an annual report on Form 10-K with in 60 or 90 days depending on market value).
- *Form 1-SA*—the new semiannual report to be filed by Tier 2 light reporting issuers within 90 days after the end of the first six months of the fiscal year (full SEC reporting companies file three quarterly reports on Form 10-Q within 45 or 30 days depending on market value).
- *Form 1-U*—the new current report to be filed upon certain events between periodic reports by Tier 2 light reporting issuers, within four business days of the occurrence of the event.

The proposal did not create a path for a Reg A issuer to become a full SEC reporting company, however. It simply provided that a company can file what is known as Form 10 following the offering to become full reporting. This is a burdensome form that can take some time to get through the SEC. It would have effectively prohibited Reg A issued stock from trading immediately on a national exchange, because they all require full SEC reporting status.

In its proposals, the SEC often includes questions for people considering making comments to consider. One such question they put in the proposal was whether they should include a simpler path to full reporting in the final rule. *Spoiler:* The final rule says that if your offering statement includes Form S-1 level disclosure, you can file a much simpler Form 8-A to become full reporting immediately upon qualification. This has opened up the current trend for Reg A+ issuers, especially in IPOs involving underwriters, to seek to trade directly onto national exchanges.

To clarify for those less in the know: How and why does one become a reporting company? In general, if a company undertakes a registered public offering, it can choose to be a permanent reporting company by filing a simple Form 8-A with the SEC within a year of going public. Otherwise the more burdensome Form 10 generally is necessary to do so. Once you are full reporting, you are subject to quarterly and annual reporting, insider ownership reporting, and trading restrictions, and the proxy rules apply as do others. It is a requirement for exchange listing and formerly was a requirement of the OTC platforms.

After a registered offering, if you don't become a full reporting company with Form 8-A, you are subject to periodic reporting obligations for one year and then no further reporting is required. Thus it was important to have a path for Reg A issuers to easily become full reporting if exchange listings were to be possible.

Another issue with light reporting related to the over-the-counter markets, the only place a light reporting company would be able to trade its stock. OTC Markets owns three key trading platforms: OTC Pink, OTCQB, and OTCQX, as mentioned earlier. On Pink, a company can be non-reporting but still have its stock trade. Previously, U.S. companies on QB and QX had to be full SEC reporting companies. To their credit, OTC Markets changed their listing standards and now allow light reporting companies to trade their stock on QB and QX following Reg A+ offerings. However, in order to trade their stock on the QB or QX, those companies must file a report for the two quarters that otherwise would not be required to be filed under light reporting.

Testing the Waters

The JOBS Act says the SEC can allow a company to test the waters with investors before filing the offering statement. This was the rule under old Reg A as well. The SEC proposal offered another gift, and expanded this to allow testing the waters both before *and after* filing the offering statement. They proposed a set of rules to implement this and to protect investors. The proposed rules required that disclaimers be placed on promotional materials and that all the materials be required to be filed with the SEC as exhibits to the offering statement.

Testing the waters with any investor is one of the principal distinguishing features of Reg A IPOs versus a registered public offering on a traditional Form S-1 IPO. With an S-1, JOBS Act Title I rules permit testing the waters only with institutions. With Reg A, you can gauge investor interest with anyone.

What exactly is testing the waters? It permits you to contact anyone in any manner to determine if they have interest in the offering. It can be to determine if it is worthwhile to go forward with the offering, to adjust the pricing based on potential investor responses, or to precondition the market for the offering. You cannot accept money or a binding subscription from an investor at that time.

As we will cover later, there are some things still unclear about what exactly constitutes testing-the-waters materials that require the disclaimer and filing. The ability to engage in this process, however, has led to a cottage industry of marketing firms and crowdfunding sites seeking to help create social and traditional media campaigns to develop investor interest. As we will also discuss, a new era of hybrid offerings combining testing the waters–based crowdfunding with traditional underwriting is creating an exciting fundraising opportunity for many companies.

Bad Actor Disqualification

As expected, the SEC proposal excluded bad actors from participating in Reg A offerings if they have some affiliation or involvement with the company or the offering. The proposal relied primarily on the standard that the SEC had previously set for Reg D offerings. In general you are limited to being called "bad" if you dealt with a securities-related legal issue. Anything more than 10 years old generally is excluded unless there is a continuing restriction on your activities. Investors in Reg A deals that have no other affiliation with the company can be bad actors so long as they do not own at least 20 percent of the company's stock.

Blue Sky Preemption and Qualified Purchaser Definition

As we have mentioned, the proposal offered the full state blue sky preemption to all Tier 2 offerings in sales to qualified purchasers. The proposal indicated that, because of all the new investor protections in the proposed to be updated Reg A, all Tier 2 investors will be deemed to be qualified purchasers. Given our previously noted concern that the SEC might have required some level of income or net worth, this was a huge relief for practitioners. Remember that we still have the requirement that non-accredited investors cannot invest more than 10 percent of their net worth or income in over-the-counter Tier 2 offerings, but again, that is not part of the qualified purchaser definition.

One side note at this point is important. The SEC indicated that states can require a notice filing by Reg A+ issuers who offer stock in their state even if it is otherwise preempted as a Tier 2 deal. Most states require notice filings in Reg D offerings, for example, which are also state registration preempted. Even though the states cannot review the filing, they can require issuers to let the state know that they are making an offering in their state and to file their offering statement with them. Most states, however, charge relatively low fees for Reg D notice filings, usually a few hundred dollars.

Many states have decided, unfortunately, to impose extremely high filing fees for Reg A+ issuers seeking to sell stock in their state (they cannot require this from companies whose stock will trade on a national exchange following the Reg A+ offering). They are using the same fee scale they use to file offerings that are going to be fully reviewed and registered in their state. Some states, as a result, are charging thousands of dollars for these notice filings. If an underwriter seeking to raise money in a Reg A+ deal wants to offer the stock in all 50 states, the notice filing fees alone could be rather significant.

It is understandable for state filing fees in a fully reviewed and registered offering to be higher. The fees have to support the overhead of examiners and others who review, process, and approve the offering. There really is no reason for such high fees when all that is happening is a bunch of paper is placed in a file. We will talk more about this later.

Access Equals Delivery

The printing companies are not too happy with the SEC these days. That is because in most public offerings there is no need to deliver a printed copy of a prospectus, or in the case of Reg A, an offering circular, to investors. The Reg A proposal (and final rule) allows an issuer or underwriter to give an investor a notice directing them to where they can find the offering circular online within two business days after the sale.

Comment Process

The SEC accepted comments to the proposal officially through March 24, 2014. Your author was quite involved in the comment process. I was active on the American Bar Association committee developing their formal comments. I also submitted my own lengthy comment letter from my then–law firm in January 2014. I am pleased to say the SEC listened: My comment letter was cited 30 times in the final SEC release, though a few times it was to say they disagreed with what I was suggesting.

Anyone can go on the SEC website (www.sec.gov) and submit comments to proposed rules. The SEC staff truly appreciates input from practitioners and companies affected by their proposals. It is not unusual for some proposed rules to receive zero comments. The SEC, however, received around 100 comment letters to the Reg A proposal. Comments came from Congresspeople, Senators, trade associations, NASAA, and a number of individual states, public companies, attorneys, crowdfunding advocates, major accounting firms, think tanks, you name it. The point is that many important people were very interested in this new set of rules.

Comments formed a wide range. There was, however, a heavy focus on issues relating to becoming full reporting, the 10 percent income or net-worth limitation, and the small $5 million limit on Tier 1 offerings. Now let us review how it all turned out in the end.

Final Reg A+ Rules

The SEC released the long-awaited final rules in March 2015, and they became effective June 19, 2015. It took a full year from the end of the comment period to finish and update the rules. As a practical matter, the SEC informally acknowledges that it continues to review comments that are submitted after the comment period ends. Roughly 30 comments were received after the deadline in March 2014. This provided additional input and may have been part of the reason it took a year to complete the final rules.

The final rules, as noted in the spoilers above, responded to a number of issues raised in the comments. As a result, Reg A+ became even more attractive than as proposed. There remain, as we will cover in Chapter 7, a number of further improvements that have been suggested, including a formal petition filed by OTC Markets (which my current law firm formally supported) with respect to some of these issues.

That said, the final rules created an exciting, attractive, and workable option for smaller companies seeking to go public. Here are the important changes made in the final rules:

- *Increase in Tier 1 Offering Size.* As noted, the SEC decided to increase the amount that can be raised in a Reg A Tier 1 deal to $20 million. If a company is willing to go through full state blue sky review, they can take advantage of the option to have no reporting obligations after their transaction and to avoid preparing audited financial statements.

  There was a feeling among some who work on smaller deals that leaving Tier 1 at the same level as old Reg A would not really effect the type of reform they believe Congress was seeking in Title IV of the JOBS Act. As noted earlier, the SEC also increased the amount that can be included from selling security-holders in the Reg A Tier 1 offering to $6 million. In Tier 2, you can include up to $15 million from selling security-holders. In both cases those amounts go toward the total cap in the applicable tier.

- *Path to Full Reporting.* Exchange-listed Reg A+ IPOs became possible because of a change in the final rules allowing a path to full SEC reporting status. The final rules permit a simple Form 8-A to be filed upon completion of the Reg A+ IPO. The SEC was comfortable doing this because they added a requirement that an issuer has to make Form S-1 (Part I) level disclosure in its offering statement to qualify to use Form 8-A. A real estate investment trust (REIT) can do the same using SEC Form S-11 level disclosure.

  Another unique requirement: The Form 8-A has to be filed within four days after SEC qualification of the offering. As previously noted, in traditional Form S-1 IPOs, a Form 8-A can be filed up to a year later. Since Form 8-A incorporates information by reference from the Offering Statement, the SEC felt that it was important that the 8-A be filed at the same time as the qualification of the Offering Statement so that the information being incorporated is current. The rules do permit a company to become qualified, get ready for a closing, and then file a post-qualification amendment, which then leads the SEC to "requalify" the offering, and file an 8-A at that time.

  Interestingly, in the Paperwork Reduction Act section of the final rules, the SEC predicted that only 2 percent of Reg A issuers will use Form 8-A. If there are 100 Reg A deals per year, let's say, they are suggesting only two will seek a national exchange listing or otherwise want to be full reporting. As we will discuss further, the current trend, thanks to these changes in the final rules, appears to be proving the SEC wrong.

  As a result, active practitioners now advise issuers and Wall Street that there is now no reason *not to* use Reg A+ for any IPO under $50 million. You can go right to a national exchange with much quicker and easier SEC review and full testing-the-waters capability. Why ever use S-1 for smaller IPOs?

- *No Limit on Accredited Investors.* In response to comments, the SEC retained the limit on non-accredited investors to invest no more than 10 percent of the greater of their income or net worth, but made a change from the proposal to exclude accredited investors from that limit. Commenters (such as your author) argued that accredited investors may choose to invest in Reg D deals with no disclosure being provided. In a Reg A+ IPO, these more sophisticated investors must receive comprehensive disclosure and audited financial statements that are reviewed by the SEC before delivery to investors.

The SEC acknowledged in the release on the final rules that accredited investors are "capable of protecting themselves" in exempt offerings such as Reg A+ and therefore removed the limit. In the case of individual non-accredited investors subject to the limit, the calculation of income or net worth is made in the same manner as a determination of accredited status for purposes of Reg D. The main thing to remember in this definition is to exclude the value and mortgage on your primary residence to determine net worth.

Importantly, the SEC also made clear that there would be no 10 percent investment limit for any investor if the Reg A+ offering will lead to an immediate listing on a national exchange. They felt the listing standards of the exchanges and greater likely liquidity were sufficient protections. Thus, in Reg A+ deals headed to an exchange, any investor can invest any amount.

The other worry that practitioners had was how the investors with limits would certify their compliance with the limit. This fear was allayed as the final rules permit the investors to "self-certify" both as to their accredited status and as to their not exceeding the limit if they are not accredited.

There was another issue with the proposal and this limit. The SEC had proposed the 10 percent limit using standards that apply only to individual investors. How do you determine 10 percent of income or net worth of an entity that invests? Some, for example, may have no income, but might have substantial revenue. And what definition of income would apply? Net income? Earnings before interest and taxes? This was not clear.

This issue was resolved in the final rules. A non-accredited investor that is not an individual cannot exceed 10 percent of the greater of the investor's revenue or net assets (as of the purchaser's most recent fiscal year end). This seems like a good deal of red tape, but these new confirmations have been built into subscription agreement forms that issuers have been using. It is not a big deal to ask an investor to confirm her compliance with the limit if it applies in an over-the-counter public offering. As we will see, this limit is a major reason the state lawsuit seeking to invalidate the rules was unsuccessful.

- *Rule 15c2-11 Information.* An apparent oversight in the proposal related to permitting broker-dealers to make markets in post-Reg A offering stocks. In general, these "market makers" cannot make trades in stocks unless they review certain information about the issuer. The light reporting obligations might not have been deemed sufficient. Thankfully, the SEC addressed this in the final rules after comments were received. The SEC made clear that an "issuer's ongoing reports filed under Tier 2 will satisfy the specified information about an issuer and its security that a broker-dealer must review before publishing a quotation for a security (or submitting a quotation for publication) in a quotation medium."

One related issue was among the relatively few disappointments in the final rules. Shares of stock become publicly tradeable if they are registered with the SEC or some exemption from registration applies. Reg A is one of those exemptions and there are others. One of these is SEC Rule 144. If stock is issued in a private offering, Rule 144 allows public resale in most cases starting six months following issuance. However, one requirement of the availability of this exemption in many cases is that there is "adequate current public information" about the company available.

If a company chooses to become a full SEC reporting company, such as if it will trade on a national exchange, this is not an issue and Rule 144 is fully available. But if a company completes a Reg A+ IPO and trades over-the-counter, is satisfying the light reporting obligations sufficient for adequate current public information? This question was raised in a number of comments to the proposal.

Unfortunately, the SEC answered in the negative in the final rules. They argued that quarterly reporting is an essential element to the availability of Rule 144. They did offer helpful suggestions, however. First, they indicated that a company would have Rule 144 available during the six months of the year that their information would be current. They further suggested that a company could choose voluntarily to submit quarterly reports on Form 1-SA for the first and third quarters, and if they did so, the company would have full availability of Rule 144.

This is important because companies completing Reg A+ offerings and using light reporting may wish to continue to raise money. They may want to do so using a Reg D private placement. Investors in those offerings wish to understand when and how their stock would become tradeable under Rule 144. If that rule would not be available, those investors might either not invest, or choose to demand that the company spend quite a bit of money to register the shares to be publicly resold, or file a further Reg A "resale" offering statement.

As a practical matter, however, this is unlikely to be a major issue for several reasons. First, any company trading on a national exchange will be a full reporting company and Rule 144 will be available. In addition, a company entering light reporting on either OTCQX or OTCQB will be required, by the rules of those trading platforms, to file Forms 1-SA for the missing quarters. Rule 144, therefore, will be available for those companies as well. The only affected companies, therefore, will be those in light reporting and choosing to trade on OTC Pink.

States' Failed Lawsuit Against the SEC

Just when we thought it would be safe to finally move ahead with Reg A+ deals, a problem arose. On May 22, 2015, less than a month before the effectiveness of the new rules, two states, Massachusetts and Montana, each filed separate lawsuits against the SEC, seeking to invalidate the new rules. The cases, brought in the Circuit Court of Appeals in Washington, D.C., were consolidated a week later into one case.

The states' arguments were, essentially, that the SEC went further than Congress intended or permitted them when they said every investor in a Tier 2 offering is a qualified purchaser. They also said the rules were "arbitrary and capricious." This is the primary standard used to attack alleged excesses of administrative agencies. They also tried to argue that the SEC somehow was not actually given the right to preempt state blue sky review of Reg A offerings by the JOBS Act.

The uncertainty of this lawsuit was a significant issue in the newly approved Reg A+ world. Should companies proceed with transactions? What if the rules are invalidated in the middle of a deal? What would happen then? What if a Reg A+ deal is approved and closed and stock is trading and the rules are later invalidated? Would the transaction be rescinded or voided? These were fair and legitimate questions being asked by actual and potential clients.

My advice to clients at the time was to move forward cautiously. If the rules are invalidated mid-transaction, we can refile as a traditional Form S-1 IPO. I also did not believe any resolution of the case would invalidate deals completed while the case was pending. Upon filing the case, the states had sought an immediate temporary order stopping the implementation of the rules during the case, but the court denied it. It seemed, therefore, unlikely that completed deals would be affected if an invalidation order was issued. I did, of course, have to advise clients that anything was possible.

We were hopeful that the case could be resolved quickly given the urgency of the situation and the fact that it was being commenced at the appellate level. Sure enough, NASAA filed a "friend of the court" brief supporting the whole thing. Did they arrange these individual filings and coordinate with the states? That is not clear.

In November 2015 the SEC finally responded to the merits of the claims in a court filing. They said that they have meaningfully increased both disclosure and reporting obligations of Reg A issuers, and imposed an investment limit on non-accredited investors in blue sky exempt Tier 2 offerings. They further reminded the court that the costly and burdensome state reviews were one of the main reasons no one used Reg A before 2012.

In July 2016, the Court dismissed the entire case. The 23-page, very well-written, clear and concise opinion started with a brief history of securities law, how it started with the states but moved to add federal oversight after the 1929 market crash. Offerings exempt from full SEC registration for smaller companies have been around for a long time, and Reg A actually was first adopted in 1936. In 1996, as we discussed earlier, with NSMIA Congress preempted state oversight of offerings involving "covered securities," at first essentially those to trade on national exchanges such as Nasdaq or the NYSE. The JOBS Act in 2012 expanded covered securities to include those issued in Reg A+ offerings to "qualified purchasers," a term the Act said was to be defined by the SEC. The SEC said everyone is qualified because of additional investor protections in the new rules.

To succeed in their challenge, the states would have had to prove (1) that the JOBS Act "unambiguously foreclosed" the opportunity for the SEC to write the rules the way they did or (2) that the rules were "arbitrary and capricious" and serving no valid economic purpose. As mentioned, the states actually tried to argue that the JOBS Act was not clear in preempting state review of Reg A+ offerings.

The Court clearly and strongly disagreed and made clear it was Congress, not the SEC, preempting the states. They also stated firmly that the SEC was given very broad power in the JOBS Act to write the definition of qualified purchaser almost entirely as they wished, regardless of prior proposals on other matters and even regardless of the plain meaning of the words. And it also noted that they added further protections such as the limit on investments by non-accredited investors and the enhanced disclosure and reporting obligations, as well as clearly demonstrating the economic benefits of the new rules. So, said the Court, they were not foreclosed by the law to act as they did and they did not act in an arbitrary or capricious fashion.

And so . . .

As a practical matter, the Reg A+ revolution really did not begin until this court ruling in July 2016. That said, a number of Reg A+ deals did close while the case was pending. Many players, however, in being briefed on the new rules as well as the lawsuit, chose to wait until it was clear that the legal challenge was over. Beginning in June 2017, the first Reg A+ deals to trade on national exchanges, starting with my client Myomo Inc., were completed.

We now had a very attractive new set of rules, a multitude of choices as to how best to utilize Reg A depending on a company's situation, and yes, some experience for practitioners to gain as they work their way through the new regime. Securities professionals, however, are used to change. The regulatory environment is an ever-evolving mosaic of laws, rules, interpretations, and so-called "no-action" letters. Anyone experienced in the field knows that it is essential to keep up on new developments.

Reg A+ remains relatively new. For a company seeking a national exchange listing and a full SEC reporting status, however, there is not that much that is different from a traditional IPO, and only improvements on the cost, timing, and hassle. For a company seeking an over-the-counter listing and either a Tier 1 no-reporting option or a Tier 2 light reporting option, some new learning is required. Upon completing that education, however, smaller companies have a significantly attractive new arrow in the quiver of financing options. Let us hope this tome provides a useful introduction to that education, starting with the next chapter outlining the preparation of an offering statement and conducting a testing-the-waters campaign.

CHAPTER 5

Offering Statement and Light Reporting Preparation; Testing the Waters

Now you are ready. The JOBS Act and SEC rules are written and finalized and the state lawsuit was dismissed. To get the job done, however, you have to understand the new rules and how they work.

For those who are not as excited about learning all the nuances of the new rules, there is good news. If your company is planning to be a full reporting company following the IPO and not planning on utilizing light reporting, you already know most of what you need to do if you have experience working with traditional IPOs and public companies.

That is because the only way to become full reporting upon your Reg A+ IPO is to include full Form S-1 level disclosure in your Offering Statement. If you have worked on S-1s, just follow the same rules you always have. Once you are public and fully reporting, you operate the same as all other companies that choose full reporting either because it is a requirement of an exchange or by choice to please analysts or other investors. Thus, for Reg A+ issuers planning exchange listings, your transaction and post-IPO reporting can work nearly identically to a traditional IPO. The one exception, as previously noted, is that the age of a company's financial statements can be more than with a traditional S-1. As long as the financials are no more than nine months old, the Reg A+ offering, even to a national exchange, can proceed.

So why bother using the new regime at all in that circumstance? There remain meaningful advantages to using Reg A+ for an exchange-listed IPO as against a traditional IPO as have been discussed. The SEC review is much more limited. Testing the waters can be as broad as you desire, whereas Form S-1 issuers are limited to testing the waters with institutions. And again, the financials can be less current.

There is a fourth benefit to a Reg A+ issuer seeking an exchange listing over a traditional IPO that has not yet been covered. As we know, one of the main advances of Reg A+ was the state blue sky preemption for Tier 2 deals. That benefit, however, only really helps companies seeking to trade in the over-the-counter markets since NSMIA already preempted blue sky review for exchange-listed companies.

There are occasions, however, where underwriters work with a company to seek an exchange listing but are not certain they will meet all the listing requirements in the end. Often this is the result of raising less money in the IPO than anticipated. There also are times when those in the listing departments of the exchanges believe a company's listing will be approved, and encourage a company to go down the road toward a listing, but the regulatory team upstairs disapproves the company later on. This may happen, for example, if a company is impressive but relatively new.

In the end, exchanges have wide latitude as to which companies to accept, even those that meet their quantitative listing standards. What happens if the exchange rejects your company after going through SEC review and other IPO readiness activities?

Before the JOBS Act, the answer would be that the IPO would get canceled. That was mainly because any attempt to "downlist" the IPO to the over-the-counter markets would require commencement of state blue sky review of the deal, which would take too long at that point. Now, since the OTC Reg A+ IPOs are blue sky preempted, a downlist is possible as long as you make simple (albeit expensive) notice filings with the states. This is a major advantage and one that underwriters are building into their plans for deals.

Let us also take a moment and examine why limited SEC review of Reg A Offering Statements as against Form S-1 review is so important, because it saves not only time but money. We certainly know the amount of time you will spend from the date of filing until SEC qualification is much less than in traditional IPOs. The SEC in early 2017 announced, as previously indicated, that Reg A deals are averaging 74 days at the SEC. Since less attorney and auditor time is spent dealing with multiple rounds of SEC comments, those professionals can and should charge less.

There is another time and money saver, and that is in the preparation of the Offering Statement before it is filed. If you seek to become full reporting and have to include full S-1 level disclosure, why should preparation be faster and cheaper? Lawyers preparing IPO filings generally focus on two sets of priorities. The first, which of course is critical, is ensuring that they have conducted full due diligence on the company and that the disclosures about the company's business, risk factors, capitalization, and the like are thorough, accurate, factually verified, readable in plain English format, not misleading, and including all required and otherwise material information.

The second priority, also very important in traditional S-1 filings, is working at length to anticipate, and hopefully preempt, what are often over 100 comments in the initial SEC review. Many comments tend to be relating to minor issues, and often there are quite a number of financial comments. The lawyers and auditors, therefore, tend to take a great deal of time looking at each and every sentence in the document to avoid as many of these small comments as possible.

Remember you already know the document is thorough, accurate, readable, and not misleading. With Reg A+, knowing your SEC review will be limited means you spend much less time focusing on the dozens of potential small SEC comments that tend to come in an S-1 filing. So far, in addition, the financial comments in Reg A+ filings have been few if any.

An analogous example is Reg D private placements. If unaccredited investors are included, or the company simply chooses to make full disclosure, a document known as a "private placement memorandum" (PPM) is prepared. The intent (and requirement if unaccredited investors are included in a Rule 506(b) transaction) is to include all the same information as would be in a Form S-1, but excluding any information that is not material.

While attorneys are very careful in preparing PPMs, the time and cost to do so is typically much less than preparing a full S-1 registration statement. So a Reg A+ Offering Statement is seen by some as essentially an enhanced PPM.

There is nothing, however, in the JOBS Act or SEC rules that requires the SEC staff to continue these limited reviews. The agency's leadership has made the decision to jump-start what they hope will be a Reg A+ boom with a swifter and more efficient process of review. This could change, for example, if a number of Reg A+ issuers turn out to include bad actors or involve fraud, or if a change in staff or commissioner-level leadership leads to greater review.

Offering Statement Preparation

Tier 2 Companies Planning Full Reporting

There is no need to review in depth the typical contents of a Form S-1, which has been around for decades and has been the go-to public offering form for thousands of companies. Thanks to EDGAR, anyone can go to www.sec.gov and view many good examples of registration statements on Form S-1.

That said, for the uninitiated, Form S-1 requires disclosure of risk factors, use of proceeds, determination of offering price, dilution, selling security-holders (if any), plan of distribution, description of securities, and interest of named experts and counsel. Then there is a full business description, including summary of the business, properties, and legal proceedings.

Financial statements follow along with the narrative "management's discussion and analysis" (often called "MD&A") section comparing financial results on a period-to-period basis. Then comes information about directors and officers, executive compensation, a chart of key security-holders, and related-party transactions.

Therefore, a company planning to become a full reporting company, which must disclose all that would be in Part I of Form S-1, does not need much further education, except to remember that the age of your financial statements can be as much as nine months old at the time the SEC qualifies your company.

Tier 2 Companies Planning Light Reporting

In addition to the concept of light reporting, the scaled narrative disclosure possible for companies not planning to become full SEC reporting companies is another brilliant balancing of investor protection and managing transaction costs to make Reg A+ public offerings more attractive.

The Offering Circular requirements for companies not planning S-1 level disclosure reduces the disclosure obligations somewhat. To start, executive compensation information is only required for the last fiscal year, instead of the last three years as required by Form S-1.

The requirements also eliminate certain politically motivated disclosure rules such as the controversial "conflict minerals" disclosure requiring information about the company's connection to "blood diamonds" from certain countries. The rules also eased disclosure regarding research and development, adopting a materiality threshold for information about time-and-dollar expenditures on R&D.

Recall, in addition, that while audited financial statements are required, they need not come from a PCAOB-registered auditing firm or be compliant with PCAOB rules as long as they comply with generally accepted auditing standards. This is not permitted with the S-1 format for companies intending to be full reporting and can help reduce costs.

In a related disclosure gift, the MD&A section of the Offering Circular, discussing details of the financial statements, can exclude a discussion of off-balance-sheet arrangements or a table of contractual obligations. The requirement to disclose off-balance-sheet information resulted from the 1990s Enron debacle, in which that company avoided extensive financial disclosure about its operations by moving assets and obligations off its balance sheet.

One other annoying part of the S-1 was eliminated in the Offering Circular rules for light reporting companies. The dreaded "dilution table," a full-page chart showing dilution caused by the offering based on net tangible book value per share of the issuer's securities, is not required. To be honest, I would be for eliminating this chart in all public offerings, as I see little benefit to investors, many of whom cannot understand the often confusing information.

Another medium hassle companies have been required to undertake upon going public through an S-1 was the creation (and disclosure) of a code of ethics and corporate governance principles. While these are somewhat standardized now, the Reg A Offering Circular rules do not require this disclosure. This offers companies the option to decide whether these additional documents, and cost to create them, are necessary.

In sum, the SEC staff took a scalpel rather than a hatchet to the S-1 disclosure regime, taking just enough away noticeably to reduce the overall level of disclosure for companies that are not planning to be full reporting. At the same time, viewed in the aggregate, the eliminated or altered items do not significantly alter the mix of material information to investors.

Tier 1 Issuers

Tier 1 issuers benefit from all the scaled disclosure rules in Offering Circulars under Tier 2 light reporting noted earlier. In addition, as previously mentioned, Tier 1 issuers can file unaudited financial statements as was the case with old Reg A. The SEC offered other scaled disclosure in Tier 1 offerings, including executive compensation information only in group versus individual format. This allows Tier 1 companies to avoid disclosing the specific compensation of their individual senior executives.

The SEC also relaxed disclosure of related-party transactions in Tier 1 deals. This relates to information a company must disclose about transactions with its officers, directors, major shareholders, and people and entities associated with them. In Tier 2 deals, the same rule now applies as to all smaller reporting companies, namely disclosure is required of transactions between the company and related parties exceeding the lesser of $120,000 or 1 percent of the average total assets at year-end for the last two completed fiscal years. Tier 1 retains the old Reg A rule requiring disclosure only of such transactions in excess of $50,000 in the prior two years, avoiding the potential lower threshold based on 1 percent of assets.

Issues Applicable to All

It is important to remember that an Offering Statement is *not* a registration statement, and as previously discussed, operates as an exemption from registration. Investors in many private companies, for example, may have traditional "registration rights," requiring a company to include its shares to be publicly resold in the filing for any registered IPO by the company.

Those registration rights would *not* apply to a Reg A+ offering unless the registration rights included the right to be included in a Reg A+ Offering Statement expressly. Investors in private companies would be wise to ensure going forward that any registration rights they are provided in their investment include rights to be included in a Reg A+ Offering Statement.

In addition, as we know, the old pre-JOBS Act Q&A format for Offering Statement disclosure was eliminated in the SEC rules, so only narrative disclosure is possible either by complying with S-1 for full reporting or the Offering Circular rules for light or non-reporting companies.

Another of the obligations in a Reg A Offering Statement is to include as exhibits all testing-the-waters materials. As we will discuss ahead, all information provided to people about the offering prior to qualification needs a disclaimer and must be filed with the SEC. Even transcripts of speeches concerning the IPO must be filed.

The confidential filing rules, as previously discussed, are a little different than in a registered offering. Remember that you must come out of stealth mode at least 21 days before SEC qualification. As with an S-1, the confidential submission is just that, a submission, and is not considered "filed" with the SEC.

Any exhibits included in a confidential submission, therefore, have to be refiled in the first "public" filing out of stealth. As a general rule, therefore, we tend not to file exhibits with the confidential submission unless we think they may be important enough for the SEC to potentially review and have an issue with. Testing-the-waters materials, for example, tend to get filed for the first time in a massive exhibit to the first public filing.

One practice tip is to make sure when you come out of stealth that all prior submissions are made publicly available as well, which is required. If this does not happen, the 21-day clock before qualification is possible does not start. This is handled with your EDGAR filer.

When is your first periodic filing due after the IPO? The SEC in the fall of 2016 clarified in interpretive guidance that an important rule that applies to companies going through registered IPOs also applies to Reg A deals. That rule, as applied to Reg A, allows you, if a quarterly or semiannual filing is due within 45 days after qualification, to make that filing up to 45 days after qualification. That same rule, unfortunately, does not apply to an annual report filing. The belief is that if you are that close to needing to file an annual report with an audit, it probably should have been included in the IPO filing.

As noted above, the SEC also has clarified that a company moving to full reporting status whose financial statements in its Reg A+ offering were more than 4.5 months old must become more current under Exchange Act rules following the offering. A missing quarterly report can be filed within 45 days after closing and a missing annual report can be filed within 90 days.

The SEC also confirmed in the Reg A rules that an important interpretation from 2007 regarding registered offerings also applies in Reg A. That interpretation allows a company to raise money in a private placement while going through SEC review of the IPO filing under certain circumstances. In the Reg A context, the key is that you can raise money in a private offering so long as you do not entice investors with the Offering Statement and the potential investor did not learn about the company through the Offering Statement.

This is a very important feature of today's IPOs. Not long ago it was nearly impossible to be able to raise money privately while an IPO was pending. With this 2007 interpretation, a company need not wait until its private placement ends to start the public offering filing and review process, which helps create an overall speedier process.

One other unique feature of Reg A Offering Statements is Part I. In this initial section, through a check-the-box and fill-in-the-blank format, the basics of the offering, company size and capitalization, bad actor information, a list of states in which the offering will be made, and costs and identification of professionals and the like are disclosed. This allows easier comparison on a deal-by-deal basis. It also includes information not normally disclosed in registered offerings. For example, the total legal fees in the transaction are included in Part I of the Offering Statement. Part I is completed online and filed as part of the Offering Statement.

The second part of the Offering Statement is the "Offering Circular." That is the same as the prospectus in a registered offering. This is the document that must be delivered to, or made accessible to, every purchaser in the IPO. It includes all the disclosure described previously.

Light Reporting Preparation

Remember light reporting applies only to Tier 2 companies that choose not to become full SEC reporting companies. Tier 1 issuers have no post-offering disclosure or reporting obligations, and their stock can trade on OTC Pink, as with old Reg A. The tradeoff as noted earlier is that Tier 1 IPOs must go through full state blue sky review and approval.

One assumes that Tier 2 companies seeking to trade in the over-the-counter markets likely will choose light reporting. As noted earlier, the "higher" tier OTC markets, OTCQX and OTCQB, amended their rules to accept light reporting companies. They also, however, require reporting for all four quarters, which has the benefit of eliminating the concern about Rule 144 availability as previously mentioned.

One also would expect that issuers and their counsel preparing these filings will use most of the same procedures as are used in full SEC reporting companies. For example, when we prepare annual filings for public companies, we ask the board members and officers to prepare updated questionnaires confirming their personal information and any activities relating to the company and its stock, as well as confirming no "bad actor" issues.

Remembering the new forms, we have Form 1-K, the new annual report, and Form 1-SA, which is the new semiannual report that also may be used to prepare filings for the first and third quarters. There is also new Form 1-U to report certain events occurring between filings. Let us review to what extent these forms differ from the typical Forms 10-K, 10-Q, and 8-K for full SEC reporting companies.

Form 1-K

New Form 1-K, the annual report, has two parts. Part I is "Notification," and Part II is "Information to Be Included in the Report." Part I is much like Part I of the IPO Offering Statement and is a form filled out online with basic information about the company. In the first 1-K following completion of the IPO, Part I will include detailed information about the offering, including how much was raised and at what price, what offering costs were, and the like.

The SEC believes that capturing key data in Part I of the Offering Statement and Form 1-K will enable it to analyze trends in Regulation A, easily compile reports about the number of completed offerings and how successful they were, and learn what types of companies are utilizing Reg A+.

One side note is that the SEC considered requiring Tier 2 companies to file a report at the time of completion of the offering to disclose information about the completed transaction and how much money was raised. They decided instead to allow the information to be delayed until the first Form 1-K filed by the company. This means the SEC will only really have detailed updated information about Reg A+ offering completions and amounts about once a year, assuming most companies operate on a December 31 fiscal year.

Part II of Form 1-K requires disclosure about the company and its business. In general the rules cross-reference to the disclosure rules in Offering Circulars, so there will be a similar regime in Forms 1-K as in Tier 2 IPOs utilizing the Offering Circular rules. In fact the SEC noted in their release that they believe companies will be able to use their Offering Circular disclosure as the basis for preparing their Form 1-K. If information was previously filed with the SEC, it can be incorporated by reference into the Form 1-K.

Topics covered in the Form 1-K include business operations, related-party transactions, beneficial ownership of officers, directors, and 10 percent stockholders (note this is 5% for full reporting companies), identities of directors, officers, and key employees, the last year of executive compensation information, and a full management's discussion section regarding financial comparisons for the last two years.

The financial statement requirements for the Form 1-K also mirror the Offering Circular rules. The report must include a two-year audit, but it can be pursuant to PCAOB or generally accepted auditing standards, and the auditor need not be PCAOB registered.

As previously noted, the Form 1-K must be filed within 120 days of the end of the company's fiscal year. Considering that reporting companies must file their annual report within 60 or 90 days, this extra time is a useful benefit indeed. The release also makes clear the filing can be amended if necessary, similar to SEC reports for full reporting companies.

Form 1-SA

It is interesting to wonder about how the new Reg A+ form names developed. I am assuming all the "1" labels on these forms were intended to track the Form 1-A, but that is just an educated guess. One also assumes that *SA* stands for "semiannual." The *K* in Form 1-K is likely meant to channel Form 10-K, the annual report for full SEC reporting companies.

Form 1-SA is filed within 90 days after the end of the first six months of a company's fiscal year and covers that six-month period. It is a filing generally limited to financial statements and management's discussion about them. It eliminates a number of items found in quarterly reports by full reporting companies on Form 10-Q. Form 1-SA does not, for example, require disclosure about quantitative and qualitative market risk, controls and procedures, updates to risk factors, or defaults on senior securities.

In addition, quarterly financial statements filed by full reporting companies must be reviewed by their auditors, even though the information is not audited. Form 1-SA provides that the semiannual financial statements do *not* need to be reviewed by their auditors. It also provides that financial statements can be supplied in condensed form. These can be real cost savings for a light reporting company.

The first Form 1-SA filing is not required until the year after the year for which full financial statements were included in the IPO Offering Statement. As previously noted, the SEC has clarified that if that filing would be due within 45 days of IPO qualification, the filing can be delayed until up to 45 days after becoming qualified.

Form 1-U

I cannot speak to why the letter U was chosen for this form. Maybe it stands for "update"? This form is used to report any of eight listed events occurring between periodic filings above. It is much more limited than Form 8-K, the current report for full reporting companies, which essentially requires the disclosure of just about every material event a company can experience between quarters.

The Form 1-U focuses on only the most significant developments. Topics include: agreements effecting a fundamental change in the business, bankruptcy or receivership, material modification to the rights of security-holders, changes in the company's auditing firm, non-reliance on previous financial statements, change in control, departure of the principal executive, financial, or accounting officer, and private (unregistered) sales of 10 percent or more of outstanding equity securities. Note that full reporting companies that are smaller reporting companies must report sales of 5 percent or more, and this was changed by the SEC from 5 percent in the proposed Reg A+ rules to 10 percent in the final as a result of comments.

There also was a bit of talk during the comment process and in the final release about what constitutes a "fundamental change" to a company. A new big customer or supplier relationship presumably would not, but a major acquisition might. The SEC sought to clarify that an acquisition only needs to be reported if it would change more than 50 percent of the company's total assets.

As with full reporting companies, the SEC made clear that you do not need to file a Form 1-U if the same information will be in a Form 1-A or Form 1-SA that will be filed within the time frame that a Form 1-U otherwise would be required to be filed (typically four business days).

Form 1-Z

Again, the speculation on form names continues. The assumption is that Z, being the last letter of the alphabet, was used for the form that involves exiting the reporting system. The exit report on Form 1-Z replaces a prior form known as Form 2-A. Tier 1 issuers use this form to report the results of their IPO to be filed no later than 30 days after completing or terminating a Tier 1 public offering.

Tier 2 issuers also will use this form if they wish to exit the light reporting system. This option can be important, because it allows Tier 2 issuers to obtain the benefit of blue sky preemption not available to Tier 1 issuers, but not necessarily be permanently obligated to continue reporting. The rules permit these companies to file Form 1-Z and stop reporting any time after completing reporting for the fiscal year in which the Offering Statement was qualified. The only condition, as discussed previously, is that the company must have fewer than 300 shareholders of record. In addition, the Reg A+ public offering must have fully ended.

Once the filing is made, the company's reporting obligations are "suspended" immediately. The process is similar to the option that SEC reporting companies have to move out of full reporting by filing simple Form 15 if the company has fewer than 300 shareholders of record.

Testing the Waters

As previously noted, the SEC expanded the opportunity to test the waters with any investor to both before and after filing the Offering Statement, so long as solicitation materials have disclaimers and are filed with the SEC. Those materials also are subject to antifraud and civil liability as with any securities offering.

As a practical matter, therefore, it seems advisable to include only information that is contained or expected to be contained in the company's Offering Statement in testing-the-waters (TTW) materials. The TTW material does not need to be filed immediately upon its use. It is filed with the company's confidential submission or the public filing of its Offering Statement. As an exhibit, of course, the material becomes publicly available. This is all the more reason to ensure consistency between the Offering Statement and TTW material.

The SEC considered requiring the pre-filing of TTW material or at least filing contemporaneous with use. They decided, however, that filing as an exhibit to the Offering Statement was sufficient. They also thought it was fair that, if a company conducts a TTW campaign and then decides not to go ahead with an offering, no TTW information would then have to be filed.

Remember that there is no limit on who can be solicited in a TTW campaign. With Form S-1 IPOs, you are limited to *qualified institutional buyers* (QIBs) and institutions. QIBs generally must own and invest and have discretionary control over at least $100 million. This broad access remains a significant benefit to Reg A+ issuers, even those headed to national exchanges.

All TTW material must have particular legends and disclaimers set out in the rules. If material is distributed after the filing becomes publicly available, the legend must indicate either the URL (the SEC's view is this must include an active hyperlink) where the Offering Circular draft can be found, a physical address where it can be obtained, or include the actual preliminary Offering Circular with the material. Most importantly, the disclaimers must make clear that no money can be accepted or subscription effected until the SEC qualifies the offering.

A quick note about post-qualification: In many Reg A+ IPOs, once the Offering Statement is qualified, a company (and its bankers if any are engaged) must go "sell" the offering, and conduct roadshows and the like to encourage subscriptions.

Materials prepared for those events no longer constitute TTW material and do not need TTW disclaimers or to be filed. However, the rules require that written selling materials distributed post-qualification are delivered with an Offering Circular or information about where an individual can access the Offering Circular, again including an active hyperlink (here providing a physical address is not sufficient). Again, it remains important even in that context where materials are not being filed to remain fully consistent with the contents of the Offering Circular.

The SEC also clarified in the rules that ongoing routine communications with customers and suppliers around the time of the Reg A+ offering constituting "factual business communications" generally will not be considered TTW material. The test is based on facts and circumstances, so be sure to get the right professional advice before doing so.

As we will discuss, there are a number of unresolved issues with the new TTW rules. How far does the definition of *solicitation of interest* go in determining what materials constitute

TTW and need legends and filing? How, for example, does one handle press and television interviews prior to qualification? As of this writing these are open issues.

What we do know is that the Reg A+ TTW regime is creating an exciting new world of social media, radio, and television advertising campaigns to promote Reg A+ offerings. Fast-talking announcers read Reg A disclaimers, and a new way to market an IPO has been born. This is a cornerstone of the view of many that Reg A+ is helping to "bring Wall Street to Main Street" and allowing average investors to participate in IPOs previously reserved for the favored customers of investment banking firms (much more about this in the next chapter).

And so . . .

There is more, but the publisher gave me only so much space. The key issues are covered here, however, and any company working with experienced attorneys and auditors who have handled Reg A+ deals already is familiar with these and other issues. For the attorneys who are here (welcome, by the way), consider this your introduction; now do some serious research and read the final rules and interpretations that have come out since.

Just as a CEO should understand how to read financial statements even if not an accountant, she should be educated about the legal framework surrounding Reg A+ deals under the new rules if that is under consideration. These rules and interpretations no doubt will continue to evolve as questions arise under this developing regime and this book may be a bit outdated almost immediately after its publication.

Let us turn now to how things have been doing in the relatively short time since Reg A+ has been live, and then examine some suggestions for improvement before moving on to other alternatives to traditional IPOs that remain active and viable.

CHAPTER 6

Early Experience with Regulation A+; Wall Street Partners with Main Street

In late November 2017, the SEC announced that, through September 30, 2017, 69 Reg A deals have closed under the new rules. These offerings raised a total of $611 million, or $8.8 million per offering. And as we know the stock of seven of those companies is now trading on a national exchange.

It appears thus far that four distinct approaches to the new Reg A have evolved. First is a large group of players in the real estate world using Reg A to raise money from the public with no intention of publicly trading their stock. Second are companies moving on their own, without the assistance of underwriters or selling agents, to file with the SEC and complete an IPO. Many of these are relying on either an existing customer or fan base of the company, or are partnering with existing crowdfunding sites to fill the offering book.

Third are traditional underwriters realizing that Reg A+ can be used to complete an IPO much like in the past but taking advantage of the speedier SEC review. The fourth and last group, potentially the most interesting, are seeking a hybrid between a traditional underwriting and crowdfunding. They combine the brave new world of social and traditional media promotion with "old school" retail and institutional brokers enticing their customers to participate.

We will examine each of these in turn, after which we will turn to a discussion of what industries appear to be or in time will be most attracted to Reg A+ offerings.

Who Is Utilizing Reg A+?

Real Estate Players

As many expected, the new Reg A+ has become very attractive to real estate investors and developers as a way to raise money to acquire and build properties. The efficiency, cost-effectiveness, and state blue sky preemption seem to be keys, not to mention the ability to raise more than the pre–JOBS Act $5 million.

Some of these companies have used Reg A+ to raise a smaller initial round of capital, and then plan a larger offering, whether or not registered, to move to a national exchange. A number of companies reported much lower legal costs, and appreciated the reduced compliance obligations under light reporting, not to mention the option to exit the reporting system if they desire.

We are also seeing some real estate IPOs as "single state" Reg A offerings in Tier 1. This allows the issuers to bring in an unlimited number of accredited and unaccredited investors with no audited financial information and no post-offering SEC reporting obligations. Because Tier 1 offerings are not blue sky exempt, the one state strategy limits that state review.

Interestingly, a number of these companies, following their Reg A+ IPO, do not even seek for their shares to trade. For example, Fundrise, which has created a series of what they call "eREITs," has developed a model to raise money for projects through a particular offering, after which the only exit opportunity for investors is a quarterly redemption option. In other words, an investor can force the company to buy back their shares at the then-current asset value, but no public trading is available.

In December 2016, it appears that two of Fundrise's eREITs each raised the maximum of $50 million under Regulation A+, the first to reach the limit imposed by the JOBS Act. Fundrise says that it believes that offering real estate investment to Main Street investors, where the investment is not locked up for years before disposition, is very attractive to smaller investors. (Disclaimer: my law firm has no involvement with Fundrise nor does it represent them.)

The eREITs appear to be remaining in, as opposed to exiting, the light reporting system. They further have the opportunity, which some of them have taken advantage of, to complete additional Reg A+ offerings within the same entity following their IPO. The rules do limit any Reg A+ issuer to $50 million in any 12-month period, but as soon as that period ends, another $50 million can be raised so long as the company has not theretofore become a full SEC reporting company.

There are several other real estate players, who had previously begun, before the Reg A+ rules were approved, promoting deals online solely to accredited investors. These entrepreneurs have seen the benefit of expanding the universe of potential investors to everyone. One thing they have found important: to have a minimum investment per investor. One player told me he had no minimum investment, and a large number of people would purchase one, two, or three shares at $10 a share. That obviously becomes unwieldy to manage administratively given the small amounts.

It does appear that the eREIT structure will both evolve and increase in popularity. They are completed without underwriters or selling agents and are marketed primarily through crowd-investing sites. Investors appreciate the tax benefits of the REIT structure and, in many cases, the relatively safer option of investing in real estate with a manageable exit opportunity.

IPOs with No Underwriter

For the first two years or so following passage of the SEC's Reg A+ rules, there were really no Reg A+ IPOs completed utilizing traditional Wall Street underwriters or selling agents to assist in raising money. The first deals involving broker-dealers were completed starting in June 2017.

The first early big Reg A+ success was Elio Motors. With no underwriter or selling agent, the pre-revenue company raised about $18 million in its Reg A+ IPO in January 2016. Elio's plan is to build a unique "motorcycle car" with three wheels and two seats, one behind the other. They had tens of thousands who had paid to preorder the car. The company simply emailed them all during its testing-the-waters campaign to develop indications of interest (known as IOIs in the trade).

The company was surprised when over 16,000 of its customers said they were interested in investing. When they finally closed the deal over 6,000 of those actually pushed the "buy now" button and gave the company that $18 million. They clearly have a long way to go before their car is built, but it gave them a big jumpstart. The company chose to trade on the OTCQX and enter the light reporting system where it currently remains. (Disclaimer: my law firm is currently representing Elio but did not represent it during its Reg A+ offering).

The Elio story, however, is illustrative of both the opportunity and challenge that underwriter-less companies face in this brave new world. The reason quite a number of companies that filed Forms 1-A ultimately were unable to raise money often comes back to valuation. Entrepreneurs, understandably, tend to view the value of their business on the high side, some even very unreasonably high. When underwriters are involved they typically bring the company some sober reality as to what it takes to get a public offering sold.

By going it alone, the job of bringing that sober reality is left to attorneys, auditors, and other advisors. Some may work to help bring a company's valuation into line. Others, however, either are not trained in understanding valuation or, frankly, just want their payday for doing the deal even if it does not close.

Underwriters also help instill confidence in investors that a professional has completed due diligence and background checks on the company and its management. Many people do not realize that the SEC does not take on this responsibility. Most law firms, like mine, run background checks on board members and officers in these situations, but frankly not all my competitors do so. The same is true with the auditing firms.

There are also times where the advisors become complicit in bad behavior. As will be discussed later, a one-time very active attorney competitor of mine recently was indicted for creating bogus public companies pretending to be operating businesses so that they could be used for reverse mergers without restrictions that apply when the company has no operations. Again, the SEC does not investigate companies or their management teams when going public; they only review the disclosure to determine if it appears to be accurate.

That said, many smaller companies are not able to attract investment banking firms interested in helping them raise money. Some Reg A+ deals involve raising only a few million dollars, or sometimes even less than that. There generally is not enough financial incentive for underwriters to step up in these situations. Others, like Elio, might attract investment banks but believe they can manage the fundraising process on their own. Clearly in Elio's case that was true.

It seems likely that the go-it-alone strategy will continue for some Reg A+ players. It is most likely to succeed for a company with a strong preexisting customer, fan, or social media base to access. One company I know, for example, makes consumer electronics and does about $60 million in revenue annually. They have a *one-million-customer email list*. They are seriously considering a Reg A+ IPO, limited to an offering to those on the list.

Some companies utilizing this strategy have brought in marketing companies that specialize in rolling out a testing-the-waters campaign. They produce a video, have an active Twitter, Facebook, and Instagram promotion, and in some cases they even run radio and TV ads. That assistance appears to have been important in the Elio Motors success, even though they also had their own crowd to pursue.

It might, in many cases, make sense for these companies to consider hiring some kind of professional financial advisor, even an investment banking firm. The firm would not be there to raise money but to advise on the valuation, structure, how much money should and can be raised, and the like. Most investment banks regularly provide this fee-based work and are happy to do so. They also can offer a "fairness opinion," which is a formal determination that the offering price is fair to investors from a financial point of view. This assistance might help offset the concern the public may have about how the IPO is developed and implemented.

It seems companies that do so, and those that have a preexisting crowd, would be the most likely to succeed in going it alone. One would hope that, over time, the marketing companies and crowdfund sites will develop more strength and help even those companies that are seeking to develop a crowd. This may mean, for example, that companies in industries like biotech, which may benefit from the traditional underwritten IPO approach ahead, may have to wait until the Reg A+ go-it-alone strategy makes sense.

Traditional IPOs Utilizing Reg A+

As we have said a number of times in this tome, there would now appear to be no reason not to use Reg A+ for *any* IPO under $50 million. The speedier SEC process and option to utilize broad testing the waters (even if you choose not to avail yourself of this) are advantages. In addition, as noted, for companies considering a national exchange listing, they enhance the opportunity to downlist the transaction to the over-the-counter markets without worrying about new state blue sky approvals if the exchange ultimately does not approve the listing. This is not possible with a traditional Form S-1, which requires full blue sky state filings and review if an IPO moves down to the over-the-counter markets. Finally, a company has the flexibility to reduce its offering costs by filing older financial information than required with an S-1.

This had led some companies working with traditional underwriting firms to utilize Reg A+. After the IPO they would be just like any other full reporting public company. The only short-term impediment has been the initial reticence of larger institutional investors to embrace the new approach. Traditional retail investors appear to have no issue, however.

Once a number of these more traditional Reg A+ deals with underwriters or selling agents are successfully completed, most believe the institutions will be right there. As mentioned, as of this writing seven Reg A+ IPOs have been completed working with underwriters or selling agents leading to immediate trading on a national securities exchange. All included testing the waters and an element of crowdfunding. We have not yet seen a traditional underwritten IPO where no additional online promotion or testing the waters campaign is employed. This should then bring high-tech, life sciences, and companies from other industries that may not have their own crowd but do have a strong group of underwriters behind them.

Biotech companies, for example, are still embracing reverse mergers in many cases to go public. It is not clear why they continue to do so other than "this is how we've been doing them" or "this is how such-and-such company did it and they were sold for $1 billion a few years later." The reverse merger seasoning rules, which we will discuss in Chapter 9, are challenging, as is the cost of the shell. If you avoid a shell by merging with a public operating business, you take on all its liabilities, known or unknown.

The small-to-middle-market underwriters seem the most likely to become involved in these smaller traditional deals. As they have begun to emerge they are finding lawyers and accountants knowledgeable and experienced in completing these offerings. They are also finding FINRA, which regulates investment banks, on board. The national exchanges are not just willing; they are enthusiastic about the Reg A+ deals that have listed with them.

It may, however, take a little more time to convince their institutional investor bases to jump on the Reg A+ bandwagon, though a few of the most recent deals now have included some institutional money. Those of us active in the space spend a great deal of time educating the Wall Street firms about these benefits. Those investment firms now will need to do the same with the pension funds and others with whom they work.

Hybrid — Wall Street Meets Main Street

As mentioned, possibly the most disruptive potential use of Reg A+ is beginning to play out as this book is being penned. Some innovative underwriting firms are working with emerging companies to combine the traditional underwriting model with a strong crowdfunded element to the deal. Someone probably should give this approach a name, but I will leave that to others (searching the word "hybrid" on www.thesaurus.com provides such helpful suggestions as "mongrel").

This approach might indeed be the clearest path to achieve the purposes of Title IV as Congress intended. One assumes that, when Congress authorized public offerings of up to $50 million, they knew that some private companies with fairly significant valuations would take advantage of Reg A+. They must, therefore, have assumed many of those deals would involve underwriting firms.

At the same time, Congress authorized, and the SEC expanded in their rules, the ability to test the waters with any investor both before and after filing with the SEC. It seemed logical, therefore, for companies and their advisors to pursue offerings combining the two.

The players utilizing this strategy essentially establish a dual track to building interest in and promoting the offering. Working with a crowdfunding site and often a marketing company, the testing-the-waters campaign is rolled out. Remember that all TTW materials need special disclaimers, must be consistent with the planned or actual SEC filing, and have to be filed with the SEC.

Separately, a traditional syndicate of broker-dealers who join a selling group is organized. Management travels around in the usual roadshow routine, meeting with the brokerage firms and their salespeople to educate them about the company and the offering. In some cases these deals are underwritings but in most cases so far the firms seek to complete "best-efforts" offerings.

Let us briefly compare and contrast these two types of offerings. In an underwriting, the underwriters actually purchase the IPO shares from the company at a discount to the planned IPO price. They then immediately resell the shares to the public at the higher price, pocketing the difference. Once the underwriters commit to the purchase they generally must agree to buy all the securities offered.

They also cannot end the deal other than due to certain major issues like a terrorist attack or market calamity of some sort. In reality, these final underwriting agreements typically are not signed until right before the actual closing. By then the syndicate members know with near certainty who will buy the securities from the underwriters once they purchase.

Underwritten deals typically involve one massive closing where all the shares are purchased by the underwriters, repurchased by the public, and cleared for trading, all within about a 24-hour period. There is a carefully orchestrated process among the company, the bankers, the attorneys, transfer agent, auditors, and the stock exchange or trading platform. Just planning the mechanics of these closings takes weeks and includes 8- to 10-page closing checklists that the team regularly updates and checks off.

In a best-efforts deal, by contrast, there is no underwriting. Broker-dealer investment banks act as agents on behalf of the company to find investors and bring them into the deal. For that they are paid a commission at closing. The "selling agents" do not promise to raise any particular amount, only to use their best efforts to do so. While underwritten deals generally are seen as more serious, reliable, and likely to succeed, many IPOs are completed on a best-efforts basis. The process also is similar, with the weeks of planning and detailed checklists.

The national stock exchanges are happy to accept best-efforts deals along with underwritten ones. As long as the company in a best-efforts situation raises at least the amount that will make the exchange comfortable, they do not really care whether the company took more risk in raising the money. In some cases, the IPOs have a minimum that must be raised to close, but others do not have minimums. All the deals have maximum amounts that can be raised.

One potential advantage of a best-efforts deal is the ability to hold multiple closings. Say a company wants to raise $20 million and plans to list on a national exchange. Its offering has a $5 million minimum but the exchange has told them it will not list the stock unless they raise at least $10 million. If the company reaches its $5 million minimum raised, it can close on that amount and start utilizing the funds to grow its business.

In that case, as the offering continues, it would not yet trade on the exchange. Investors would need to understand that a downlisting might be necessary if they raise only $5 million. The company then can continue, and if in a second closing they raise the additional $5 million, they then can start immediate trading on the exchange.

One advantage of an underwritten deal is what is known as an "overallotment option." If you seek to raise $15 million but you would like to raise more if possible, you can build in an option to sell more if there are oversubscriptions. The option is often called a "green shoe" because the Green Shoe Manufacturing Company (now known as Stride Rite) was the first company to use it. Real pros often just call it "the shoe."

Green shoes are not permitted in best-efforts deals, but they are in underwritten ones. There is generally a limit of 15 percent of the total offering size. This option allows underwriters to address unexpectedly high demand without increasing the official size of the deal. This can assist in optics; if the shoe is not exercised but the deal is otherwise "fully subscribed," it is generally considered a success.

Reg A+ rules do permit companies to amend their offering circular to increase the size of the deal up to 20 percent post-qualification. In a best-efforts deal this can provide a method to deal with surprising demand, but is somewhat awkward compared with the simplicity of implementing a previously approved shoe.

In the summer and fall of 2017, the first group of these hybrid deals were closed, and all are trading on national exchanges. The first to close was our firm's client Myomo Inc., which now trades on the NYSE American exchange with the symbol MYO. The trading in the first few months following these deals has been challenging at times, so time will tell how these companies will fare in the longer term.

Early indications regarding these hybrid deals are that players will evolve and improve their techniques in implementing this new approach, especially regarding the crowdfunding piece, which so far has not been a homerun success. The further hope is that smaller investors will become more and more aware of these opportunities and seek out more information. And, as noted above, the institutions have yet to arrive as of this writing.

It appears that the most likely to succeed in the initial years will be those who have a strong fan or customer base and wish to combine that crowdfunding piece with a strong, primarily retail (as opposed to institutional) effort using an underwriter or selling agent. The early efforts to build crowds that previously did not exist for a company have been challenging.

The SEC disclosed some telling information at a recent conference. Without being too specific, in reviewing the public company investing habits of those who are not accredited investors, the numbers were somewhat sobering. They discerned that a very low percentage of those with lower levels of income, say below $100,000, actually invest in public companies, and when they do the amounts are very small. Those just below accredited status, however, with incomes in the mid- to high-$100,000s, have much higher levels of both investment and amounts.

It appears that the opportunity for hybrid players is to target these just-below-accredited-type investors rather than cast a very wide net seeking any and all investors at all income levels. These investors have been left out of most Reg D deals, since those deals almost always are limited to accredited investors.

Attractive Industries

It would be easy to be somewhat disingenuous and say, "Reg A+ is for everyone." It is not. First, as we discussed in Chapter 1, a company needs to determine whether going public is right for it.

Assuming a determination is made that a public trading stock makes sense, the next very important question is which method of going public will be the most effective in that company's situation. As we will see in later chapters, there are situations where a reverse merger, self-filing, or even Rule 504 offering may be attractive. There is no one-size-fits-all approach to going public.

How does a company navigate the maze of these different options? Most ensure bringing on experienced advisors who are knowledgeable about the advantages and challenges of each approach to going public and how they might apply to a particular company's situation.

Questions we typically ask include,

"How quickly does money need to be raised?"
"What is the company's stage of development and expected growth trajectory?"
"How much money do you really need in the short and then intermediate term?"
"Does the company have a strong fan or customer base that can be accessed for investment?"
"Are other public companies in your industry faring well in the stock market?"

As far as Reg A+, it does appear, as noted, that companies that bring their own crowd may fare best, along with those pursuing traditional underwritings with no crowd component. The real estate players additionally appear to have found a workable niche to exploit by offering everyday investors the opportunity to invest in properties.

It seems, therefore, that consumer products companies may be the path of least resistance in these early years of Reg A+ implementation where a crowd component to the offering is desired. Given the investment statistics above, the best might be those whose products cater to the higher end of the middle class, making over $100,000.

In addition, much of the crowdfunding marketing efforts take place online. It might be easier, therefore, for companies whose target market for their products focuses more heavily on younger, more Internet-savvy investors to be successful with a crowdfund piece to their Reg

A+ offering. As the millennials begin to marry and have children, companies selling products like home goods, baby products, and the like may find success. Of course social media and entertainment companies also may benefit from crowdfunding their IPO to millennials.

There also is a strong opportunity, as noted earlier, for traditional underwritten deals to move to Reg A+ where less than $50 million is being raised. Here, there is no concern about the crowd, just the advantage of a much speedier IPO process and the possibility of using more aged financials. Most believe the underwriters and even institutional investors will begin to realize and become comfortable with this over the next few years. This opens up opportunities for whatever industry may find itself to be hot in the IPO market. This could include energy, high-tech, biotech, and social media (which also may access the crowd as noted earlier), just to name a few.

Given the lower cost and faster process in these straight underwritings, the hope is that the investment banks will be interested in doing more small-cap IPOs following their still mysterious death around 2000 as we have covered. With tick sizes hopefully beginning to increase and significantly lower offering costs and delays, some of the issues that plagued the small-cap IPO market may be ameliorated.

And so . . .

It is both an exciting and stressful period for those who are pioneering the first group of Reg A+ deals. No question there is some trial and error taking place, and many who could add to the discussion have chosen to remain on the sidelines until more successful deals are completed.

That said, nearly 70 companies already have raised over $600 million dollars, most without the help of underwriting firms. Getting them trading has taken a while, but their ability to help finance their growth with the help of these new rules has been amply demonstrated.

The eREIT concept also is showing its ability to succeed and allow investors to benefit from seemingly favorable returns along with a reasonable path to exit. Promoters can keep their offering and compliance costs reasonable, which further enhances those returns. Avoiding the uncertainties of the trading markets also could work to their benefit as investors' exits focus only on the value of properties held by the company as opposed to the vagaries of the stock market.

The jury is still somewhat out with respect to the hybrid and straight underwriting approaches. One assumes that both will find their place for the right companies as noted earlier. Let us hope that this market and this book are successful enough to bring you another edition in a few years that reports on how these began to take off right after this book was published.

There are some issues with Reg A deals and the rules that have arisen that, if addressed, might improve the attractiveness of this approach. Let us turn now to review some ideas for enhancing this already well-crafted and increasingly popular public offering method.

CHAPTER 7

Potential Changes to Regulation A

It is important to repeat that JOBS Act Title IV and the new Reg A rules adopted by the SEC were brilliantly crafted and if left alone should not materially impede the success of this new and modern approach to public fundraising. The noticeably reduced offering disclosure in Reg A+ deals headed to light reporting, plus the much more scaled, less frequent, and later filed light reporting obligations have led many smaller, and some not so small, companies to enter the Reg A+ world. The very limited SEC review of these filings and unlimited testing-the-waters capabilities also have been of significant benefit to issuers.

As we have noted, it is clear that, in developing the Reg A rules, the SEC sought to design an approach that would be very attractive to issuers and underwriters while retaining strong investor protections for smaller offerings. The SEC adopted many improvements from their original rule proposal after the comment period, most notably including a path to full reporting that is enabling companies to go right from their Reg A+ offering to trading on a national exchange.

As with anything new, however, both a little hindsight and education by experience are developing useful and practical suggestions for improvement. Some are ideas that were proposed in comments but which the SEC did not adopt initially. Others arose as deals were progressing and either language in the rules could be clearer, or rules applicable to registered offerings weren't clearly applicable in Reg A+ deals. In other cases, new ideas arose to further improve the process.

The members of the SEC staff, especially those in the Office of Small Business Policy, have been extremely responsive and have done their best to be helpful to practitioners seeking clarification or explanation of issues that have arisen. In some cases they have issued guidance, known as "Compliance & Disclosure Interpretations" (C&DIs), resolving questions that had been raised, and we will review a little of that here plus a number of suggestions for improvements that have been made.

OTC Markets Petition

On June 6, 2016, OTC Markets Group Inc. submitted a petition for rulemaking with the SEC. As we know, OTC Markets owns and operates the over-the-counter trading platforms, including OTC Pink, OTCQB, and OTCQX. My law firm also submitted a letter in full support of the petition. Several issues are addressed in OTC Markets' request for change.

Allow Reporting Companies to Utilize Reg A

The petition makes the case that it appears there is no particular reason, other than history, to restrict the availability of Reg A just to companies that are not full SEC reporting issuers. This restriction was in the earlier versions of Reg A and the SEC simply retained it. There is nothing in the JOBS Act restricting the SEC from allowing reporting companies to utilize Reg A.

Expanding Reg A use to reporting companies would allow existing public companies to take advantage of the faster review and expanded testing-the-waters capability, not to mention the blue sky preemption for OTC issuers. As the rules stand now, once a company decides to move to full reporting, any public offering thereafter must go through full blue sky state review if the company's stock is trading on the OTC markets.

It also would be beneficial for companies trading on national exchanges to be able to utilize Reg A. Again, the speedy review and TTW capability could clearly enhance companies' ability to raise capital while keeping transaction costs reasonable. It is true that nationally listed and reporting companies, after being public for a year, usually can utilize short registration Form S-3. This is a very simple form that is approved quickly by the SEC. Form S-3, however, is not available for a company that filed any periodic report late in the last 12 months. The larger benefit, however, of allowing reporting companies to use Reg A likely will go to those that are trading in the OTC markets and have chosen full reporting.

The SEC also made clear in a C&DI in 2015 that a full reporting company can, if eligible, complete a filing (called Form 15) to suspend their reporting obligations, and thereafter be eligible for and utilize Reg A as a non-reporting company. Some OTC companies that have been full reporting have been considering this option to allow them to conduct a new public offering, avoid blue sky review, and enter light reporting.

As to companies currently completing Reg A+ deals without becoming full reporting, they generally are remaining in the light reporting system. As such, they are able to continue utilizing Reg A+. In the end, therefore, while it could be helpful to allow reporting companies to utilize Reg A, there may be only a relatively small number of companies that would benefit from it.

A bill which passed the U.S. House of Representatives in September 2017 by a whopping 403-3 margin would direct the SEC to permit reporting companies to utilize Reg A+. A company would be deemed to satisfy its post-offering reporting obligations so long as they continue with full quarterly and other reporting required of most Exchange Act reporting companies. As of this writing it is not clear if the Senate will take up this bill or whether President Trump would sign it, though clearly on the House side it has wide bipartisan support.

Allow "At-the-Market" Offerings

The Reg A rules prohibit so-called "at-the-market offerings," also called ATMs. In these deals, the company offers investors the right to invest in company stock at the same price as it is publicly trading. The investor gets the same freely tradeable stock as if she bought it from an existing shareholder in the public market, and the company gets the money for the purchase price.

As an example, if the company's stock is trading at $7.00 per share, and the company has an SEC-approved ATM offering, investors can purchase shares for $7.00 directly from the company instead of in the public market. Unfortunately, the SEC felt that only fixed price offerings should be permitted in Reg A deals. They left the door open in the final release, however, potentially to revisit this issue.

The OTC Markets petition suggests that allowing Reg A to be used for ATMs would be good for issuers and investors. There would seem to be no particular reason to prohibit these types of offerings.

Blue Sky Issues

One would think that Title IV and the new rules, along with the dismissal of the two states' lawsuit, would put to bed the blue sky issues in the new Reg A world. There remains, however, one issue raised during comments and several that have arisen since the implementation of the new rules.

Blue Sky Preemption of OTC Resale of Reg A Securities

The JOBS Act and SEC rules make clear that state blue sky registration and review of Tier 2 Reg A+ offerings is preempted under NSMIA. That covers the initial sale of securities by issuers. The public *resale* of those shares, however, also would have to be preempted, or some other exemption from state registration would have to be available. To be clear, the resale of securities listed on national exchanges is preempted from state blue sky review, so this issue relates only to OTC trading.

Without preemption, OTC issuers must find an exemption. The most common is called the "manual exemption" and is recognized by nearly 40 states. With this exemption the company must be listed in a recognized securities manual such as Moody's. There is a cost and medium hassle associated with getting and maintaining this manual listing. Another exemption, which Elio Motors has been relying on, is called the *unsolicited broker transaction*. In this exception, the company cannot be a party to the transaction and there must be an unsolicited order or purchase completed through a broker.

Commenters to the original SEC proposal, including the American Bar Association, requested that resale be clearly preempted. In the final release, as with ATMs, the SEC noted that no resale preemption is "more appropriate at the outset" but indicated a willingness to reconsider the issue after they see how things go under the new rules. They also have issued a C&DI reconfirming that resale of Reg A+ securities is not preempted from state review.

One would hope the SEC will take another look at this issue before long and allow the resale of OTC Reg A+ shares to be preempted from state registration to close the loop on providing the full benefit of minimizing overlapping state involvement in Reg A+ deals.

State Notice Filings

As previously noted, the SEC made clear that states can require Tier 2 issuers, though pre-empted from state registration and review, to make notice filings of their Reg A+ offerings. This is the exact language from the final release:

> We see no reason why state securities regulators could not continue to rely on the multistate coordinated review program as a mechanism to allow Tier 2 issuers to make notice filings of their offering statements with the states . . . . In this regard, notice filings of offering statements of Tier 2 issuers would be available to the states for a period of time prior to the qualification of the offering.

There are two issues with the state notice filings. The first is how the states have implemented them, namely in many cases with extremely high filing fees as has been previously noted. When states require offerings to be registered, reviewed, and approved, as is the case in Reg A Tier 1 offerings, many charge a percentage of the offering amount, typically with a cap. That cap can be as much as several thousand dollars.

Unfortunately, many states have decided that Tier 2 notice filings should require that same high fee. This might make sense where the fee helps offset the cost of examiners and such. Instead, however, a Tier 2 notice filing simply places the company's offering statement in its electronic filings. No humans (or, these days I guess we need to say, potentially, robots) are required to review the document.

A comparable example, as discussed, is Regulation D. As we know, Rule 506 offerings are preempted from state review like Tier 2 Reg A+ deals. States do require notice filings of these offerings, however. The filing fees for Reg D deals generally are a few hundred dollars per state. This is much different than the thousands some are charging for Reg A+ notice filings.

The SEC should consider a rule requiring states to charge only reasonable fees for notice filings or even cap them potentially. This also may be something Congress could take up if necessary in a Reg A fix bill.

The second issue that may have been overlooked by the SEC is whether notice filings should be permitted in Tier 2 offerings that will be listed on national securities exchanges. NSMIA clearly states that no notice filings or fees can be charged by states in connection with offerings intended to be listed on an exchange. This seems to technically conflict with the SEC's language quoted earlier.

Companies that completed Reg A+ offerings to national exchanges thus far have not made state filings in reliance on NSMIA, to the author's knowledge. It would seem appropriate, however, for the SEC to clarify this issue, possibly with a C&DI, and hopefully confirm that no state filings can be required in Tier 2 deals headed for a national exchange.

Testing-the-Waters Issues

The new Reg A+ rules on testing the waters are not that long or detailed. In old Reg A, as we know, companies could only test the waters before filing their offering statement. Now that the SEC has permitted TTW activity post-filing, the rules were enhanced to clarify how that would work. They added information that must be included in disclaimers and required that recipients of TTW material must receive the then-current preliminary offering circular or a URL (which the SEC says must include an active hyperlink) or physical address where it can be obtained and reviewed. And all TTW material must be filed with the SEC, including transcripts of oral presentations and radio and TV ads.

The rules do not tell us certain things, however. For example, what about media interviews? If a CEO, having filed an offering statement, gives an interview to the *Wall Street Journal* about her IPO, what then? Presumably you cannot force the newspaper to add your disclaimer, and the material may be copyrighted and not permitted to be filed with the SEC without permission.

Broadcast interviews are similar, but potentially more manageable. If you are going on CNBC, maybe they would add a crawl under you that includes the disclaimer. Or you can tell the interviewer you have to read a disclaimer before the interview starts. You still may have the copyright issue, however, in seeking to file the transcript of the interview.

We understand the SEC is considering providing some guidance on this. They might say you cannot do media interviews without the disclaimer and ability to file without violating copyright. They also could exempt media interviews since they are not actually materials created by the company, although in fairness they are completed with the participation of company officials. In the meantime, company executives should consult with their counsel before engaging in media interviews concerning their Reg A+ offering.

Another TTW issue is simply defining what actually constitutes appropriate TTW material. New Rule 255 says any time before qualification a company may "communicate orally or in writing to determine whether there is any interest in a contemplated securities offering." Those communications are to have disclaimers and be filed.

What is not defined in the rule is which company materials actually constitute testing-the-waters material and are intended to gauge interest in a contemplated offering. As an example, a client of ours that had filed an offering statement issued a press release concerning the addition of a new senior executive. The move had nothing to do with the IPO. There was one sentence in the release noting that the company had filed an offering statement regarding a contemplated IPO. A week later the SEC contacted the company and insisted that they amend the release to add TTW disclaimers.

Another example might include offering materials for a pre-IPO private fundraising under Reg D. If the securities issued in the private financing convert into the IPO at a discount, does that make the offering materials in that private round all TTW? Does that include every investor presentation and meeting regarding that private offering?

The SEC has not provided any guidance yet on these points. It is easy to say, when in doubt just add the disclaimer and file it since it is relatively easy to do and not a significant burden to file them now that EDGAR filing services often complete an entire Reg A IPO for a fixed price. If the goal of new Reg A+, however, is to reduce the burdens on issuers and streamline the process, then adding more hassle with TTW would seem to go against that goal.

Some questions have been raised about a few issuers whose radio and other ads pre- and post-qualification were alleged to be misleading. One touted huge players in their industry and encouraged investors to "get into the next [name of large player]." There is no question all in the industry must work hard to ensure that both TTW and post-qualification offering activities are consistent with their offering circular and not misleading.

Other Issues

Raising the Limit

As mentioned previously, the SEC has the right to increase the $50 million limit that a Reg A+ issuer can raise in a 12-month period. They must assess this under the JOBS Act at least every two years and report to Congress only if they do not raise the limit, and explain why they have not. As we know, since the passage of the JOBS Act in 2012 the limit has remained unchanged.

Given that FundRise and apparently others have successfully raised multiple $50 million Reg A+ IPOs, many believe the SEC should consider offering more companies the opportunity to take advantage of the benefits of Reg A+. I had a client planning a $75 million IPO. They will be burdened by the TTW restrictions in traditional Form S-1 offerings and have to endure much more comprehensive SEC review for what appears to be no particular reason. As noted above, the Financial CHOICE Act, passed by the House of Representatives in June 2017 on party lines, would mandate an increase in the Reg A+ limit to $75 million. I recently had a call with a group of attorneys who represent IPO underwriters who said a change from $50 to $75 million could significantly increase their clients' potential interest in Reg A+. That increase also was recommended by the 2017 Conference.

The argument for keeping the limit in check, however, appears to be that the SEC is willing to risk greater fraud in smaller deals, allowing them to feel comfortable with the much more limited review of Reg A+ offering statements. If Reg A+ were to increase to, say, $200 million, the risk obviously becomes greater. The context of this view is worth exploring in a little detail.

The SEC has made clear in recent years that they wish to use much more of their enforcement resources to prevent the next Bernard Madoff or Enron. For those less in the know or not as grizzled as your author, both were multibillion-dollar frauds. In the case of Madoff, a former Wall Street pillar was convicted in 2009 of a massive Ponzi scheme in which he kept raising new money to pay back to prior investors what appeared to be tremendous gains in investments.

The allegation was that over $16 billion was stolen or paid back illegally. Roughly $9 billion of it was ultimately recovered and returned to investors. Madoff had stolen, however, from his high school buddies and friends. Many lost their entire life savings. The lesson one hopes many learned was never to place all your eggs in one basket, and also that in many cases when something sounds too good to be true it probably is.

Enron was one of the largest U.S. companies in the oil industry. In order to make their performance look better, their crafty CFO moved certain key assets (and related liabilities) off their balance sheet through complex, ultimately proven to be illegal, machinations. In December 2001, the company filed for bankruptcy as a result of the fraud, and several key executives ended up in jail. Market and job losses were gargantuan.

Many blamed the company's auditing firm, Arthur Andersen, for being too cozy with management, auditing the firm while also doing consulting for them, and looking the other way as the fraud developed. The firm, one of the then–"Big Five" accounting firms in the United States, was ultimately convicted of criminal activity, and in 2002 it gave up all its licenses to practice. This led in part, in SOX, to the prohibition on accounting firms serving as auditor and consultant for the same company, and the rotation rule requiring that a new audit partner take over each client every five years.

The Commission did deal with a backlash after the Madoff scandal, since some commentators felt the regulators in general did not do enough to prevent his scheme or stop it sooner. Some also blamed the SEC indirectly for Enron, since they could have placed similar restrictions on public auditors as SOX ultimately did.

As to Madoff, there had been multiple whistleblower complaints about him in the years prior to his ultimate arrest. He was finally outed when his longtime secretary broke her silence to a reporter, which led to Madoff allegedly informing his sons about the crime, upon which they reported him to authorities. Prior to that, however, there had been a formal investigation in the early 1990s of his alleged amazing investment returns, and at least two other times the SEC made inquiries of his brokerage.

During these inquiries and investigations, the SEC requested documents from him, rather than delivering subpoenas. They did not raid his offices as is common to try to obtain documents. They simply relied on what he and his team chose to send in response to requests for documents. As a former chairman of the Nasdaq, many could not believe such a well-respected senior Wall Street veteran could be capable of such crimes. It turned out that much of what he delivered voluntarily to the SEC when they inquired was completely bogus and fraudulent. Some believe that, as a result, Madoff continued to steal from innocent investors for much longer than he should have.

The SEC's internal Office of Inspector General later did a review of how the SEC handled the Madoff situation and its failure to uncover his crime. The report reviewed, but did not see, any conflicts of interest among SEC staff, which had been alleged (an SEC enforcement staffer had been dating Madoff's niece). It did, however, make other startling findings, and the key language from the OIG's report from August 2009 is worth quoting:

> The OIG investigation did find . . . that the SEC received more than ample information in the form of detailed and substantive complaints over the years to warrant a thorough and comprehensive examination and/or investigation of Bernard Madoff and BMIS for operating a Ponzi scheme, and that despite three examinations and two investigations being conducted, a thorough and competent investigation or examination was never performed. The OIG found that between June 1992 and December 2008 when Madoff confessed, the SEC received six substantive complaints that raised significant red flags concerning Madoff's hedge fund operations and should have led to questions about whether Madoff was actually engaged in trading. Finally, the SEC was also aware of two articles regarding Madoff's investment operations that appeared in reputable publications in 2001 and questioned Madoff's unusually consistent returns.

There were other massive scandals during the same period. Telecom giant WorldCom in 2002 got caught treating millions of dollars of expenses as "capital investments," grossly exaggerating their profit by over $1 billion. The CEO of blue-chip conglomerate Tyco, Dennis Kozlowski, stole hundreds of millions he managed to siphon out of the company, and ended up in jail.

This backdrop may lead one to have a greater understanding of the SEC's shift of focus since these scandals to preventing and stopping large frauds. It would take 320 $50 million Reg A+ frauds to match one Madoff. It is somewhat ironic since Congress and the SEC spent a great amount of time in the 1980s and 1990s trying to combat fraud in the microcap markets, as will be discussed in greater detail later.

If the SEC, therefore, were to increase the cap on Reg A+ to, say, $100 million, you are only down to 160 Reg A+ frauds equaling Madoff. It is a difficult line to draw certainly. When I spoke at an SEC conference on microcap fraud in the mid-2000s, a speaker put it thus: "If you assume the regulators cannot stop all fraud, the question in making enforcement priorities is, what fraud is okay?" For now it seems the answer, indirectly at least, is that small frauds are more okay than big ones.

How all this will change under new SEC Chairman Jay Clayton is unclear as of this writing. His background is as a mergers-and-acquisitions transactional attorney at one of the country's most prestigious law firms. He does not come from a regulatory, enforcement, or political background as many of his predecessors did. He also does not have a background, it appears, in working with smaller public and private companies. He has, however, expressed dismay over the dwindling number of public companies and support for improving the IPO market to reverse this trend.

International Companies

As noted previously, there was no particular reason given in the final Reg A rules as to why the SEC chose to maintain the limitation on use of Reg A only by U.S. and Canadian companies. Many foreign companies seek access to U.S. capital and trading markets every year. They already have certain relaxed reporting and disclosure rules compared to U.S. companies, if they choose to operate in the United States as a "foreign private issuer." So why not allow these companies to use Reg A?

It is not likely we will learn the reason, but one might speculate it has something to do with China. As we alluded to earlier and will discuss more in Chapter 9, hundreds of Chinese companies went public in the United States through reverse mergers in the 2000s. The Chinese rules had been sufficiently relaxed to allow foreign ownership of these companies, and many took advantage. Investment banks dove in, raising hundreds of millions for these companies.

As we know, smaller company IPOs had ended, so these Chinese so-called SMEs (small and medium enterprises) generally did not qualify for traditional U.S. IPOs at the time. Thus, reverse mergers were the path. Underwriters, attorneys, and accountants presumably did their due diligence. As we will discuss, however, they generally had to rely on local Chinese professionals to confirm legal, financial, and business information.

As discussed, several dozen of these companies were accused of fraud around 2010. This led to the SEC issuing a warning about reverse mergers and ultimately asking the national stock exchanges, in 2011, to implement the *seasoning rules* for shell mergers requiring trading of post-merger company stocks on the OTC markets for at least a year following the merger.

If this was the main reason behind the SEC's unwillingness to expand Reg A geographically, presumably they could have simply excluded Chinese companies. As a practical, political, and possibly legal matter, however, one assumes this was not doable.

Some foreign companies have considered relocating their headquarters to the United States to qualify. In 2015, the SEC issued a C&DI that says if the "officers, partners or managers primarily direct, control and coordinate the issuer's activities from the United States or Canada," then the company qualifies as able to use Reg A. Thus, operations can be anywhere as long as the top management is in North America. The company also has to reincorporate into a U.S. or Canadian jurisdiction.

I have had many conversations in the last few years with foreign private companies that could have benefited from having a Reg A IPO as an option in their bag. For example, the interest of Israeli companies in going public in the United States has been increasing. It would seem worth the SEC reconsidering this limitation. Maybe foreign companies can have a lower limit to what they can raise than North American ones, to reduce the risk of the size of any potential fraud.

Conforming to Registered Offerings

The SEC has worked to allow rules or interpretations that benefit registered offerings to apply to Reg A deals as well. There are several we know about at this time.

Periodic Filing After Qualification

If you are completing a registered offering, and your registration statement is declared effective, and a quarterly report on Form 10-Q would be due very soon thereafter, an SEC rule allows you a full 45 days from when your registration goes effective to get that filing done. There is no similar rule for an annual report on Form 10-K, but the quarterly guidance is helpful to avoid a mad scramble from newly public companies.

The SEC has issued guidance making clear that Reg A issuers can rely on the same guidance.

Private Offering Concurrent with Public Offering

Another interpretation previously limited to registered offerings, issued in 2007, related to how to conduct a private securities offering at the same time as a public offering is occurring. It provides, essentially, that as long as you can show that the investors in the private offering did not find out about the private offering or the company by reviewing the company's registration statement, and the company did not use the registration statement to entice the investor, then the private offering can proceed and will not be deemed an improper part of the public offering.

The SEC has issued guidance making clear that Reg A issuers can rely on the same guidance.

Avoiding Unnecessary Financial Disclosure

A third helpful issue also has been resolved. In the 2016 Fixing America's Surface Transportation (FAST) Act, emerging growth companies, as defined in the JOBS Act, were provided some relief in their registered public offerings. Namely, if when you file initially with the SEC there are financials that have to be filed at the time but you reasonably expect they will not need to be included at the end of the process, you are allowed to omit those financial statements from the initial filing. This might include, for example, quarterly information that will likely be subsumed into annual audited financial statements yet to be prepared but likely to be included at the end of the process.

The SEC in November 2016 issued guidance making clear that Reg A issuers can rely on the same guidance.

And so . . .

With every "A" grade I came home with in high school, my mom would always say, "What, no A+?" (Yes I realize the irony of the A+ reference, which didn't hit me until I typed it.)

The point is, everything that is good, or even excellent, can be improved. Maybe when some of these changes are implemented we will start calling it Regulation A++.

Clearly we are just beginning in the exciting new world of Reg A+. These chapters have merely scratched the surface in summarizing the benefits, challenges, and process of determining if Reg A is for you, and then getting the deal done.

Much will depend on continuing the education of both Wall Street and entrepreneurs about this very well-crafted new regime. One hopes that this overview of Reg A+ has shed some light on the topic for those who seek to better understand its benefits. That said, it does appear true that, as we have said a number of times, there now appears no reason not to use Reg A+ for any public offering under $50 million where a company qualifies to use the new rules.

We move next to reviewing and updating information that was in the author's first two books on reverse mergers and other IPO alternatives. These options remain viable under the right circumstances and also should be considered as a company examines the best way to go public once it determines that a public stock is the way to go.

Finally, our "Experts Speak" chapter brings many of these issues to a head as we discuss some of the greatest opportunities and challenges in today's financing world with some very experienced and well-respected thought leaders on Wall Street.

CHAPTER 8

Basics of Reverse Mergers

As exciting as the potential for Reg A+ is, it may not be the best option for all companies considering the benefits of having a publicly trading stock. Over the last few decades, Wall Street has discovered that there are more ways to go public than through an IPO. Of course we know the benefits of being public, including access to capital, growth through acquisition, and incentives for management through stock options.

Having various options for going public therefore is good news to many smaller companies, especially those that do not fit the typical profile investment banks use when deciding which companies can successfully accomplish an IPO, even under the new Reg A+. Now we will explore a number of these alternatives beyond an IPO, starting here with reverse mergers.

Berkshire Hathaway, Occidental Petroleum, Turner Broadcasting, Texas Instruments, Jamba Juice, and American Apparel are just a few well-known companies that went public through a reverse merger. To the uninitiated, a reverse merger is a deceptively simple concept. Instead of pursuing a traditional IPO where, in many cases, an investment bank serves as underwriter or selling agent, a company arranges for its stock to be publicly traded following a merger or other similar transaction with a publicly held shell company. The shell company has no business other than to look for a private company with which to merge.

The shell may be the remnant of a bankrupt or sold organization or specially formed for the purpose of investing in a private company. Either way, the basic maneuver is the same: A private company purchases control of a public one, merges or combines with it, and when the merger is complete becomes a publicly traded company in its own right.

As previously mentioned, after small-company IPOs virtually disappeared around 2000, reverse mergers stepped in as a viable alternative. The technique had been around for decades, but only gained significant popularity in the 2000s. An average of over 200 reverse mergers were completed in most years between 2000 and 2010. In many cases a contemporaneous private placement (generally under Regulation D) was completed at the time of the reverse merger, providing needed financing.

As will be discussed, the market also was somewhat controversial following a period in the 1970s and 1980s during which a number of shady operators used reverse mergers as a means to dupe and fleece investors. A number of players (your author included) worked to bring the technique into legitimacy and transparency to great effect, especially in the second half of the 2000s.

The process generally is quicker, cheaper, simpler, less dilutive, and less risky than most IPOs, but has its own unique risks and challenges. Currently, for many companies, Reg A+ may indeed offer a more effective alternative. This is especially true given the addition of *seasoning rules* in 2011 that made reverse mergers less attractive to many, as will be discussed in the next chapter. Reverse mergers also are complex transactions with traps that even otherwise experienced practitioners with limited knowledge of the technique can easily fall into. When done correctly, however, these hidden dangers can be avoided and the process can move forward quickly and smoothly.

Let us explore how reverse mergers work and the history and current status of this unique approach to going public.

Overview of Reverse Mergers

A *shell company*, as the SEC defines it, is a public reporting company with no or nominal assets (other than cash) and no or nominal operations. Other SEC rules refer to a "blank check" company as a development-stage company with no business plan, or whose business plan is to acquire another business. Some of these rules overlap, at times causing some confusion. The distinction also has been used to skirt some of the shell restrictions as we will discuss. The industry refers to both types as "shells."

A reverse merger simply is a method by which a private company merges or combines with a shell and becomes public without a traditional public offering. The private company's shareholders generally receive the majority, if not all or nearly all, of the stock of the shell company, depending on the factors above and the value of the private company merging in.

A shell tends to be valued based on whether it has cash, whether it is fully reporting with the SEC, the size of its shareholder base, how "clean" the shell is if it has had past operations, and whether its stock is trading, and if so, on what exchange or platform. Values rose significantly through around 2007 and then dropped dramatically thereafter and through this writing.

In some cases a shell is purchased for cash. In those cases, either all existing shareholders are bought out, or more commonly only the control shareholders' shares are purchased, with the remaining publicly trading shares continuing to trade. In other cases the merger is completed with no cash to existing holders of the shell, who simply hold their shares in a company that now will have operations. In effect the shareholders go from owning 100 percent of nothing to maybe 5 percent of something.

The most common structure to complete this process is called the *reverse triangular merger*. In general, a direct merger between a shell company and a private company requires shareholder approval of both companies. In the case of a public reporting company (i.e., the shell), this requires preparation, filing, mailing, and seeking SEC approval of a somewhat complicated proxy statement. This is an expensive and time-consuming process.

The reverse triangular merger is one way around this that the SEC has recognized as legitimate. In this transaction, the shell company creates a wholly owned subsidiary. Then the subsidiary merges into the private company and disappears. Shares of the private company are exchanged for shares of the shell company. As a result, the private company becomes a wholly owned subsidiary of the shell, with the owners of the formerly private company owning the majority of the shares of the shell following the deal's closing. If the shell trades on a major exchange such as Nasdaq, however, any reverse merger—even a reverse triangular merger—requires shareholder approval and a full proxy under exchange rules.

Another common structure for these transactions is a simple exchange of shares or a direct asset acquisition by the shell. The share exchange is a simpler method of completing the business combination, because the shell does not have to create a new subsidiary and merger materials do not need to be prepared and filed in the state in which the shell subsidiary and private company are located. In a share exchange, the owners of the private company simply agree to swap their shares for new shares of the shell, taking it over.

The potential problem with the share exchange is that every shareholder of the private company has to agree to sell his or her shares. If there is a concern that a few small holders might object, or if a company has a large number of owners and finding them all and obtaining their signatures might be challenging, the reverse triangular merger is preferable. This is because the merger structure requires only a majority of the private company's shareholders to approve. In most states, dissenting shareholders in a merger have a right to be bought out if they choose.

In a situation, however, where a private company is owned, say, by just four active shareholders, all of whom favor the transaction, a share exchange is a simpler method to complete the business combination. In that circumstance, however, each shareholder becomes a "seller" in the share exchange agreement and may become personally liable for representations and warranties they provide about their stock and the company. This generally is not required in reverse triangular mergers, in which the representations and warranties are made only by the company itself.

People often ask why these transactions are called reverse mergers. The reason is that the smaller public shell, which is really being swallowed up by the private company, survives the merger and remains the parent company. The accounting industry calls these *reverse acquisitions*. There actually are many examples of reverse acquisitions by major companies that went public by acquiring a smaller public operating company rather than a traditional IPO. Examples include the New York Stock Exchange, Kohlberg Kravis Roberts, Burger King, and others. When public companies Merck and Schering-Plough merged, for various reasons the smaller Schering survived that merger.

IPOs versus Reverse Mergers

When management of private companies enter my office having concluded that they see real benefit to being public, we explore all options. Comparing reverse mergers, self-filings, and IPOs has changed quite a bit in the years since my first book on reverse mergers was published in 2006. There may, however, still be benefits in considering a reverse merger as against even a Reg A+ IPO.

Many companies simply are not good IPO candidates, either because investment banks are not interested or there is a concern about how to raise money in a Reg A+ IPO without an investment bank. Others are working with investment banks that believe it easier to merge with a shell, complete a contemporaneous private placement, and then do a "secondary" public offering after the reverse merger.

There are challenges to that approach following the addition, in 2011, of the seasoning rules, which we will cover in the next chapter. These rules require a post–reverse merger company's stock to trade only in the over-the-counter markets for at least one full fiscal year before looking to uplist to a national exchange. An exception to the rule is if a secondary public offering raises at least $40 million in a *firm commitment* underwriting. But many companies are not large enough to attract that kind of financing.

Advantages of a Reverse Merger versus an IPO

Reverse mergers generally provide six major benefits when compared to IPOs: lower cost, speedier process, they are not dependent on the IPO market, they are not susceptible to underwriter changes, they are less time-consuming for company executives, and there generally is less dilution. Let us explore these briefly:

1. *Lower cost.* Reg A+ IPOs thus far appear to have cost much less than traditional IPOs in most cases. Traditional S-1 IPOs are expensive, indeed. The reverse merger cost also includes the cost of the shell, however, which can add to the price. But in general, the total cost of a reverse merger is likely to be less than an IPO.
2. *Speedier process.* As much as the SEC proudly touts that Reg A+ IPO filings are going from initial filing to SEC approval in around 74 days, which is much quicker than most S-1 IPOs, reverse mergers do tend to be quicker than both. In addition, before the SEC filing of an IPO disclosure document there are several months invested in preparing the filing. The main advantage of a reverse merger is that no SEC involvement takes place prior to completion of the transaction. Therefore, as quickly as you can negotiate a merger or share exchange agreement your private company can be public.

   In most cases you do have to prepare a disclosure document, known in the industry as a "super" Form 8-K, with much of the same information as would be in an SEC registration statement, within four business days of completing the merger. That includes audited financial statements and comprehensive information about the company, and the preparation of this document can slow the transaction somewhat. That said, reverse mergers at times can be completed in a matter of weeks, though most take around two to three months.
3. *Not dependent on IPO market for success.* Many believe that the market for Reg A+ IPOs will not be and so far has not been significantly affected by the overall IPO market. There are times when IPOs generally are very popular, and others, at times even during stock market surges, when they are not. During these times, the IPO "window" is said to be "closed." As we have discussed, IPOs all but disappeared during most of the 2000s. The window opens and shuts without warning and often at extremely inopportune times. Numerous dot-com companies were left with uncompleted IPOs after the market crash of April 2000. In 2008, as the financial crisis hit, more than a hundred companies pursuing IPOs changed their minds and pulled out.

   Reverse mergers generally tend to continue in all markets. In down markets companies see it as a viable alternative. In up markets many companies still choose reverse mergers because of speed, cost, and the other benefits described herein.
4. *Not susceptible to underwriter changes.* One of the trickier aspects of most IPOs is that an underwriter can decide to terminate the deal or significantly change the share price of the offering at the last minute. Unfortunately, much of the success of an IPO depends upon the state of the securities markets during the week that the stock begins to trade.

As previously noted, many hope that Reg A+ IPOs will remain less market sensitive. Reverse mergers generally are less affected by current market conditions. This is in part because financings accompanying reverse mergers generally require the investors to hold their securities for up to six months, with less concern about immediate liquidity.

5. *Less time-consuming for company executives.* Private company management teams generally spend less total time preparing a Reg A+ offering statement than a typical S-1 as has been noted. That said, we still go through multiple fairly long drafting sessions to get the disclosure right. Then the team must deal with SEC comments, roadshows, and the like. In a traditional S-1 IPO, a management team can find itself spending up to a year away from building the business to pursue an IPO. In general, the time that management needs to spend to complete a reverse merger is much less as most of the work can be handled by a capable CFO working with counsel and auditors.

6. *Less dilution.* It is not uncommon in IPOs for an underwriter essentially to force a company to take more money than it may need in the foreseeable future. They do this because they are paid based on what is raised. Of course, legitimate investment banks work toward what is in the company's, versus their own, interests, but that potential conflict remains. In reverse mergers, the related financings are often smaller than most IPOs. That said, Reg A+ deal sizes are in many cases similar to those seen in reverse mergers. There is, however, less dilution as a result of raising less money. This allows a private company's management, founders, and prior investors to retain a greater percentage ownership.

Disadvantages of a Reverse Merger versus an IPO

IPOs have three significant advantages over reverse mergers. First, IPOs tend to raise more money. Second, the IPO process makes it easier to create market support for a stock. Last, IPOs are not restricted by the seasoning rules affecting reverse mergers.

1. *Less funding.* A company completing an IPO, including a Reg A+ deal, is more likely to raise more money than in a typical reverse merger. When the capital markets are strong this is less of an issue for a post–reverse merger company since it can proceed with a subsequent public or private offering. However, as noted below, the seasoning restrictions make it tougher for these companies to raise their next round until the seasoning period ends.

2. *Market support is harder to obtain.* After a reverse merger, most stocks trade "by appointment" because there is no real buzz about them. Analysts tend not to follow stocks trading over-the-counter or that are trading below $5 per share. Therefore, building market support leading to a higher volume of trading is more difficult. In a typical IPO, the underwriter seeks to create this buzz and obtain analyst coverage and the like. This support issue also has been a bit of a challenge for the handful of Reg A+ IPOs completed thus far.

In some cases, however, this may be less important to a company going public. They might care more about how the stock will trade after they complete a larger secondary public offering. It is, however, a real challenge in reverse mergers and requires a different attitude focused more on building market support over time as opposed to requiring it immediately. Post–reverse merger companies also can and do take steps to increase support for their stock, including engaging capable and reputable public and investor relations firms. A good mantra is that Wall Street's attention should be earned and not manufactured!

3. *Seasoning restrictions.* As we will discuss in the next chapter, in an IPO, a company can go directly to a national exchange, or start trading in the over-the-counter markets and uplist relatively quickly. After most reverse mergers, unfortunately, the company now is required to trade only on the OTC markets for at least one full fiscal year. This is one of the reasons many started pushing the SEC and Congress to look at other alternatives such as reforming Reg A.

It should also be noted that Reg A+ holds two additional advantages over reverse mergers. First, Reg A+ issuers can test the waters through general solicitation and online promotion of their offering. Second, Reg A+ allows more aged financial statements than are required in the post-reverse merger "super" Form 8-K.

A Little History, Rule 419, and Subsequent Rulemakings

In the 1970s and 1980s, the reverse merger technique was effectively discovered and put to immediate and extensive use. During this period, a number of unsavory players got into the market and began engaging in fraudulent practices by forming new blank-check companies, raising money in IPOs of the blank checks, and simply taking the money as fees for themselves rather than finding merger candidates for the newly created shells. Other abuses, including manipulative trading of the stock of the shells, were rampant. At the same time, a small number of legitimate players emerged who formed shells but did not take fees unless a merger candidate was found.

This was part of a broader pattern of fraud and abuse during this period in what is known as the penny stock market. Throughout the 1980s, the penny stock market was regional and a number of boiler-room-type brokerage firms engaged in enormous amounts of fraud in the over-the-counter markets. For example, a firm would buy a large amount of an undervalued, thinly traded penny stock, float a false rumor about a proposed transaction, watch the price rise, and then sell its holdings, only for the new shareholders to find the stock falling back down when the rumor turned out not to be true. These were called "pump-and-dump" schemes.

We all recently were reminded of this era with the release of the 2013 movie, *The Wolf of Wall Street*, based on the 2007 book written by infamous criminal Stratton Oakmont leader Jordan Belfort. It took until the late 1990s for Stratton to be shut down and Belfort sent to jail for 22 months for securities fraud in pump-and-dump transactions. He got a lighter sentence in exchange for testifying against many of his partners and subordinates.

Belfort emerged from jail in 2006 as a motivational speaker and author focusing on the art of selling. The movie, starring Leonardo DiCaprio as Belfort, to some extent sadly glorifies the criminal direction Belfort's life took. Also sadly, pump-and-dump schemes continue to this day and the SEC and U.S. Justice Department have done their best to shut down Stratton-type boiler-rooms, which still exist.

Adoption of Rule 419

Following the rough period in penny stocks in the 1980s, Congress took action by passing the Penny Stock Reform Act of 1990. That law directed that the SEC pass rules to treat registrations of shares by blank-check companies differently. The SEC then passed Rule 419 under the Securities Act of 1933 in 1992.

Rule 419 sought to eliminate the four major concerns about abusive blank checks: promoters milking the shells for cash, abusive trading practices, the fact that no time limit existed to find a reverse merger candidate, and the fact that investors were not typically offered an opportunity to review or vote on a proposed merger.

Rule 419 has three main components. First, it provides that a blank-check company going public through an IPO must take all money raised in that public offering (minus up to 10% for expenses and underwriting commissions), as well as the shares issued in the offering, and place them in an escrow account until a merger is undertaken. This way, unscrupulous players cannot convert those funds, and no improper trading is possible because there is no trading prior to a merger.

Second, the management of the blank check must find and complete a merger within 18 months after the IPO, or all remaining funds must be returned to investors. Following this period, under some circumstances the company could continue as a shell company and get a second life, but it would do so without the IPO investors' money.

Third, the investors in the blank-check IPO have the right to opt out and get their money back (minus any expenses and commissions taken) if they do not like the proposed merger. This opt-out feature requires the blank-check company to prepare, file, get SEC approval of, and distribute to investors a prospectus-like document providing detailed information (including audited financial statements) about the company proposed to be merged in.

If investors holding at least 80 percent of the blank check's shares do not approve the merger, it cannot be completed and all money is returned to investors, minus any deductions previously taken. If more than 80 percent opt in, those voting their shares against the deal still get their money back, but the transaction can be completed. At that point, the money and shares are released from escrow.

There also are specific requirements a merger must meet to qualify for release of the funds, including that the value of the private business merging in must be equal to at least 80 percent of the amount raised in the blank check's IPO.

Rule 419 does *not* apply to a blank check that has $5 million or more in assets prior to its IPO, or that seeks to raise at least $5 million in a firm commitment IPO underwriting. Thus, these companies are free to operate much like pre-419 blank checks, without escrow arrangements, trading restrictions, or time limits. This exemption created the opportunity for special-purpose acquisition companies (SPACs) to develop, which we will discuss in more depth ahead and in Chapter 11.

Aftermath of Adoption of Rule 419

The adoption of Rule 419 had a dramatic and almost immediate purgative effect on bad actors in reverse mergers transactions, eliminating, at least for a time, most of the abuses from the market. In the next chapter we will explore some of the more creative, and ultimately in some cases illegal, workarounds that players utilized. At the same time, the new rule also hurt many quality players, and initially there was much concern that this might mean the end of reverse mergers.

A number of professionals attempted to create legitimate new blank checks under Rule 419. It became clear, however, that the SEC intended to make this extremely difficult. Initial IPO filings of these blank checks were met with hundreds of SEC comments, substantially delaying the process. This, combined with the knowledge that there was a short time limit to find a deal and the cost and delay associated with shareholder approval of the merger, ultimately led virtually all market participants to seek other paths.

Three major trends then developed, starting in the 1990s, that continued somewhat successfully through around 2010, effectively vitiating the potential impact of Rule 419. First, given the apparent unattractiveness of Rule 419, many players moved to acquire or merge with shell companies that had been created through the sale or liquidation of an operating public company. These shells are not restricted by Rule 419. They also often had the added attraction of a larger shareholder base and a trading market. However, they typically needed to be scrubbed to make sure there were no problems in their past.

The second trend was the development of SPACs, which we will discuss in more detail in Chapter 11. By raising as much as $40 million to $1 billion in an IPO of a blank check, promoters avoid the proscriptions of Rule 419. Shrewdly, however, as we will cover, SPAC sponsors voluntarily adopted a number of the Rule 419 protections in order to market investments in the SPAC and ease SEC scrutiny.

A newer wave of SPACs that started around 2010 adjusted those somewhat as we will discuss. In general, however, in SPACs all the money (in some cases minus some expenses) is placed into escrow. Investors can opt in or out of the deal with full disclosure before that decision is made. There generally is a short window to complete a merger, or else all money is returned. Each SPAC typically has an industry or geographic focus, but most current SPACs have the flexibility to go beyond their stated focus. They generally include a high-caliber board selected to approve deals.

Unlike Rule 419 shells, however, the stock (and associated warrants) of the SPAC is permitted to trade, earning commissions for the promoters and affiliated investment banks, and allowing investors to trade out of the stock (and retain their warrants) even before completion of a merger. For investors, SPACs have been perceived as relatively low-risk investments, because investors have the right to opt out if they are unhappy with a proposed merger. Consequently, these vehicles became, and remain, very popular with structured-finance and hedge fund investors.

The third trend to emerge, but ultimately dissipate following adoption of the seasoning rules in 2011, was the use of Form 10 shells. A legal way around Rule 419 when forming a blank check is to simply file SEC Form 10 under the Securities Exchange Act of 1934, rather than conduct an IPO for the shell that would be subject to Rule 419.

Form 10 is a voluntary request to become a full SEC reporting company. No offering is conducted, except perhaps a private offering that is not subject to SEC scrutiny. After the Form 10 is declared effective by the SEC, the shell company is public and is obligated to file periodic and other reports, but the stock does not and cannot trade until a merger and a process of registering individual shares of stock with the SEC have taken place. A reverse merger then can be completed, shares can be registered, and trading can thereupon commence.

A number of players, including hedge fund investors and investment banks, formed hundreds of Form 10 shells primarily for use in their own transactions. A common structure, effectively ended by the seasoning rules, was to complete a reverse merger using a Form 10 shell with a contemporaneous private placement, followed by a small public offering and an application to a national securities exchange. Thus, a company would go from being a simple Form 10 shell to being traded on a large exchange.

Two groups of companies still utilize Form 10 and other shells in reverse mergers, even after the seasoning rules. One group includes those that have no problem with allowing their stock to trade in the over-the-counter markets until the seasoning restrictions lapse, easing into public company status with lower governance and compliance obligations than on large exchanges.

Another group, consisting primarily of life-sciences companies, uses the merger-then-public-offering approach previously noted, but raises above the $40 million threshold required by the seasoning rules to bypass the requirement to trade over-the-counter. The number of these deals, however, is significantly lower since the passage of seasoning restrictions in 2011.

SEC 2005 and 2008 Rulemakings

In June 2005, the SEC finalized a set of rules intended to close several loopholes widely used by those pursuing reverse mergers. Prior to these new rules, a post–reverse merger company had up to 71 days to disclose its pro forma financial statements, and did not need to complete comprehensive disclosure about the merged company until its first annual report on Form 10-K, which could be as much as a year after the merger.

Some shell managements also abused Form S-8, used to easily register and allow public resale of shares issued to consultants and employees, to compensate questionable players involved in pump-and-dumps. There also was a real concern about the creation of bogus shells, which we will cover in more detail in the next chapter.

The new rules created a new definition of *shell company* as noted in the beginning of this chapter. It then required a full registration–level disclosure filing immediately following a combination with a shell company, through filing of the "super" Form 8-K, eliminating the long delay before disclosure. Finally, the rules prohibited shell companies from using Form S-8 for anything.

A famous footnote in the 2005 rules, footnote 32, noted that the Commission was aware of a practice where people were taking apparent operating businesses public without employing the protections of Rule 419 as an effort to get around the rule's restrictions. These companies and their promoters had an undisclosed intention to find a reverse merger quickly and then shut down or sell back the operating business to its owner. The rule made clear that those also would be considered shell companies. Implied as well was that this might be considered a violation of securities law and possibly even criminal (more about this in the next chapter).

Another very important change in the 2005 rules required *every* SEC reporting company to check a box on their public filings to indicate whether the company is a shell company. This allowed, for the first time, tracking of shells and reverse mergers and a much better sense of the breadth of use of the technique has been possible since then.

In 2008, the SEC adopted broad changes, mostly positive, to SEC Rule 144. That rule allows privately issued securities to be publicly resold, as an exemption from registration, as long as they have been held for a long enough time period. The rule generally shortened those periods from the prior restriction.

The 2008 rules also adopted special rules for shells and former shells. First, they reversed a series of letters that previously prohibited the public resale under Rule 144 of shares issued by a shell while it was a shell, even after it completed a merger. The 2008 rules did prohibit the use of Rule 144 in most circumstances while the company is a shell. Thereafter, however, while the normal holding period for non-shells is six months, they applied a period of the longer of six months of holding and one year from the reverse merger and filing of the super Form 8-K. This permitted for the first time, however, shell shareholders to use Rule 144 at some point after ceasing to be a shell.

Last, the rule provided that Rule 144 is not available to shareholders of former shells at any time that the company is not current in its SEC filings, and that restriction continues *forever*. For companies that were never shells, after a holder has their stock for a year he can publicly sell under Rule 144 even if the company is not current.

This caused a serious issue for attorneys and others trying to release shares for sale in the initial years after the rulemaking. Since then, however, there has been an easing of the burden, and shareholders' restrictions can be removed after one year so long as they represent that they acknowledge they cannot sell if the company ceases to be current in its filings at some point.

The Importance of Due Diligence in Reverse Mergers

There is enough material to write a book solely on the challenges of due diligence in reverse merger transactions. Yet too many players choose not to spend sufficient time or resources completing thorough due diligence in these deals. This can and has led to significant losses and even litigation.

The basic topics that generally are covered in performing due diligence on a shell company include, among other things, the corporate structure and history, management and their backgrounds and compensation, SEC filing history, details about any prior operating business in the shell and potential undisclosed liabilities, litigation or threat thereof, any prior attempted reverse mergers, identity of the auditors and whether the company has changed auditors, recent and historical trading patterns, identity of key shareholders, and press releases.

Most companies want a "clean" shell—companies with well-kept, organized records and no history of unsavory activity. These are few and far between and can only be identified after careful investigation. Form 10 shells tend to be among the cleanest since they are formed from scratch as shells.

We tend to categorize shells that are not clean either as "dirty" or "messy." A messy shell is one in which no shady activity is suspected but recordkeeping is disorganized, so it is difficult to determine what actually has been going on in the shell. A dirty shell is one in which involvement of some questionable players or occurrence of some questionable actions is found. Here are some of the distinguishing characteristics of each type.

Messy Shells

In a messy shell, although certain agreements may have been made, no one is able to locate a copy of the agreement, or the only copy is not signed by the parties. It may or may not be clear that the company's actual bylaws are the ones provided. Older records of when people acquired shares may not be available or may be incomplete. Information comes in from the shell owners in dribs and drabs and is not organized.

On one occasion, for example, a shell was messy because it had previously entered into a reverse merger but unwound the deal after about six months, selling the assets back to the owners. All owners, in giving up their shares of the shell, signed seemingly identical agreements in which they released the shell and ceased to be shareholders. However, one of the agreements contained a hidden clause indicating that if the shell were to complete another reverse merger, the former shareholder would receive a cash payment equal to 5 percent of the value of the reverse merger!

Some law firms would not have reviewed all 15 agreements as thoroughly as my then-associate did, but instead would have presumed them all to be identical. I am proud of my team's work in this instance. My client approached the controller of the shell to find out more about this arrangement. The controller said that this individual had been "long gone" and was unlikely to resurface to claim his prize. My client (now defunct and bankrupt) decided to take the risk and closed the deal anyway.

Some messy shells are behind in their SEC filings. In other cases it is not possible to verify how board members were elected. Sometimes messiness relates to the ownership of shares. The hope is that messy shells can be "scrubbed" and become cleaner. This requires cooperation of the shell's management, attorneys, and auditors. In many cases that cooperation does not come, because many shells are operated by individuals seeking the simplest, quickest, least complicated transaction they can find. Feel free to pick up my book, *Reverse Mergers, Second Edition,* to read about the "messy shell nightmare scenario."

Dirty Shells

The next chapter discusses the issue of dirty or bogus shells in much more detail. Suffice to say that dirty shells can be more challenging to dissect. In these circumstances, we believe that possible abuses have been taking place and bad actors are either present or lurking in the background. The challenge, of course, is tracking the information. If you do find a dirty shell, the general advice is *run*, don't walk, away from it.

And so . . .

Through most of the 1990s and especially the 2000s many of us in the small- and microcap world were extremely active in reverse mergers and worked hard, as noted earlier, to make them legitimate and transparent. My initial text on the subject, originally published in 2006, sold out three printings, was translated into Chinese, and led to a second edition in 2009 that shockingly is still regularly selling well. In fact, a new client came to me in early 2017 because they had read the book and sought to contact me. This was not the first time, but frankly it had been awhile. The unavailability of IPOs, along with strengthening the regulatory environment, not to mention the SPAC movement, led the charge.

We will next turn to the unfortunate series of events that led to the current near-death of reverse mergers as of mid-2017. Some of those developments, fortunately, are directly responsible for the movement that led to the Reg A+ amendments and a very positive current outlook for small companies considering going public. We also are seeing greater interest in self-filings and other IPO alternatives such as Rule 504, as we will explore in later chapters.

The headline in a recent article in an industry newsletter was "RIP Reverse Mergers." After reading the next chapter one might think that is indeed mostly true. I completed, however, two reverse mergers in late 2016 and early 2017. I believe the technique might indeed be on life support, but may still be attractive in certain situations. Maybe it is not time to pull the plug just yet.

CHAPTER 9

Troubled Industry: China, Seasoning Rules, Bogus Shells

Rereading the second edition of my book, *Reverse Mergers*, in preparation for this effort, I realized how dramatically the world of shell mergers has changed since its 2009 publication. The market was frenzied and largely unsupervised by the regulators. Many exciting and legitimate deals had been completed, including quite a number of life-sciences companies such as Puma Biotechnology. That company completed a reverse merger with a Form 10 shell in 2006 and sold to Johnson & Johnson just three years later for almost a billion dollars.

Some SPAC successes had been riding high around 2009 as well, including Jamba Juice and American Apparel, though the SPAC market then was taking a pause right after the 2008 market meltdown. Our work to enhance the legitimacy and transparency of these transactions was truly bearing fruit, and Wall Street had come around.

At the same time, however, the stock market in general hit a nadir in early 2009 as the country was still reeling from the economic and market calamity in the second half of 2008. It was around this time that my second edition came out. It seemed at the time, however, that the shell merger market would get through it, Chinese deals were continuing, and frankly the SEC had done little to stop the questionable players at that time. This was not good for legitimacy but did increase the numbers of mergers and financings being completed.

Also around that time the seeds were being sowed for all of it to pretty much fall apart not too long thereafter. A devastating trifecta of sorts hit the market over a period of about five to six years starting in around 2010. First, the once-booming China reverse merger market came to an abrupt halt. Second, the SEC responded with new, significant, ill-conceived restrictions on reverse mergers. Last, the SEC and Department of Justice began aggressive enforcement actions against alleged bad actors in the shell space.

As we have discussed, it was as these developments were occurring that a number of us began to realize that an alternative path was going to be important. This led to our efforts to suggest, encourage, and then support, the successful overhaul of Reg A that is the subject of the first half of this book. There also continues to be both a present and future for reverse mergers to be covered in the next chapter. Let us now, however, examine the events that induced the continuing near-coma for the reverse merger market.

The China Bubble Pops

So much had changed between the 2006 first edition and the 2009 second edition of my reverse mergers book that I knew the incredible China phenomenon had earned its own chapter. This is how I opened it in 2009: "Who could have imagined even five short years ago the impact that the People's Republic of China (PRC) would have on the U.S. capital markets, and on reverse mergers in particular? Certainly not this humble observer."

In many ways that observation still holds in 2017, but clearly for very different, and not so good, reasons. The "yuan rush," as I called it in a brief description of an emerging trend in 2006, evolved into a crescendo of dealmaking in the late 2000s as well over 300 Chinese companies went public in the United States. Sadly, allegations, many of which came from active stock short sellers, that dozens of these companies had committed fraud or other crimes, ultimately brought an end to the long Chinese march to the U.S. capital markets through reverse mergers.

As is often the case in both law enforcement and the media, mere accusations, regardless of veracity, can have the same ultimate economic effect as if the alleged bad actor was indeed guilty. Dealmakers and stock investors did not wait to see how these dozens of cases alleging fraud were going to end; they simply bailed. This was understandable, however, given the apparent widespread bad activity. Let us examine briefly what led to the start of the China phenomenon, the nature of allegations made, and the question of which party or parties involved with deals, if any, fell down on the job.

Genesis of the China Phenomenon

Starting around 2003, China began to relax its rules, making it easier to allow foreigners to own a controlling interest in a Chinese company. This allowed ultimately hundreds of Chinese SMEs (small and medium-sized enterprises) the chance to go public and raise money in the United States. It had only been since the late 1970s that any private ownership of businesses was permitted in China.

The government surmised, in furthering its development of a "market economy," that encouraging foreign investment into the country would be good. The savings rate among Chinese individuals had not been high, and their ability to invest in growing companies was extremely limited. They traded this ceding of local control of these companies for a new influx of capital.

China's State Administration of Foreign Exchange (SAFE) issued a series of rulemakings starting around 2005 ultimately requiring local registration of all deals with foreign *special-purpose vehicles* such as shell companies. In 2006 they made it tougher for foreigners to acquire companies in certain sensitive industries or that included a well-known Chinese brand. They also required much more scrutiny of larger deals, generally with a value in excess of $125 million. Very few reverse mergers were larger than that at the time. There also were at times limitations on the amount of funds that could be taken out of China at one time.

The flurry of regulations continued through 2008, often requiring practitioners to pivot mid-deal and restructure things to comply with changing rules. Terms such as the *slow walk* and the SINA model mattered then but sadly do not now. A contingent of U.S. lawyers, accountants, and investment bankers focusing heavily on this bubble kept close tabs on the regulatory environment working with Chinese-based players. Many of these American deal-makers found themselves making the arduous journey to China almost every month. I made seven trips myself during this time.

There were real challenges in completing Chinese reverse mergers, including due diligence, language and cultural barriers, and the financial audit. With very few exceptions, American attorneys and auditing firms had to rely on assistance from Chinese attorneys and accountants. My firm, for example, had no way to independently confirm if a Chinese company was validly existing, or if a particularly important contract was proper and enforceable under Chinese law. We took guidance from Chinese lawyers on these subjects.

Does the company really own the assets it says it does? Do we really understand all its liabilities? Are its bank balances proper? U.S. auditors did not have it easy to confirm these things, not to mention that Chinese accounting principles differ markedly from the United States.

Chinese business culture also tends to resist disclosure. This does not mean the company has done anything improper. The "lift-the-veil" comprehensive disclosure system in the United States did not come naturally to many Chinese executives. Instead of asking a company to simply tell us everything, specific questions were needed to which they would provide specific answers. Dealmakers developed approaches to ensure a belief that there was indeed full compliance in due diligence and disclosure.

Most active U.S. players in the space employed Mandarin-speaking attorneys, accountants, and investment bankers to work on their transactions. Still, it was better when at least one key person in the Chinese company spoke English. Too many things would get lost in translation, or a hired interpreter would "summarize" a ten-minute back-and-forth conversation in 30 seconds. This was a challenge for sure.

The Chinese business culture also is very different from the United States, as Chinese are very plodding in making key decisions. They tend to examine an opportunity or issue from all different angles before making a commitment. As I noted in the 2009 book, if Americans are indeed cowboys (and cowgirls, of course), Chinese businesspeople are more the "Whoa, Nelly!" type when looking at business deals. This can make it a little frustrating at times for get-it-done-type American dealmakers. That said, the Chinese were extremely welcoming and genial hosts to their American guests.

Despite these challenges, over 300 Chinese reverse mergers were completed. Many followed a common path: (1) Combine with a shell, (2) raise $X in a private placement at the same time as the combination, and then (3) file shortly thereafter for a $5X public offering and application to a national exchange. Investment bankers perfected this approach that allowed the company to raise meaningful cash quickly at the time of the merger, and then complete a "secondary" public offering and list the stock on an exchange.

The X above was usually around $3–5 million, so the 5X was usually around $15–25 million. Some were larger. These numbers will become important when we examine the impact of the seasoning rules ahead.

My conclusion in 2009 was that the China outlook was good. To show you how wrong I can be, it is worth reprinting the last few paragraphs of my China chapter in 2009:

> My two cents: The China phenomenon is exciting. I have enjoyed being a part of it. Much like other stock market bubbles, such as the Internet boom, at some point the valuations will come down to earth, and to some extent that has already begun to happen. But that does not mean that companies in China will stop wanting to be public. Even though Internet stocks crashed, the Internet as an industry continued to thrive, especially after the Google IPO several years ago.
>
> As long as the Chinese government allows it, and we all work hard to keep the charlatans from taking advantage of the challenges in these transactions, Chinese reverse mergers appear to be here to stay.

Allegations of Fraud

Things began to unravel in 2010, not long after I published the passage above. An article on *TheStreet.com* in December of that year reported, "The Securities and Exchange Commission is investigating allegations that U.S. firms and individuals have joined with partners in China to steal billions of dollars from American investors through stock fraud, according to people familiar with the probe." The same article noted that three Chinese companies already were facing investigation at that point and included reviews of a dozen more that faced other challenges and suits.

The article further noted that the SEC was targeting U.S. investment banks, auditors, law firms, and stock promoters. One challenge the regulators had was obtaining jurisdiction over alleged bad players based in China, so they were focusing on American players. At the time, some of those U.S. dealmakers were quoted as saying the allegations were overblown and involved only a few companies. Even if the ultimately 30 or so companies that faced allegations and class action lawsuits all were guilty, that would still suggest over 300 Chinese companies that went public in the United States faced no such allegations at all.

None of that mattered of course; the appearance was everything. The alleged fraud took one of several forms as has been discussed. One, simply, was the CEO stole everything and had disappeared. Cash or other assets were gone and no one could locate the founder.

The next form of alleged fraud suggested that Chinese executives bribed employees at their local bank branch. The employee could not easily change opening or closing balances on accounts, but could manipulate everything in between, allegedly creating a false increase in both revenues and expenses, making companies look bigger. Following this, auditors seeking confirmation of Chinese bank balances obtained it only from the bank's *headquarters,* but the damage was done.

Yet another method Chinese companies allegedly used to defraud investors was in the reconciliation of their financial statements to American accounting principles. In a number of cases it appeared that the financial statements filed with the Chinese tax authorities were different, even when adjusted, from those filed in the United States with the SEC. Some quietly noted that the penalties for filing a false tax return in China are extremely low, and companies therefore feel incentivized to cheat on their Chinese tax returns to lower their tax burden.

A number of these financial statement cases ended up dismissed or withdrawn. To succeed, plaintiffs had to prove first that the financials were indeed different after reconciliation, which was hard enough. Then, if they overcame that hurdle, they had to prove that the incorrect financials were the ones filed with the SEC as opposed to the ones filed in China. This, plaintiffs found, would be very difficult to prove.

Another alleged ploy suggested that Chinese companies claimed they had important and valuable contracts that either did not exist or were not legally binding. Other suggested bad behavior involved hiding the involvement of certain particularly questionable U.S.-based players who were either secretly controlling companies or indirectly owning stock that should have been but was not reported.

Who Was Responsible?

The authorities and plaintiffs' attorneys, going after the U.S. players who put these deals together, asked: Where was the due diligence? Were you only focused on the payday and did you do nothing to confirm these companies were real? If these companies did proper IPOs, they would have been more careful. That is what they said.

What more, however, could American investment banks, lawyers, and auditors have done if these allegations were true? And would it have been different in an IPO, considering so many of these companies indeed completed full underwritten public offerings following their reverse mergers in which full and careful due diligence generally is the same as in an IPO?

Take the example of the allegation of different financials filed for tax purposes than in the United States. Is it really the responsibility of auditors of U.S. public companies to check the tax returns and filings in their home countries? Most auditors I have spoken to believe it is not.

The bribing of the bank employee, if it happened, also is problematic to uncover. When an official letter from the actual bank that is holding company funds is delivered to the U.S. auditors confirming the balances and transactions during a month, would any reasonable auditor (before all this) really wonder if the bank branch employee phonied up the official letter?

When a CEO orders the transfer of company assets to his personal account but the accountants do not discover that until afterward, frankly there would have been no realistic way for them to have done otherwise. Auditors do not have access to every bank transaction as it occurs. They take financial statements prepared by other accountants and then come in and check things. If a contract turns out not to be enforceable, or not to be real, the U.S. attorneys representing the company would not have had responsibility to confirm that other than to ask their Chinese counterpart to do so.

Not really any of this was something that traditional investment banks in an IPO would have been responsible to check. They do business and financial due diligence but rely heavily on the auditors with regard to financial issues. It is not their job to check if a contract is legal or if the bank balance is right or if the company files things properly with the Chinese tax authorities.

Early on in this mess, a particularly active auditing firm discovered the "bribe the bank employee" problem and immediately (and rather publicly) resigned from four public Chinese clients. All four happened to have been taken public by the same investment banking firm, also very active in China deals. Both of these firms were, in your humble scribe's opinion, unfairly vilified and thus began the finger pointing.

In the end, while no one I am aware of has completed a thorough analysis, it appears that the 30 or so cases brought in 2010 and 2011 were all either settled (in many cases with insurance) or dismissed or led to the dissolution and liquidation of certain companies. It appears that most of these companies did not think it wise to spend years in litigation leading to a trial.

The damage, however, had been done. The public valuations of all the post–reverse merger Chinese companies plummeted. A number of them went private and gave up their public status. Zero new deals were completed. It was over. It is important, however, to go through this analysis, though it would now seem moot, because it is the hysteria that followed, implying that greed on behalf of U.S. dealmakers overtook care when it is not at all clear that was the case, that led the SEC to pass the seasoning rules that effectively all but ended reverse mergers.

The responsible parties, assuming the truth of the allegations (remember only a few companies actually admitted any liability), were the fraudsters themselves. For good or bad, smart criminals sometimes get away with it despite normal safeguards. In this case, again assuming the truth, they did not, ultimately. Most of the U.S. parties involved in these deals were experienced, diligent, and yes, careful practitioners. Unfortunately, their need to rely on Chinese confirmation of what ultimately turned out in some cases not to be true made it more difficult.

The SEC Responds with Draconian Seasoning Rules

Not long after the China mess began to unravel, the SEC took action. Technically, the action was taken by Nasdaq and the NYSE. It was, however, widely acknowledged that the SEC requested that they do so.

The Rules Are Adopted

In June 2011, Nasdaq floated its seasoning rule proposal. The NYSE (along with the NYSE American exchange, then known as NYSE Amex) followed with theirs in August 2011. The concept would be to require companies merging with shell companies to *season* on the over-the-counter markets for a certain period before being permitted to apply to uplist to a national exchange.

The justifications offered as to why these actions were necessary were these: According to the NYSE proposal, it was (1) allegations of accounting fraud, (2) suspension of trading or registration of some reverse merger companies, (3) an SEC enforcement action against an auditing firm involved with reverse mergers, and (4) the issuance of an SEC bulletin on reverse mergers.

The Nasdaq proposal added a few more reasons, including: (1) concerns raised that certain promoters have regulatory histories or are involved in transactions that are "disproportionately beneficial" to them, (2) the PCAOB has cautioned accounting firms having "identified issues" with audits of these companies, and (3) Nasdaq's being aware of situations where it appeared that efforts to manipulate prices took place to meet Nasdaq's minimum price.

The proposals suggested that seasoning would be the best response to this because it could provide greater assurance of reliable reporting, time for auditors to detect fraud, the ability to address internal control weaknesses, and time for market and regulatory scrutiny of the company.

The proposals differed a bit from each other and from the final approved rules. In the end, the exchanges adopted, and the SEC approved, virtually identical seasoning restrictions in November 2011. In each case, a post–shell merger company must season on a market other than the larger exchange for at least one full fiscal year of the company (and file its annual report on Form 10-K with the SEC for that year). In addition, the stock must trade for a sustained period at the minimum level required to list before uplisting, and a "firm commitment" underwritten public offering with gross proceeds of at least $40 million allows a company to bypass seasoning on any of the three exchanges. In addition, SPACs that trade over-the-counter would also be subject to seasoning after they complete reverse mergers.

Reaction to the Rules

A few months after the rules were adopted, in March 2012, I published commentary on this development in the *Harvard Business Law Review*. To summarize, I questioned both the basis of why restrictions were needed and challenged the notion that seasoning would somehow reduce or address these issues. At the time I also was working with Congress on the new JOBS Act and Title IV. But we had no idea whether it would pass and if so whether the new Reg A+ would catch on.

The seasoning restrictions clearly were a direct response to the allegations of fraud in Chinese reverse-merged companies. A number of those companies, however, did not even go public through reverse mergers. For example, Longtop Financial, whose underwriter was Goldman Sachs and the auditors Deloitte, did a traditional IPO. Longtop was accused of bribing their bank to create phony cash balances. My argument: Reverse mergers did not create or make easier any fraud.

I further noted that trading suspensions do not imply fraud. Companies completing reverse mergers are generally earlier stage. Some do not succeed, run out of cash, and cease their SEC filings, leading to these suspensions. As to the questionable backgrounds of promoters, I argued that the exchanges already have broad discretionary authority to examine the regulatory histories of and financial arrangements made with these individuals. In any event, it was unclear to me how seasoning would reduce the risk of this problem.

It also seemed that imposing these restrictions in part because the SEC issued a bulletin warning people about reverse mergers and the PCAOB had identified issues with reverse merger audits was not sufficient substantive support for this extreme reaction. Further, the fact that there had been one enforcement action against one auditing firm does not suggest any sort of systemic problem.

It further made no sense to me that both the NYSE big board and its smaller sister, the NYSE American, imposed the same minimum $40 million offering amount to bypass seasoning given that all other listing criteria are lower on NYSE American than on NYSE. I suggested $15 million might be sufficient for NYSE American.

In sum, I felt that, unlike in the 1980s when fraud was indeed rampant in the reverse merger space, here the alleged fraud took place, if at all, in a narrow and potentially severable corner of the space, and where the same alleged fraud may have occurred in IPOs and transactions where full public offerings took place.

Our entreaties fell on deaf ears. I submitted a formal proposal to the SEC to make some changes. When I ran into a senior SEC staffer at the 2012 Conference and reminded the official that I had sent the letter, the response was, "Well, this really just isn't the time for anyone to go to the Commissioners and say we want to help people with shell companies." And that was pretty much that.

Aftermath of Adoption of Seasoning Rules

Surprisingly, the new rules did not completely end reverse mergers. It did mean the end of the very successful model of merger and PIPE followed immediately by a $15–25 million public offering and exchange listing. Most reverse merger candidates simply are not big enough to attract a $40 million public offering to bypass the seasoning speedbump.

As previously noted, however, two buckets of deals continued undeterred as we will discuss in more detail in the next chapter. First were companies that had no problem starting their trading in the over-the-counter market. The second group of companies, almost entirely in the life-sciences space, were large enough in value to complete that $40 million public offering and bypass seasoning.

Two other interesting developments also followed. First, some of us noticed a drafting error in the seasoning rules, which only applied after a merger with "an SEC reporting shell company." A number of shells, however, trade on the OTC Pink market and are non-reporting. One assumes the SEC did not mean to intentionally exclude them and allow companies merging with non-reporting shells to freely uplist, but the words are very clear. When I queried an SEC staffer about it, the unofficial answer was, "I guess it says what it says."

It took some effort but Nasdaq did agree to do one deal this way and let a company (Lipocine Inc.) uplist and trade in March 2014 after a reverse merger with a non-reporting shell in July 2013. A few months later the SEC apparently got wind of this and the word came down: There will not be a second deal done this way. The rules were not changed but it was clear the exchanges simply were not going to allow it going forward.

A more interesting development involved more interest in private companies merging with smaller public operating companies that are not "checking the box" as a shell company. These mergers generally would be exempt from the seasoning restrictions. The rules do, however, have interesting language stating that the exchange has the right to consider a very small operating company as the equivalent of a shell company for purposes of seasoning even if it does not technically qualify as a shell under SEC rules.

A number of companies have, however, now successfully completed reverse mergers since the adoption of seasoning and promptly uplisted because their reverse merger was not a shell merger. This was problematic as will be discussed ahead since questionable so-called "footnote 32 shells" were used in some of these deals. As noted previously, these are apparently operating companies taken public and commencing trading with an undisclosed intention immediately to find a merger candidate and spin off or shut down the business operations.

Some reverse merger deals, therefore, continue to be completed despite the challenges of the seasoning rules.

Bogus Shells and Prosecutions

The third piece of the trifecta attack on reverse mergers was in a number of ways a good thing. Both editions of *Reverse Mergers*, published in 2006 and 2009, included a full chapter on shady tactics and how to spot them. It carefully laid out the improper schemes being used to mislead people and avoid Rule 419 and other reverse merger restrictions and how to steer clear or look for signs of trouble.

It is true that the SEC issued famous footnote 32 in 2005. It followed a meeting that I held with senior enforcement officials at the SEC in 2004. In that meeting, which they requested, I explained what we were witnessing in the marketplace by questionable characters. The "operating company" gambit was in full swing, and the footnote sought to put folks on warning about it.

The problem: Throughout the 2000s, the SEC brought only one tiny enforcement action related to this practice and fined a player $25,000 in that one action. This seemed to embolden the bad actors. In fact within the industry these became brazenly known as "non-shell shells."

There were several reasons constructing bogus shells was attractive. First, they avoid any restrictions of Rule 419 and can complete any merger they like with no shareholder approval. In addition, unlike under Rule 419, their stock can trade. The only legitimate way left to create a shell and avoid Rule 419 was with Form 10, but stock does not trade, which was a major disadvantage.

The second advantage of creating bogus shells was avoiding seasoning. If you are an operating company, as noted, you can merge and apply right away to uplist if you qualify since seasoning would not apply. Thus, while these footnote 32s had become somewhat popular before seasoning, they really took off after that.

Another interesting development occurred because some of these bogus shells were outed by the exchanges and treated as shell equivalents as permitted by seasoning. Some players, therefore, gave up on bypassing seasoning but took *pure startup companies* public, relying on another footnote (172) in the 2005 SEC rulemaking.

These startups admitted they were shells because they had no operations or assets, but correctly avoided the *blank check* definition of Rule 419 and therefore could go public without the 419 restrictions, have trading, and take as long as they liked to complete a merger without a shareholder vote. They would merge with private companies not seeking a near-term uplisting and comply with seasoning.

I am not sure, but I believe they did this because they were finding it difficult to find dozens of true operating businesses with at least some revenues of some kind. I admit it was clever and required quite an esoteric knowledge of the reverse merger legal landscape.

What ultimately made these companies bogus, it turned out, went way beyond just failing to disclose their true intention to seek an immediate reverse merger. When I would encounter companies like this, the promoters would say, "Who knows what their real intentions were when they went public? I guess their intentions changed."

What we did not know was that in many cases the bad actors hid their identities and did not disclose their control, in some cases, of dozens of non-shell shells. In addition, they would bring in straw CEOs to run companies that in fact were not real at all and had no actual or intended operations despite the flowery language in their "self-filing" registration statements, which is how many went public (we will cover self-filings in more depth in Chapter 12).

These companies also were required to have at least 40 unaffiliated shareholders to qualify for the commencement of trading. Almost all these companies followed the same path of issuing a lot of stock to the "CEO," then doing a small private offering to 40 individuals, often all foreigners, and then filing an S-1 resale registration as a self-filing to allow the shares held by the 40 stockholders to be publicly resold.

In many cases, however, the stock certificates, along with signed but undated blank stock assignment forms signed by the stockholders, sat in the drawer of the promoter ready to be sold to the purchaser of the shell. We have also learned in some cases the "stockholders" were completely fictitious people.

Some of the CEOs were someone's housekeeper's 19-year-old brother in the Bahamas, clearly with no background or knowledge in the industry in question. There were (and are) many other telltale signs of trouble. As mentioned, however, there remained no enforcement activity. This made it difficult for legitimate advisors to steer clients away from these questionable shells. They would ask the risk that the SEC or criminal authorities would come after them, and we would have to admit the risk was low.

That changed, rather dramatically, starting with the indictment of a well-known Las Vegas–based reverse merger attorney in the summer of 2014 (note I will not be naming any individuals charged in the various cases I will describe).

The indicted attorney was connected to a group that was accused of creating bogus shells and engaging in pump-and-dump schemes related to reverse mergers and aiding and abetting their efforts. Of course her clients and others also were charged in an apparent $300 million fraud scheme that also involved the ex-husband of a well-known celebrity. The case appears to be continuing currently with no resolution.

Four other major cases, also including indictments of prominent reverse merger attorneys, followed. In May 2015, a New York lawyer who ran a law firm and investment bank was sentenced to 18 months in jail when he, along with a contact, were involved in illegal trading activities in post–reverse merger companies.

In November 2015, a New Jersey attorney and several others were indicted and alleged to be part of the $300 million scam above. The U.S. Attorney announcing the indictment said these individuals were "entrusted to be gatekeepers to the securities markets but instead perpetrated one of the largest manipulation schemes ever, and by doing so, preyed upon unsuspecting and elderly investors." In October 2017 the attorney, along with another individual, pled guilty to one count of conspiracy to commit securities fraud. As of this writing they have not been sentenced but each faces up to five years in prison and a fine.

In May 2017, another well-known New Jersey attorney was indicted after being sued civilly by the SEC in 2016. This case directly targeted the creation of nearly a dozen bogus shells with alleged bogus CEOs, fictitious shareholders, and the like. The lawyer also was alleged to have coached witnesses to lie to the authorities during the investigation. The authorities say that the scheme was elaborate and included the attorney assisting in hiding the involvement and identity of the ringleader client of the attorney. Again, there is no resolution yet. The rumor mill indicates that more indictments may not be not far away.

In October 2017, two lawyers, from Florida and California respectively, were charged by the SEC with working with three already convicted individuals to create 22 bogus shells and issue false opinions so shares could become tradeable. One also was criminally indicted.

Now, therefore, I can speak much more strongly to clients about the risk of becoming involved in questionable non-shell shells. There are good-quality public vehicles available for reverse mergers as we will cover in the next chapter. They include shells created from the carcass of a legitimate public company that was sold or went bankrupt and operating businesses that sold off part of their business but retain a small amount and do not see a benefit in remaining public. And yes, Form 10 shells are still attractive in certain situations. Each of these public companies is legitimate and can be utilized for a speedy path to public status without a concern about questionable players and activities.

And so . . .

What a difference eight years makes. Despite the 2008 market meltdown, in my 2009 second edition it truly appeared that the reverse merger market would stay solid and China would help drive that success. I like to tell colleagues to watch me. When a bubble is happening and I finally enter it, you should get out because it means it is about to pop.

When one door closes, as they say, another one opens. I am heartened that the authorities are finally making a serious effort to jail bad actors in this space, though I am of course saddened on another level to see fellow attorneys whom I have known for many years arrested in front of their children. I am also pleased that the challenges described in this chapter led rather directly to the effort to reopen the SEC's front door through the changes in Reg A.

The period from 2008 until the implementation of the Reg A+ rules in mid-2015 was rough for those working to take smaller companies public even as the markets were recovering rather strongly. Reverse mergers were much more difficult and we did not have an alternative. Thankfully, as Reg A+ begins to take hold, we are all hopeful that dark period is behind us. As we will also see in the next chapter, there remains a place for shell mergers as well.

CHAPTER 10

The Future of Reverse Mergers

It certainly appears that, absent a dramatic change in the regulatory environment and investor perceptions, there will not be a return to the heyday of legitimate shell mergers that we saw in the 1990s and 2000s. The China scandals and imposition of seasoning requirements have significantly hampered the interest in this technique. As indicated earlier, however, advantages to these transactions remain in certain situations.

As we also have noted, part of the reason for this decline has been and will be the increasing attractiveness of a Reg A+ IPO as a more appropriate front-door alternative to a traditional IPO for many companies. The facts that total transaction costs are very similar in both and that a Reg A+ deal will not take much longer than a reverse merger are major reasons many believe Reg A+ will supplant most of what would have been shell combinations.

The true test of this thesis may not come until the next bear market. As of this writing in fall 2017, the stock markets have been enjoying continuing record highs amid a slowly but steadily growing economy. There also remains continuing hope among investors, despite the looming Russia scandal and failure to pass a repeal and replacement of Obamacare, that President Trump will succeed in his goals to enhance deregulation, pass tax reform, tackle our infrastructure problems, and strengthen trade.

Will Reg A+ IPOs be tied to the overall IPO market or be more like reverse mergers, which have tended to be less sensitive to market conditions? This is something we do not know enough about yet, and will not until the next closing of the IPO window. If Reg A+ deals pause in a down market, will more companies turn to reverse mergers? Again, this is unclear. Thus, as noted, we should not close the coffin on the humble shell merger.

We also should remember that shell mergers and Reg A+ IPOs are not the only options available to companies seeking a publicly trading stock and having reasons not to pursue a traditional IPO. As we will cover in the chapters ahead, special-purpose acquisition companies (SPACs), self-filings, and other methods, including the recently amended Regulation D Rule 504, remain very attractive options, depending on a company's circumstances.

The future of reverse mergers, therefore, remains somewhat uncertain. Yet companies continue to pursue them, albeit in much fewer numbers than in the past. The attraction of reverse mergers going forward should continue for companies that are content with over-the-counter trading, companies that are confident in their ability to raise $40 million in a public offering and avoid seasoning restrictions, and companies combining with legitimate public operating companies where seasoning would not apply. Let us review each of these and then discuss the real risks of getting involved with bogus shells and the future of the supply, pricing, and market of shells and "non-shell shells."

Reverse Merger, Then OTC Trading

Some smaller companies do not plan a listing on a national exchange when they go public, or they plan to uplist at some point down the road. This might occur when a company simply is not large enough to meet the exchange's initial listing standards. Other situations could include a management team that is relatively inexperienced in running a public company that wants to take advantage of the lower compliance and disclosure obligations that the exchanges require. They can ease into public status with a bit less intensity.

Some biotechnology companies also prefer OTC trading at first. This might be true, for example, if they are going public but expect to reach a major business milestone (such as a successful Phase III trial that can lead to FDA approval) down the road and would rather wait until that milestone is achieved before splashing their way onto an exchange.

Most biotechs had historically waited until the completion of their Phase II trials before going public. We are now seeing, however, some seeking a publicly trading stock as early as completion of Phase I trials. Reasons for this trend include frustration with the collars and restrictions with later venture capital rounds and the desire to reward executives with stock options. These companies also have a bit easier time raising additional rounds of capital once public, even if on the OTC.

Some of these earlier stage biotechs are seriously considering a Reg A+ IPO, but others are looking at shell deals, knowing they will trade over-the-counter initially. Part of the credit for the interest should be given to OTC Markets Inc., which runs OTCQB, OTCQX, and OTC Pink, and its leader, Cromwell Coulson. Cromwell has succeeded in dramatically improving the image of U.S. over-the-counter trading by adding more transparency and accountability from companies trading on their platforms.

I think even Cromwell would admit, however, that the quality and volume of trading in most cases is stronger on the national exchanges. Analyst coverage typically is unavailable on the OTC, and institutional investors generally are prohibited from purchasing these stocks. Many OTC companies, however, do enjoy heavy volumes of trading and solid stock prices. Cromwell also boasts with pride about how many OTC-traded companies successfully graduate to larger exchanges, and that is the right attitude. You will hear some of Cromwell's thoughts in Chapter 14.

A number of legitimate advisors to OTC companies can assist in strengthening market support for their stock. Experts in investor and public relations, along with active market makers and investment banking firms, enjoy the excitement and, frankly at times, the volatility of trading in the OTC markets. Investors who purchase a stock at 5 cents that goes to 10 cents have just doubled their money! How easy is it to do that investing in IBM or Google?

Of course the opposite scenario also exists with sometimes dramatic downturns in these stocks. Short sellers, who make purchases betting a stock will go down, often create self-fulfilling prophesies when the market sees them arrive, especially with relatively thinly traded stocks. Short sellers claim they serve an important purpose when they alert the market of their concerns with management or a company's plan or financial condition. There are times, however, where short sellers get involved where no such negative conditions exist because they believe they can, simply by shorting, cause the stock price to go down and make money.

As we recall, the seasoning rules require a company completing a reverse merger with a shell company to trade somewhere other than the national exchange for one complete fiscal year, among other things. For a number of companies, this is just fine.

Bypass Seasoning with $40MM Public Offering

As we know, the seasoning restrictions can be avoided with a $40 million firm commitment underwritten public offering. A number of companies, principally life-sciences companies, since the rules were adopted in 2011 have completed a reverse merger and a subsequent large public offering to bypass seasoning. These companies are able to continue the previously very popular approach that existed before seasoning, where a reverse merger and contemporaneous PIPE would be completed, followed by a public offering and immediate uplisting to a national exchange. Prior to the seasoning rules, however, as we have noted, those public offerings usually were in the $15–25 million range. Post-seasoning, unfortunately, most companies seeking a reverse merger simply are not mature enough to attract a larger public offering.

One wonders, however, if a private placement followed by a Reg A+ IPO would not achieve the same goals without the challenges that shell mergers bring. There were some deals where the secondary public offering following the reverse merger exceeded $50 million, so Reg A+ would not have been available. If your public offering fundraising goals are $50 million or less, however, it may be that the shell component is no longer necessary.

The counterargument to this suggests that the PIPE completed with a reverse merger looks different because the PIPE investor is putting his money into an already public company, which may allow a bit higher valuation. In Reg A+ deals so far, however, private placements preceding the IPO have been successfully completed.

As previously noted, in some cases it appears that the shell merger model is continuing for these companies because "that's what we've always done." They point to prior successful deals in their industry and feel they should continue that approach. The attorneys, auditors, and others are familiar with the process, have their favored methods of acquiring shells, and can mostly take documents from prior deals and just change the names.

This might make sense if there is no real downside to continuing this way. Even if you are able to avoid seasoning, however, shell mergers face challenges that a company would avoid in a Reg A+ IPO. For example, as we noted there are restrictions on the use of Rule 144 to publicly sell shares that were previously restricted if your company was a shell at any time in the past. Some believe there is also still a taint on a company that has merged with a shell. Finally, if the shell has had past operations, there is a risk that unknown liabilities from the past may surface, and most shell operators sell the entities as is, with no post-closing indemnities as to prior obligations.

This last risk can be avoided with a Form 10 shell, which is formed from scratch as a shell and never has operations. Even companies merging with Form 10 shells, however, face the taint and 144 issues. In addition, as we will note later, the supply of Form 10 shells has dwindled substantially.

In time, many believe that, just as it took a little time for companies to understand the benefits of reverse mergers and start on transactions, the same is likely to happen with Reg A+ when compared to a shell deal.

Merger with an Operating Public Company

We did examine the unfortunate creation of many bogus shell companies masquerading as public operating companies whose stock could trade and avoid all issues of shells. As we now know, thanks to the multiple prosecutions, merging with a public vehicle with the signs of bad actors involved is to be avoided.

This does not mean, however, that there are not legitimate public companies with operations that could be good candidates for a reverse merger. There have been quite a number of these over the years. An example might be a company that sold its assets but remains licensee of its former technology and has an employee whose job it is to monitor the license and collect royalties. A company might be failing and getting ready to liquidate but instead first sells the public vehicle then shuts down. A small company might have determined that being public was not valuable, and after a merger with a larger company, that small company is sold back to its owners.

There also have been reverse mergers involving public operating companies going through Chapter 11 bankruptcy reorganization. The bankrupt company would sell off its assets to the creditors but complete a simultaneous reverse merger with a private company that takes over its public status.

This can be a double win for the private company. First, the buyer knows that it is acquiring a public entity with no liabilities post-bankruptcy, since they are wiped out by court order generally. Second, shares issued in connection with a bankruptcy are exempt from SEC registration and freely tradeable immediately upon issuance. Normally in a reverse merger with an operating public company the shareholders of the former private company acquire restricted stock that must be held for at least six months under Rule 144.

All these opportunities are few and far between, however. Most going through bankruptcy do not even think about or realize the possible sale of their public status. Struggling public companies are more likely just to shut down or file to stop being a reporting company if possible. There are brokers who work to find and offer these entities to private companies. Most are legitimate and well-intentioned but do not necessarily do the same thorough due diligence that a buyer and their counsel would. This often requires going through a number of different public entities before finding one that could work.

Then of course there are the elusive "shells with cash." A public company is sold, say for $50 million. All but $5 million of that is distributed to the shareholders, and a minuscule continuing operation legally avoids a shell designation. It then offers its public status, along with the $5 million, to a private company. The challenge many have found in these situations is that the public vehicle owners tend to view the value of their cash in excess of the value of their cash.

As has been mentioned, some very large companies have chosen to go public by merging with smaller public operating companies. These include Burger King, Kohlberg Kravis Roberts, and the New York Stock Exchange. None of these companies went public through an IPO.

One of the most famous reverse mergers, Warren Buffett's Berkshire Hathaway, was the mid-1960s acquisition of the smaller shirt company still bearing the diversified holding company's name. Interestingly, at one point I wrote to Mr. Buffett to see if he might be willing to assist in our efforts to improve the regulatory environment for reverse mergers. They say he responds to every letter. His assistant wrote back, "Berkshire Hathaway did not go public through a reverse merger." She attached the company history, which actually does not explain how the company went public.

To the extent vehicles are available, acquiring a legitimate operating public company can be an efficient method of going public. None of the shell restrictions such as seasoning and Rule

144 issues apply. As with shells that had former operations, however, careful due diligence must be conducted to ensure that no surprises await post-closing.

The Real Risks of Using Bogus Shells

We discussed earlier the fact that the risk is greater in getting involved with shells or non-shell shells that have earmarks of being fraudulent than it was in the past. Recent prosecutions directed squarely at this practice bear this out. The likelihood of a problem developing is now clearly higher than a few years ago.

What, however, is the problem that will arise? If a legitimate private company merges with a shell that turns out to be bogus, which parties have what risks in that situation? Much of that depends on the extent of complicity in that bad behavior on behalf of the private company.

For this analysis let us assume that we have a shell, or more likely a company pretending to be operating or actually operating with an intent to shut down or spin off the operations shortly after going public. Let us further assume that the public company has indeed materially misled the public about either the true extent of its operations or the plan to find a merger partner and then shut down or spin off its operations.[st

We also assume that it is likely that a single individual or group has engineered the creation of this entity and probably many more such vehicles and has hidden their involvement as control persons. Let us also sadly implicate attorneys who knowingly assisted in taking these entities public knowing not only their bogus nature but also the secret control of third parties.

In this situation, if there is an SEC and/or Department of Justice investigation into the matter, the control promoter, attorneys, and the puppet CEOs all face potential civil liability and criminal risk. Sometimes other players appear in these schemes, including investor relations types, who fully understand the improper nature of the plan or who in any event engage in pump-and-dump-type crimes. They also could find themselves in trouble.

In some cases it turns out that the CEOs did not really understand what was going on and therefore may have no criminal intent. If you are on the board or an officer of a public company, however, you have fiduciary duties that could lead to civil liability for negligence or breach of fiduciary duties if there is something you did not but you *should have known* with reasonable investigation.

The more complicated question is to what extent a private company that merges with such a bogus public entity, or its principals, board members, and officers, faces potential liability. When I am asked as an attorney about that, the answer frankly is not easy and is very fact-dependent. Of course there is some risk if the private company's leaders are told point-blank all about the scheme and the hidden control persons. Even then, though, it might be possible to argue that prior to a merger these individuals have no particular duty to do anything about that information.

In general, additionally, a board member is not held liable for actions taken before that individual came on the board, unless the board needs to take some action to prevent further harm to a company thereafter. So what risk exists then for the private company individuals if they do *not* know that the company is bogus and has secret controllers, or only that it appears to have the earmarks of an illegal scheme but there is no actual direct evidence?

Again, these questions are very difficult. If, for example, it could be shown that in the face of "inquiry notice" where some red flags appear, the private company did not in fact inquire further, some risk could attach. For example, the private company negotiates its entire deal with an individual who is not a formal or disclosed advisor, shareholder, director, or officer of the company. If no questions are asked about the role that person has, some risk may be created.

The promoters generally have pat answers when those questions do come. I own stock but less than 5 percent, so it is not disclosed (private company can ask for the shareholder list if this claim is made). I'm a paid consultant but it doesn't need to be disclosed because it's not a material contract (almost anything is material in a near-shell or shell). I'm friends with the CEO and work with him/her on other things and I'm just helping out here. I plan to buy some shares from the existing shareholders before the deal and I will be compensated that way (again the tax issue discussed earlier).

More commonly, however, the promoters stay in the background and do not get directly involved in the negotiation. In one alleged scheme, the attorney helped the promoter create an email account *in the name of the CEO* so that the promoter could communicate with merger candidates appearing to be the puppet. They usually develop well-crafted stories about why this tiny company with operations in Romania consisting of one small retail store needed to be public in the United States and how it got exactly 40 Romanian individuals to be shareholders, just enough for trading, and how shortly after going public something changed and they suddenly did not want to be public anymore.

It is generally advisable at least to arrange a direct phone call, or ideally meeting, with the public company's executives. Of course this also could be staged, but with greater difficulty than simple email exchanges. How much such due diligence is necessary to satisfy oneself not only that the company is not bogus but that it cannot be later claimed that the due diligence was not sufficiently thorough? That is difficult and usually needs to be assessed on a deal-by-deal basis.

If you therefore assume no or little real liability risk as the principals and executives of the private company merging in, why worry if the risk is to the shell promoters? The first answer is that there might be some risk, as noted earlier, to the private company players. Second and more important, even if they are completely risk-free, their merged company faces the risk of a multiyear, expensive, distracting, and potentially company-killing SEC and/or DOJ investigation and possible lawsuit as well. Even if the private company individuals did nothing wrong, the regulators likely will assume the opposite at first and insist on subpoenas not only for reams of documents but multiday interviews and depositions.

It is therefore the *litigation risk* as opposed to the liability risk that may be greatest for the post-merger company. As we also know, the SEC has the power to destroy companies and individuals merely by accusing them of bad behavior. Several clients of mine who had been in the reverse merger space found themselves arrested at 6 A.M. in front of their children one day. Two years and a half-million dollars in legal fees later, other players involved in deals with my clients went to jail but *all charges were dropped against my clients*. The story is obviously much longer, but this is the DOJ acknowledging the case never should have been brought. As one client said to me afterward, "Now where do I go to get my good name back?"

If faced with some evidence of what appears to be a bogus shell, therefore, it would seem much safer in most cases simply to find another option as opposed to taking any of the kinds of risks previously described. In the end, however, my job as an attorney is merely to lay out the risks upon which my client decides his or her path and risk tolerance.

The Future Supply and Cost of Shells

As with all things economic, the value of shells is all about the relative levels of supply and demand. The basic price to acquire a trading, high-quality, full reporting, electronically trading eligible shell with a large number of public shareholders (these generally being considered the most valuable type of shell company) has varied widely over the years. Prices have ranged in recent decades from the low $200,000s to well over $1 million during the periods of greatest demand.

Other shells tend to be priced lower, including Form 10 shells, non-reporting shells trading on OTC Pink, and trading, reporting shells with a small shareholder base and no actual trading despite technically having a ticker symbol.

Unlike other products in the economy, however, there are only three legitimate ways to manufacture a shell company. The first is complying with Rule 419 and completing an IPO of a shell. As we learned earlier, players quickly learned this process would be difficult, time-consuming, and expensive, and the Rule 419 restrictions very burdensome. The second method is to create a shell raising over $5 million, which allows you to avoid the Rule 419 restrictions. Now known as SPACs, we will cover them in the next chapter.

The third approach to forming a shell is through Form 10. As noted, Rule 419 does not restrict a shell from voluntarily subjecting itself to the SEC reporting requirements. These shells' stock does not trade until after a reverse merger and subsequent registration of shares with the SEC. It took a while, but Form 10 shells really caught on in the second half of the 2000s. My clients alone created and completed deals for over 300 of these shells. There was a time I had two full-time lawyers in my shop doing nothing but creating and maintaining Form 10 shells for our clients.

There are, however, no active players this writer is aware of seeking to create new Form 10 shells currently. Nor have there been since the adoption of the seasoning rules. I currently have one remaining client with one Form 10 shell and that is it. To the extent that demand increases at some point, it will take four to six months for the creation of new Form 10s.

The other types of shells we have noted as likely to be attractive in the future, including former and currently operating public companies, cannot be manufactured. They come about randomly depending on the progress of the already public company. Most believe the period of bad actors creating bogus shells pretending to be operating essentially is over thanks to the recent prosecutions. The supply of shells, therefore, currently is both limited and unpredictable. There remain some of the clearly bogus operating public vehicles around, and some less suspecting players may well acquire them.

On the demand side, as we have noted there are many fewer reverse mergers than before the seasoning rules, so few that there is no longer an industry publication, known as the *Reverse Merger Report*, that tracked the deals on a monthly basis. The SEC does not regularly release statistics on reverse mergers, though thanks to the check-the-box requirements imposed in 2005 they could do so.

A good old-fashioned Google search of "reverse mergers 2017" does lead to a number of deals apparently being completed, most of which appear to be biotech companies. It does seem that these will continue for now, but over time one assumes the increasing notoriety of Reg A+ will draw the attention of dealmakers and investment banks.

Where does this lead shell cost? Of course it remains to be seen. It is also true that asking "What is market?" for a shell is like trying to get 50 cats to stand straight in a line. Some players manage to sell shells well above what others achieve around the same time for a similarly comparable shell. Some shells are sold for cash while others are sold for equity or a combination. The more equity is in the consideration, the higher the price generally.

Another recent trend involves a shell source finding a shell (or operating vehicle) and agreeing to put up or raise the money to acquire the shell from its existing holders at the same time or right before the actual reverse merger. The shell source gets to buy the shell for a much lower price per share than the private company will charge for the issuance of new shares to investors in a private placement that will close upon the merger. Thus, the shell source's shares rise substantially in value almost immediately.

The private company accepts this in order to avoid paying cash for the shell. This also acts indirectly to compensate the shell source for his efforts, and he receives no other pay for finding and negotiating the deal with the shell. If this is indeed the case, however, this structure could create tax issues if some of the difference between the price paid by the shell source and the price paid at the same time by new investors is deemed compensatory.

And so . . .

Reg A+, reverse mergers, self-filings, and SPACs all will have their use in the years ahead. Reverse mergers will continue to be used when OTC trading is acceptable, a $40 million public offering can follow, or where the public company is not a shell.

The market for shells likely will remain fickle and uncertain. The supply, as well as the demand, has gone way down. Prices likely will remain roughly where they have been since seasoning came along, unless something changes to affect demand.

Remember the most important advantage of reverse mergers is speed. There will always be certain deals where a company needs money sooner rather than later, say in two to three months, and the source of financing requires the company to be public to be funded. Those situations lend well to reverse mergers. Even a Reg A+ deal cannot be completed that quickly.

Now we go on to SPACs and other interesting options private companies may consider.

CHAPTER 11

Special Purpose Acquisition Companies (SPACs)

As mentioned in previous chapters, there are two ways to create a shell. One method is to use the public entity remaining after an operating, publicly traded company is sold, liquidated, or goes out of business. The other method is to create a shell from scratch, as many players chose to do, especially in the second half of the 2000s.

The major reasons at the time for the proliferation of newly formed shells were the high cost of purchasing trading shells from former operating businesses, and the difficulty of finding a clean shell even if cost is not an issue. By creating a shell, a deal promoter structures it according to his needs and ensures that it is clean.

A significant development in the shell creation business since 2000 had been the proliferation of special purpose acquisition companies (SPACs) and Form 10 shells (previously discussed). Unfortunately, in March 2008 the pace of creating and taking public new SPACs came to a virtual halt for a variety of reasons, which we will discuss. In the last four to five years, however, as we will note, SPACs have made a strong return.

SPACs have been around since the 1990s. In the mid-1990s about a dozen SPACs were formed. They stopped being popular later in the decade when the initial public offering market boomed. SPACs returned with a vengeance in 2003 when the initial public offering (IPO) market hit the doldrums and, even after recovering, remained inaccessible to smaller companies. That particular SPAC rush continued until 2008. According to *Wikipedia*, about $1.2 billion was raised in three deals *in one day* in December 2007, which was the one-day record for that. We all know what happened to the markets in 2008.

There were some new SPACs around 2010–11. When the reverse merger seasoning rules were passed, SPACs trading over-the-counter were forced to comply, making those SPACs less attractive. The latest SPAC rush started around 2014, and of course they now are all listed on national exchanges to avoid the seasoning issues. Over $5 billion was raised in SPAC IPOs in 2014 and 2015. As of this writing in mid-2017, the SPAC market remains extremely active.

One brief note on names and categorizations: Often, outsiders and industry professionals alike talk about SPACs and reverse mergers as if they are separate topics. In truth, a SPAC is a shell company like any other and it engages in a reverse merger like any other shell would. It is simply a special type of shell. Therefore, SPACs should be considered part of the reverse merger landscape, not something separate from it.

Introduction to SPACs: The GKN Experience

David Nussbaum, of boutique investment banking firm EarlyBird Capital, was essentially the founder of the SPAC movement. It is important, though, to note that he had some help from prominent lawyers (in particular, David Alan Miller at Graubard Miller) and his partners at the time.

In the mid-1990s, while heading up brokerage firm GKN Securities, Nussbaum saw an opportunity. The IPO market was suffering. The Internet boom had yet to occur. The nation was just coming out of a recession, but things were beginning to look up. President Bill Clinton was balancing the federal budget, the economy was starting to improve, and companies were growing to the point where being public could provide some benefit. Yet they had no way to get there through traditional means.

Nussbaum took advantage of an exemption under Rule 419. This exemption provides that any company with $5 million in assets, or that seeks to raise $5 million in a public offering (the SEC views this as requiring a "firm commitment" and not a "best-efforts" underwriting), need not comply with any of the restrictions of Rule 419. The thinking, apparently, was that 419 was meant to restrain smaller players, because those who can raise $5 million are more likely to have other methods of protection for investors.

Under this exemption from Rule 419, one can complete an IPO of a shell with $5 million much like one could during the pre-419 days. This means there is no requirement to put money in escrow or restrictions on the use of the money, no time limit to complete a deal, no shares in escrow (so there can be trading in the shell), and no shareholder reconfirmation prior to closing a reverse merger, which theoretically allows a quicker transaction.

But Nussbaum saw a different opportunity. He would conduct a firm commitment underwriting for a shell of $5 million or even more. (Most of his SPACs in the 1990s raised between $15 million and $20 million.) Instead of staying free of the Rule 419 restrictions, however, he voluntarily adopted a number of them, primarily to help attract investors to his shell vehicles, but also to convince the SEC not to put unnecessary roadblocks in the way as they did for those who tried to create shells under the Rule 419 regime.

So, even though the SEC did not require it, his SPACs (as he started calling them) put all the money raised in escrow, except a small percentage for operating expenses and commissions paid to the investment bankers. The SPACs at the time required investor reconfirmation and vote to approve the deal, with a full disclosure document approved by the SEC. More recently this has been replaced with a tender offer allowing investors to opt out of a merger and redeem their investment, but they no longer have a right to vote for it.

GKN put a time limit on finding a merger partner, but they allowed more time to close a merger than did Rule 419—up to two years instead of 18 months. This period has been shortened in some of the newer SPACs. Most importantly, Nussbaum arranged for a trading market for the stock of the SPAC as well as for warrants sold to investors in the IPO. This would not be permitted in a 419 shell that did not raise at least $5 million.

In addition, as a twist for marketing purposes, Nussbaum declared that each shell would specialize in an industry or geography—one for telecommunications, one for entertainment, one for China, and so on. Newer SPACs might have a focus but give management the right to complete a merger with a company outside that area of focus. Then he would attract a blue-ribbon management team (known as "sponsors") that would be in charge of finding the right deal for the SPAC. The management would be compensated primarily with a hefty chunk of stock, but their experience and eye for deals would be valuable, and in some cases each sponsor would also personally invest in the SPAC's IPO. (Later these investments became typical.)

Investors snapped these up. Why not? They purchased a unit consisting of a share of stock and a warrant to purchase more stock later, or sometimes two warrants. Ninety percent of their money would not be touched and would earn interest while the SPAC searched for a merger target. Later these percentages were even higher, with some escrowing a full 100 percent of investor dollars or, in a few cases, even more than 100 percent.

If investors did not like the eventual deal that was proposed, about a year or two later, they would likely receive 92–95 percent of their original investment back (the escrow funds would earn interest). Again, more recently these percentages went even higher. This was because more investors seemed interested in simply pocketing this extra spread rather than investing in the ultimate operating company. Unfortunately, this also led to some investors looking to vote down deals, which was beginning to be a problem in 2007 and 2008. This led to the elimination of voting as noted earlier.

In most cases, when a deal was announced, and the stock moved back up, investors could simply sell their shares and make 100 percent of their money back, holding the warrants to see how the deal would ultimately go. Others would sell the warrants and hold the stock. Others might like the deal and simply let their money ride.

Although the investment was in a blank check, the money was protected and the investor had a legitimate means to opt out when the deal was presented. In other words, a SPAC offered many of the protections that 419 offered, but stock and warrants of the SPAC were permitted to trade. Essentially, the only risk for investors was the opportunity cost of investing the money elsewhere.

In the meantime, Nussbaum and his firm earned commissions on the money raised. They also earned commissions on the trading of the stock while they waited for a merger. Later SPACs required the investment banks to defer large chunks of their banking fees until a merger was completed.

Companies also liked the SPAC concept as a way to get public. In general, a company that otherwise might have considered a smaller IPO saw the SPAC as guaranteed cash, less risky than an IPO, in which there is always a chance that the underwriter will not be able to raise the desired amount of money. Plus, some companies took advantage of the self-imposed expiration date on the SPAC and cut favorable merger deals in the waning days of the two-year time limit. All in all, the companies that merged with these initial SPACs generally fared well, and the technique worked.

There are several reasons why some companies prefer a SPAC to a more traditional reverse merger. First, the SPAC has cash (although some traditional shells have cash, too). Second, the SPAC has a relatively active trading market, which most shells do not. Third, the SPAC is totally clean and not burdened, as are many trading shells, with a history from a prior operating business in the shell.

In the late 1990s, as the IPO market picked up, Nussbaum moved away from SPACs. Also, some state regulators were beginning to have problems with allowing the aftermarket trading of SPAC stocks. As mentioned, SPACs seemed to move countercyclically to the IPO market for small- and mid-cap stocks. Thus, as the IPOs of Netscape and America Online helped usher in the gold rush now known as the Internet boom, GKN returned to more traditional IPO work.

The First SPAC Resurgence—Bubble and Bust

In 2003, Nussbaum, then running EarlyBirdCapital, determined the time was right to bring back SPACs. I do not think he could have known what he was starting. Although he is still one of the more prolific players in the market, he had helped create a cottage industry. Many brokerage firms specializing in small- and mid-cap stocks completed a SPAC transaction or actively participated in one.

Nussbaum's biggest challenge in the new millennium was convincing Nasdaq, then overseeing the OTC Bulletin Board, then the main over-the-counter trading platform, to allow the stock of the first new SPACs to trade there (the Financial Industry Regulatory Authority, or FINRA, runs it now). In the 1990s, shells routinely were granted the right to trade over the counter. In the early 2000s, however, an unofficial ban on allowing new shells onto the then-OTC Bulletin Board went into effect. That changed, and shells were permitted to trade on it. The "OTCBB" has all but gone defunct though it still technically exists. Over-the-counter stocks now are traded on the platforms of OTC Markets as previously noted.

Although I do not know the details of Nussbaum's discussions with Nasdaq, my understanding is that it required quite a bit of high-level arm twisting to convince Nasdaq that, primarily because of the large amount of money being raised and the high quality of management, the legitimacy of the SPAC and its anticipated trading market should be respected.

To Nussbaum's credit, these discussions opened the door for all others to follow. Later, many SPACs were permitted to trade on what is now the NYSE American exchange (then the American Stock Exchange) as well. Nasdaq also now lists SPACs. This is significant because no state blue sky review of an IPO is required if a company is going to trade on the NYSE American (or Nasdaq for that matter), because Congress preempted that regulation in NSMIA as we know. Later this offered another benefit: avoiding reverse merger seasoning restrictions put in place in 2011.

In case you were wondering, the new Reg A+ rules expressly prohibit the use of Reg A+ by shell companies, or we might have seen some SPACs use the technique. We tend to see two groups of SPACs, one that raises between $35 and $50 million, and the other that raises well over $100 million in each SPAC IPO. That first group might have benefited from Reg A+, but the SEC did not feel it appropriate to extend that opportunity.

The 2003–2008 batch of SPACs certainly were different from Nussbaum's one-man industry in the 1990s. First, those SPACs raised significantly more money as noted earlier. Second, SPAC investors became more savvy and forced bankers to retool the commissions they received for raising money. As a result, as noted, more underwriters of SPACs agreed to back-end a portion of their commissions until a merger with the SPAC actually was consummated.

Third, major players, including Deutsche Bank, Merrill Lynch, and Citigroup, became active in the SPAC market. Their involvement brought much greater legitimacy to the space. In fact, the venerable underwriter Goldman Sachs planned to do a $350 million SPAC, called Liberty Lane, with great fanfare in early 2008 (not great timing!). They were hoping to bring a new type of investor to the vehicle. They proposed some changes in the structure to benefit investors, including giving management about one-third of the upside normally seen, but also cutting the amount of money they had to put in. They also reduced the number of warrants in the deal, making it less attractive to the hedge funds that invested in SPACs.

In a rare Goldman failure, only two weeks after it went to market, the deal was shelved. But the fact that they even pursued a transaction in this area suggested that there is virtually nowhere left on Wall Street where objections to reverse mergers as a concept remained. Of course this was before the China trouble and seasoning.

Fourth, SPAC management teams began to look like business A-lists. People like Steve Wozniak, one of the founders of Apple Computer; famed investor Mario Gabelli; Revlon chief Ronald Perelman; former Vice President Dan Quayle; former CIA Director George Tenet; and billionaire Nelson Peltz joined SPAC teams. For a short while, SPACs were the hottest topic on the Wall Street cocktail circuit. Interestingly, as strong as the current SPAC wave is, there is much less press hoopla about it than there was during this period.

By 2009, over 150 SPACs had become public and over 70 had completed business combinations. It is interesting to distinguish between SPACs raising less than $100 million and those raising more than that amount. About 90 of the SPACs in this generation raised less than $100 million. The remaining 75 or so raised more than that. But while there were more smaller SPACs, the larger ones began to dwarf them in amounts raised.

In 2007, the biggest year by far in both categories, about $1.6 billion was raised by smaller SPACs, but over $10 billion was raised by SPACs raising more than $100 million. When things died down in 2008, those numbers dropped to $288 million and $4.3 billion, respectively. The current wave of SPACs is strongly dominated in number of deals and dollars raised by the larger IPOs.

The SEC did make life a little difficult for this newer generation of so-called "SPAC-meisters" in the 2000s. The examiners of SPAC registration filings tried different tactics to put roadblocks in the way of this technique. All registration reviews were temporarily halted in early 2005 when a SPAC by the name of International Shipping Enterprises announced a merger deal only a couple of months after having gone public. The SEC believed that this meant conversations must have taken place with the target company prior to the SPAC's going public.

Since SPACs must confirm in their filings that they have had no discussions with possible merger candidates before going public, this raised red flags at the SEC. If the SPAC had had such a target picked out in advance of going public, then disclosure of the target, its business, risk factors, and so on, might have been required. After a brief investigation, the SPAC sponsor was able to demonstrate that they did not meet their target until after their IPO was completed, and SPAC registrations were allowed to resume.

In addition, in 2006 the SEC tried to question the treatment of warrants that are purchasable by management, potentially creating another barrier to taking such deals public, although the rules for handling these warrants ultimately were resolved with an SEC no-action letter. Key SEC officials confided in me at the time that, while SPACs are totally lawful, they still dislike any shell company with a trading stock.

Nevertheless, the bankers and their attorneys generally have fought off attempts to stand in the way of SPACs, and the industry has survived the various regulatory setbacks. The involvement of larger banks, and the simple fact that the SPACs are legal and permitted under SEC rules, means that, in the end, the SEC had to allow them to continue. It appears now, in 2017, there remains no meaningful concern at the SEC with the SPAC market.

Who won in the group of SPAC deals from 2003 to 2008? Underwriters, of course, who saw as much as 7 percent of the money raised winding up in their pockets (some of which could not be paid until a merger was completed, in most deals), along with commissions from trading the stock of the SPAC. Service providers such as lawyers, auditors, EDGAR filing preparers, and transfer agents also benefited. The lawyers got a double benefit—first a fee to bring the SPAC public (this involved two law firms, one for the underwriter and one for the SPAC itself), and then another fee when the SPAC negotiated a merger and prepared a disclosure document that had to be approved by the SEC. It should be noted that average legal fees in the latest round of SPACs generally are much lower than those during the SPAC rush in the 2000s.

SPAC management teams benefited as well. They received some stock for their efforts, but they also often put their own money into the SPAC in order to have some skin in the game, as Wall Streeters like to say. That became a de facto requirement in the last year or so of the 2003–2008 SPACs and this remains true in the current round of SPACs. Roughly 2–3 percent of money raised was put in by management, and this was money they would stand to lose if no deal was completed.

Investors also won in these SPACs. They have very little downside risk prior to a merger. Hedge funds and institutions appreciated this facet of the structure. Also, there was real potential upside, because some SPACs did very exciting deals, such as the merger that took public the retail chain Jamba Juice.

Private companies looking to merge with SPACs can win because they see the ready cash. They also often benefit from the guidance and advice of the SPAC management team. Many times the company merging retains some people from the former SPAC management to assist in building their company.

So why did the SPAC market dry up so suddenly in early 2008? Most agree it was a combination of difficult market conditions, simple saturation, and the generally underwhelming performance of many former SPACs' stock after their business combination. The hedge fund and institutional investor community was attracted to the vehicle for a variety of reasons. The most attractive of these was the ability to park their investors' money in a trading vehicle and count the money as "invested." At the same time they had virtually no downside risk and an opportunity to look at the deal subsequently found by the SPAC and determine whether to invest.

The investors represented a relatively limited community, and as the SPACs got larger and, some would say, greed set in, there simply were not enough investors to go around. Some with even more cash to invest decided to park their money elsewhere when some merger deals were held up by lengthy SEC reviews of their proxy statements. On top of this, the stock market had been badly hit by the credit crisis by that time; this also had an impact on the SPAC market.

Lastly, many of that era's SPACs did not fare well in the stock market after their combination. Why was this? First and foremost was the poor performance of the equity markets overall. Other factors were the dilution of investor ownership because of possible exercise of the many warrants in the deal, as well as additional dilution resulting from the meaningful percentage of the SPAC sold to the management sponsors. In addition, some incentives were added to bring investors in, but the incentives tended to attract those interested in a more short-term investment.

SPACs' Recent Return

As previously noted, it took a few years but SPACs returned, mostly after the seasoning rules kicked in. The current SPAC iteration seeks to address many of the issues that challenged the last round. As a result, there has been a new wave of SPACs that mostly began around 2014. Many believe it was a combination of the strengthening equity markets generally and a change in SPAC structure, ultimately approved by the national exchanges, that helped bring back these deals. One significant risk with the prior generation of SPACs always was the uncertainty as to how the SPAC shareholders would vote on the deal. Many private companies stayed away from SPACs because of the risk that, many months after starting the process, the deal could be killed by a negative shareholder vote.

In fact some investors, not as fundamentally focused, learned their return could be enhanced by voting against a deal in certain circumstances. This trend was increasing around the time SPACs took a break in 2008. The new SPAC-meisters changed this, as noted earlier, by replacing a shareholder vote on the deal with the right to opt out of the merger through a tender offer. The problem was that the exchanges had required the shareholder vote when they first allowed SPACs to list there. The exchanges relented, however, and agreed that investors were equally protected with an opt-out and tender offer that included full disclosure about the potential merger.

The other important difference in the newer SPACs is the elimination of the requirement to complete a transaction in a particular industry or geography. Some do not even pretend to have a focus, and others have one but leave management the right to change it. The industry limits required SPAC sponsors to predict what would be hot or popular on Wall Street more than a year after they commence the process. This was becoming difficult.

Another problem with the 2000s-era SPACs was that too high a percentage of SPACs had to liquidate without finding a transaction. This led to an assurance in the newer deals that a full 100 percent of investor money, at least, would be in escrow and earning interest. The sponsors put up sufficient money to cover the cost of the SPAC going public. There is no question this puts the sponsors at real risk. However, when a billionaire private equity player I know put $5 million into a SPAC it was frankly not a big risk for him.

Another change adopted by some SPACs was to include "cornerstone" investors who put money in before the IPO and promise not to redeem their shares even if they disapprove of the proposed merger. This is a feature that has drawn some major private equity players into the SPAC orbit.

The average size of the SPACs also is growing, to over $200 million in 2015. The number of smaller deals has decreased as a few of the underwriters focusing on that size deal have refocused their efforts on other investment banking activities in the steadily rising market we have seen since 2009. In March 2017 the SEC approved allowing the big board, the New York Stock Exchange, to list SPACs with the tender offer approach instead of shareholder approval.

What Is the Future of SPACs?

In the final chapter of this book, we will hear more from experts as to what may come next. In the reverse merger books, I discussed the concept of a "junior SPAC" that I had reviewed with several clients. Even while SPACs were hot, these underwriters were not able to pursue interesting smaller deals, especially as the SPACs grew so rapidly in size. This is especially true today with the average SPAC size continuing to grow. To pursue these smaller deals, some SPAC underwriters created Form 10 shells and used them successfully. Reg A+ now is becoming an additional viable option; in fact it is expressly tailored for smaller deals, and the investment banking community is expanding its learning curve as of this writing. Others discussed with me the possibility of a different kind of SPAC, though to my knowledge no one has pursed this.

The idea is to take full advantage of the Rule 419 exemption provided by the SEC. Form a SPAC not with $20 million or $50 million or $100 million, but with the minimum $5 million necessary to claim the exemption, or a little bit more than that. One way to do this is to raise the money privately, with the underwriter serving as placement agent, before the shell goes public. Then the private shell has the money in the bank as an asset and claims the exemption by filing a Form S-1 resale registration for the investors. One could use a Reg A+ filing for the resale, but there are certain limitations that for the time being make S-1 more attractive.

In this case, no company public offering is involved; therefore, the FINRA compensation review is not undertaken, state blue sky review is streamlined, and the process is a bit simpler. In addition, the placement agent can own part of the shell, which is much more difficult for it to do when it serves as an underwriter of an IPO of a traditional SPAC.

The other approach is to do an IPO of a shell, much like a SPAC does, but only raise $5 million or a little more. The advantage here is that investors have tradable shares immediately, but FINRA, SEC, and state reviews are more difficult, and the investment bank will have more difficulty owning stock. As we mentioned, unfortunately the SEC prohibited shells from accessing Reg A+, and that includes SPACs.

Either way, the key to what I have been calling a "junior SPAC" is to eliminate most of the SPAC and Rule 419-type protections, because the SEC does not require them. The placement agent, now also the promoter of the shell, goes to its closest investors to raise the money—those that it trusts not to act improperly, and that have invested successfully with it in the past.

I have suggested to several clients the following approach to structuring a junior SPAC:

1. The money raised (approximately $5 million or more), minus deal and operating expenses, is placed in escrow, much like in a SPAC.
2. The stock is permitted to trade just like that of a SPAC. It is not clear that the OTCQB or OTCQX will permit this, but OTC Pink will.
3. There is a self-imposed time limit to complete a deal, but it is longer, possibly two and a half years or even three years.
4. No shareholder reconfirmation or ratification of the deal is sought or required. However, see ahead regarding my suggestion for a disclosure and opt-out feature.
5. There is no industry or geographic focus. SPAC management puts in a small amount and receives 10 percent or less of the stock.
6. The size of the merger deal would not have to be related to the amount of money raised. By contrast, in a SPAC the merger deal must have a value of at least 80 percent of IPO proceeds.

I also have suggested that clients consider providing a full disclosure document concerning the company proposed to be merged in, including full financial statements much like those in the "super Form 8-K" required upon closing the reverse merger. This document would not be reviewed by the SEC, and would be mailed to all investors, who would have a certain period, say 20 days, to either opt into the deal or opt out and get their money back. This eliminates the frustrating three-to-five-month delay in getting a proxy, or more recently a tender offer document, approved by the SEC.

Companies can make arrangements similar to the current spate of SPACs, offering backstop protection in case some investors opt out. In this structure, the investment bank assures that it will raise enough money to replace that which is leaving, and the deal does not close without it. In other cases, a company may not need all the money in the SPAC. For example, if only $3 million is needed, but there is $5 million in the SPAC, and $2 million drops out, the merger would still be completed.

The SEC should not be able to stop the underwriters from pursuing this structure, because we remember that any entity raising more than $5 million is fully exempt from all of Rule 419. Will they try to stand in the way if someone attempts this? That is a different question. I am hopeful that they will determine that the junior SPAC structure described earlier still provides sufficient and meaningful protection for investors.

My books have included this suggestion for over 10 years now. I surmise that, despite many conversations with underwriters, there simply are insufficient commission dollars for the investment banks to justify this structure. I believe, however, as noted before, that underwriters would have the ability to increase their equity stake in the ultimate merged entity by forming a new company, issuing stock to itself, and then waiting six months to pursue the $5 million IPO or private placement. Then in any future public offering the underwriters' compensation review at FINRA would be unaffected by the stock since there is a six-month window for that calculation to be made.

Placement agents routinely raise $5 million in private offerings, so this might be a way to think about adding another arrow in the quiver of potential approaches since, like a traditional SPAC, the junior SPAC would have cash ready for the merger partner.

Will the current strength of SPACs continue? The largest investment banks currently are playing in the space, including Goldman, Deutsche Bank, Citigroup, and others. Investors in SPACs now include more institutional players, not just family offices and hedge funds, which increases the potential investor base, a limit that plagued the 2000s-era SPACs. Clearly, time will tell.

And so . . .

Back in mid-2005 when I first wrote about SPACs, some began to wonder if the SPAC market already was saturated with pre-IPO deal activity. I think most were surprised that the growth not only continued, but practically exploded, through early 2008. It was not a surprise to see the technique take a pause when the market tanked, but it frankly was a surprise to this writer when they came back with such strength in the last few years.

As we see also with Reg A+, the legislators and regulators have real power to help or hinder the process of capital formation. SPACs would not exist but for the small exemption in Rule 419 for capital raises above $5 million. Reg A+ only came about because Congress noticed our recommendations from the 2010 Conference.

In the first edition of the reverse merger book, published in mid-2006, I wrote, "It looks to be a fascinating few years ahead in this dynamic area of finance." In the 2009 second edition, after noting this prior quote, I added, "I guess I was right on that one—and I believe that this quote applies today as well."

I find that when someone on Wall Street looks at a trend and says, "This could last forever," that is usually a good time to head for the hills. People said that about Internet stocks in 1999, about Chinese reverse mergers in 2008, you name it. Could SPACs last forever? No one I know is saying that, at least not yet. And given history, we know the market can explode and then suddenly take a pause.

That said, I think it is safe to stick to my 2006 and 2009 pronouncements that we are headed for a fascinating few years ahead in this dynamic area of finance. But wait, as they say on TV, there's more. We move on to self-filings next.

CHAPTER 12

Self-Filings

This chapter describes how to complete a self-filing, also known as a direct listing, through the use of Form S-l or Form 10.

Self-filing with a Form S-l may be appropriate for companies that do not wish to go public by merging with a shell or for whom a Regulation A+ IPO may be inappropriate for some reason. Raising money during the process is slightly easier with Form 10, but in general Form S-l provides the greater benefit with little restriction. As we will see, the SEC rules on Reg A+ place heavy limits on how self-filings can be done, making S-1 or Form 10 generally more attractive for this option.

Self-filings through an S-l, or through Form 10 for that matter, have not yet become very popular and remain somewhat emerging techniques. This has begun to change as several important biotech companies chose this route over a reverse merger or IPO. In addition, in 2017 music giant Spotify, flush with billions in cash, announced it is likely considering going public through a self-filing since it does not need additional funds from an IPO but sees benefit in going public. The New York Stock Exchange as of this writing is seeking approval from the SEC to allow companies to go public on the big board through this technique, which the Nasdaq already permits.

The 2008 changes to Rule 144, which imposed some negative consequences for having been a shell company at some point, along with the seasoning requirements imposed on reverse mergers in 2011, have led some players in the industry more seriously to consider self-filings. In these transactions, a company avoids the need to enter a transaction with a shell company and does not raise money through a public offering.

How Do Shares of Stock Become Tradable?

Once a company is public and has a trading symbol, its shares can be traded publicly through a broker if the appropriate SEC regulations are followed. The basic rule is that the shares to be sold must be registered with the SEC unless an exemption from registration applies.

Registration of Shares

Companies and shareholders with stock to sell publicly can register their shares with the SEC (or qualify shares through the exemption from registration that is Regulation A+). If a company's first registration is for the public sale of stock by the company, it is called an initial public offering (IPO). Subsequent registrations are called follow-ons or, sometimes, secondary offerings.

Shareholders whose shares were not registered when they acquired them also can complete a registration known as a *resale registration*. They may undertake to register the shares when they need liquidity and the ability to sell the shares publicly and cannot wait long enough for an exemption to apply. For example, one exemption, under Rule 144, allows public sale of shares in a company that was never a shell without registration after the shares have been held for either six months or one year, depending on certain circumstances. Another exemption permits public resale without registration if the shares were issued pursuant to a bankruptcy reorganization.

In most private investment in public equity (PIPE) transactions, investors acquire unregistered shares that bear a legend prohibiting transfer except upon registration or an available exemption from registration. They do so with the understanding that the issuing company will effect a resale registration on the investors' behalf, generally within 90 to 120 days. This is usually preferable to a secondary offering because the completion of fundraising can happen more quickly and involves fewer regulatory hurdles.

The resale registration generally is not reviewed by the Financial Industry Regulatory Authority (FINRA) and is subject to a much less stringent state securities law (or blue sky) review than an IPO. Of course, in exchange the company generally raises money in the PIPE at a discount to the stock's trading price, because the investor takes a short-term liquidity risk.

Registration takes time. Someone must write the public offering prospectus or offering document, which is included as part of the registration statement filed with the SEC, making sure that it includes the information the SEC requires. Much like the offering circular for a Reg A+ offering, a prospectus included in a registration statement must include at least two years of audited financial statements, a year-to-year comparison of results, executive compensation, business description, review of litigation, risk factors, a full capitalization chart, a detailed discussion of dilution, disclosure of related-party transactions, and a whole host of exhibits, including material contracts, corporate charter, and bylaws. Other elements of the registration statement include a summary of prior securities offerings and certain promises the company must make to the SEC in order to complete the registration.

This registration statement (including the prospectus) is filed and then reviewed by the SEC's staff of examiners in the Division of Corporation Finance. The SEC must respond to the filing of an original or amended registration statement within 30 days. It is not unusual to go through three or four iterations of the filing before it is approved, upon which the SEC declares it "effective" and it can be used to sell shares publicly.

In an IPO registration (remember, Reg A+ is an IPO but is exempt from registration and so is distinguished from this), a prospectus must go to the buyer the first time each newly registered share is sold. SEC rules, however, stipulate that shares sold in resale registrations do not have to be accompanied by a prospectus as long as one is publicly available. The registration must be kept current until all shares registered under that registration statement are sold by the selling shareholders. This may require quarterly and other updating, but that is usually not difficult to do.

To make this a little easier, in 2016 the SEC adopted rules permitting smaller reporting companies (as long as they are not considered penny stocks) to "forward incorporate by reference" their future SEC filings into the resale prospectus to keep it current. Therefore, there is typically no longer a need to constantly update, supplement, or amend the registration after effectiveness. The theory is that potential purchasers of the stock being resold should look at all the SEC filings of a company before investing. The SEC was required to adopt these rules under the Fixing America's Surface Transportation (FAST) Act of 2015.

Exemptions from Registration: Rule 144

As mentioned earlier, stock must be registered with the SEC before it can be sold publicly, unless an exemption applies. A number of exemptions are available, depending on the circumstances and facts of a particular situation. For example, as mentioned before, certain issuances in connection with a bankruptcy reorganization are exempt from registration, and shares issued may, in certain circumstances, be immediately resold if there is an existing trading market for them.

The most popular exemption from registration is Rule 144. As previously discussed, shares can become freely tradable without registration as long as they are held for a certain period of time. In general, a nonaffiliate shareholder of a full SEC reporting company must hold unregistered shares for six months. During the following six months the company must remain current in its SEC filings if a Rule 144 sale is to be available. After shares have been held for one year, they are freely tradable by nonaffiliates without these restrictions.

If the holder is an affiliate of the company, meaning an officer, director, or other control person (this is generally presumed if one owns over 20 percent of the outstanding shares or has the ability to effect policy change in the company), no shares become freely tradable for six months. After the six-month period, the affiliate can sell up to 1 percent of the company's outstanding stock (or 1 percent of the average weekly trading volume, whichever is higher) for as long as the holder remains an affiliate, and for 90 days thereafter. If shares are purchased from an affiliate, a new holding period begins (as if the affiliate never started his own holding period). Thus, an affiliate cannot allow a purchaser to *tack* his holding period.

As mentioned before, these holding periods are adjusted in the case of shells so that sale under Rule 144 is available following a reverse merger, starting the later of six months from acquisition of the shares or one year after the reverse merger and filing of the super Form 8-K. Also recall the *evergreen requirement*, which does not permit a sale of stock in a former shell under Rule 144 if the company has not been current in its SEC filings for the 12 months prior to sale. In addition, Rule 144 is generally not available for the resale of shares issued while the company is a shell.

Another Rule 144 wrinkle relates to derivative securities such as warrants or options. If one receives an option on a certain date and holds it for a year, then exercises the option for the cash purchase price, a new holding period begins after that cash purchase. If, however, the option or warrant simply is traded for common stock without any cash payment, an exception in the rule allows what is known as *tacking* of the holding period from the day the option or warrant was issued. In other words, in so-called cashless exercise transactions, the holding period relates back to when the original derivative was received.

Cashless transactions work as follows. Imagine a warrant to purchase 100 shares of stock. It has a $3 per share exercise price and was issued on January 2, 2017, when the stock was trading at $2. This warrant is known as being *out of the money* because the warrant exercise price is above the current market price and it does not make sense to exercise at that time. A year later, on January 2, 2018, the stock moves up to $6 a share, making the warrant *in the money*, because the holder can exercise the warrant for $3 when the stock is selling in the market at $6.

A holder can exercise the warrant for cash at $3 per share, upon which a new holding period begins. Now he must wait at least another six months under Rule 144 to sell the shares. Alternatively, if permitted by the terms of the security, the holder can exercise a warrant for 50 shares by turning in the warrants for the other 50. In other words, the holder returns 50 warrants, which now have a net value of $3 per share (the $6 market price less the $3 exercise price), which becomes the purchase price for the other 50.

The negative side of the cashless event is that the holder must give up a portion of his holdings. The positive side, besides avoiding the use of cash, is that the holder can tack the holding period and has the immediate ability to sell the underlying shares under Rule 144. PIPE investors typically receive cashless exercise warrants as part of their investment. They like this cashless exercise feature, which protects them from the risk that the company will not succeed in completing the registration of its primary stock holdings purchased from the company. (After a registration, Rule 144 will not be needed.) At least they know that one year after closing the PIPE transaction they will be able to sell some of the shares underlying their warrants, as long as the warrants are in the money and there is a liquid market for the shares.

This same analysis applies to preferred stock or convertible debt. In both cases, the security usually can be exchanged for common stock on some basis, without payment of additional cash. Under Rule 144, because one security is exchanged for another, the holding period relates back to the date of acquisition of the preferred stock or convertible debt. Again, in PIPE transactions involving these securities, an investor utilizing this cashless feature has some protection if the resale registration is not completed.

Self-Filing Through Form S-1 Resale Registration

SEC Regulation S-K sets out the disclosure rules for all public companies and includes a definition of *smaller reporting company*. A smaller reporting company has to have a public float of less than $75 million. If public float does not exist or is zero, the company must have less than $50 million in revenues.

Smaller reporting companies do not need to do everything larger companies do in terms of disclosure. The major difference is that a smaller reporting company only has to provide two years of audited financial statements, whereas a larger company has to provide three years unless it qualifies as an "emerging growth company" under Title I of the JOBS Act, in which case two years is sufficient. Most companies pursuing self-filings are likely to be smaller reporting companies, but that is beginning to change as noted by the Spotify example.

Using the Form S-l resale registration method of self-filing, a privately held operating business "goes public" by effecting a resale registration of shares that have been issued but, under Rule 144, cannot yet be publicly resold.

Private Offerings During Registration

Until 2007, one of the basic no-no's of a primary offering or resale registration was that, with narrow exceptions, one could not pursue a private offering of company securities when a registration is pending with the SEC (this was also true at the time for Regulation A IPOs). In a famous no-action letter, the SEC had ruled, again with very few exceptions, that the only private placement one could pursue during a registration was an offering to qualified institutional buyers (QIBs), as defined in SEC Rule 144A.

Qualified institutional buyers are (1) entities that, either acting for their own account or others, own or invest on a discretionary basis at least $100 million in securities of issuers not affiliated with the company selling securities to the QIB, or (2) securities dealers who own and invest at least $10 million in securities not affiliated with the company. Therefore, many usual sources of financing—angels, venture firms, and accredited investors—were unavailable while a registration statement was pending. Occasionally, depending on circumstances, the SEC would allow an exception.

This interpretation prior to 2007, which prohibited most private placements during a pending offering or resale registration, existed to make sure that one of the provisions of Regulation D Rule 506(b) was not violated. The provision, as noted earlier, says that when a company wishes to complete a private placement, it may not engage in a "general solicitation" of investors. The offering documents filed pursuant to the registration are publicly available during the SEC review process.

In 2007, as part of a rule proposal relating to Regulation D that appears to have been otherwise abandoned, the SEC issued immediately effective new guidance that mostly eliminated the restriction previously noted. The new interpretive guidance makes clear, essentially, that any otherwise legitimate private offering of securities may be able to move forward, even while a Securities Act registration is pending, *so long as the investor was not solicited using the pending registration, and the investor was not directed to the company as a result of the pending registration.* The actual language is more technical, and I urge you to consult with counsel in specific circumstances.

In the final rules on Regulation A+, the SEC confirmed that this same approach applies to public offerings there. A company can complete a concurrent private placement, even if it prohibits general solicitation, so long as investors are not solicited or directed to the company by the Form 1-A or any testing-the-waters materials.

One major benefit of the S-1, however, is that if a company has many shareholders whose shares would not become publicly tradable under Rule 144 if it went public through Form 10 (which does not register individual shares and relies on enough shareholders being able to sell under Rule 144 without registration), the S-1 effects the removal of all trading restrictions on the shares being registered to be resold.

Mechanics of Form S-1 Self-Filing

The beauty of the SEC's integrated disclosure system is that almost regardless of the type of filing being undertaken, much of the same information needs to be prepared; it just has a different context. The basic process of completing an S-1 resale registration in a self-filing involves (1) engaging the necessary professionals to assist; (2) identifying the shareholders whose shares will be registered; (3) preparing and filing the document; (4) dealing with SEC (and possibly FINRA) comments and revisions; and (5) establishing a trading market. A brief examination of each follows.

Engaging Professionals

A cadre of expert professionals is necessary for the timely completion of an S-1 filing. Necessary experts include auditors, legal counsel, a transfer agent, SEC electronic filing services, possibly printers, and others. As stated earlier, it is a good idea to engage an investment banker or other Wall Street veteran to assist you in selecting these professionals. Indeed, the professionals may advise that an S-1 is not the most advantageous route for a particular company.

Identifying Shareholders

The next decision, given that this is a resale registration, is determining which shareholders will have their shares registered. The first question to ask is which of the company's shareholders may already have the ability to sell their shares publicly under Rule 144. (Remember, technically a resale registration is made on behalf of the selling shareholders, not on behalf of the company.) Some shareholders—those who are not affiliates of the company—will have owned their shares for six months. Under Rule 144, in most cases these shares may be traded without prior registration and would not need to be included in the resale registration.

Equally, the company or its investors may wish to restrict which shareholders will have the right to have their shares registered. For example, a key member of management who may have held shares for a short time may wish to have his shares registered, but investors may feel it is not desirable for a member of management to have the ability to cash out his company ownership.

At this time, an analysis of the timing of the financing makes sense. If the company is considering a PIPE or other financing before it goes public, it can include the investors' shares in the S-1 registration and will be tradable as soon as the registration becomes effective. Those who invest early, however, take a risk that the S-1 or other going-public event will never occur and they will be left with illiquid securities.

The flipside of limiting who gets to register has to do with the float. The larger the number of shares and shareholders available to resell in the public market, the stronger the potential that a robust and liquid trading market will develop, thereby creating a reasonable float in the outstanding shares of the company.

Here it is appropriate to explain how the Reg A+ rules address resale filings. Unfortunately, in most cases these rules do not permit the use of a Form 1-A to allow the public resale of shares unless there is a concurrent public offering of new shares by the company. The SEC requires that the dollar value of shares being resold cannot exceed 30 percent of shares being sold in a Reg A+ public offering for a company's first Reg A+ filing and for the first year thereafter. This requires a contemporaneous public offering. As an example, in order to publicly resell $10 million in securities there must be an IPO for at least $33.3 million at the same time.

Therefore, while a potential Reg A+ issuer could conduct a Reg D offering before its IPO and promise public resale as part of the IPO process, it cannot complete a Reg D offering and go public solely through the resale as is possible with a Form S-1. Therefore we would not tend to call these filings "self-filings" since they would merely accompany an IPO.

In its release, the SEC stated that they did not want to encourage allowing the use of Reg A+ when no new funds are being raised. If the interest in self-filings grows, however, so might the drumbeat for the Commission to reconsider this restriction. If the prospect of a Reg A+ resale filing helps raise money in a Reg D private placement prior to filing, the same goal is achieved.

Preparing and Filing the Document

The preparation of the contents of the S-1 filing is similar to the preparation of a super Form 8-K following a reverse merger. Usually, the attorneys, with help from management, take the lead in putting the document together. The basis of the filing is a well-written business plan prepared by management, which is then transformed into a prospectus.

The auditors must complete their two-year audit, as well as assisting management in preparing the MD&A. In this section, management must describe, line item by line item, what changed from year to year and from quarter to quarter (if it is the middle of a year), and why it changed.

Once the filing is ready, it is sent for "Edgarization" under the SEC's Electronic Data Gathering, Analysis, and Retrieval system (EDGAR). As we have discussed, EDGAR is the electronic filing system that the SEC fully implemented in 1996.

Once all the approvals of the Edgarized version of the filing are obtained, a company authorizes the EDGAR service to push the button and file. The filing date is the same as the day the files were sent, as long as this occurs before 5:30 P.M. Eastern time. The filing date can be important, as the financial information in the filing must be current, in most cases no more than 135 days old. If the financials go stale, it may be necessary to input updated information and then file.

The FAST Act in 2015 added another helpful change. It provides, essentially, that if at the time of your initial SEC filing you reasonably expect that certain financial statements will not need to be included in the final effective filing, then you can exclude those financial statements from the initial filing. If, for example, your initial filing is made in early January 2018, you would have had to include full annual audited financial statements for 2015 and 2016 (assuming your fiscal year is a calendar year).

However, after mid-February 2018 in this scenario, you would have to include annual audited financials for 2016 and 2017, and you no longer would need 2015. Since it is likely that you will not complete the SEC review process by mid-February, the new law allows you to exclude the 2015 audit from that initial filing since it will not be required at the end of the process.

We should note that the SEC has confirmed that this flexibility also applies to Reg A+ filings even though the law technically limits itself to registration statements. This change has provided some helpful relief in allowing companies to avoid wasting time on preparing financial information that ultimately will not be needed.

SEC (and FINRA) Comments and Revisions

After filing comes waiting. Sometimes the response from the SEC arrives in less than 30 days, but not usually. The company typically receives a formal comment letter from the SEC examiner who reviewed the filing. FINRA may need to review the document as well, to determine if any interest held by those individuals or entities who are selling shares violates the limits on underwriting compensation. FINRA's review has no specific time frame and can take quite a bit of time.

Most professionals rank SEC comment letters by the number of comments received. "We only got forty comments" is a common happy response to a first filing. I think, though, that quality of comments is more important than quantity. I once received 72 comments on an initial filing, and felt very unhappy. But as I went through the comments, it was clear that very few of them were substantive, and the great majority were cosmetic or minor. That, to me, is better than receiving 40 difficult comments to address. In contrast, recall that recent Reg A+ filings generally have received fewer than 10, almost always very minor, comments. It should be noted that the SEC examiners, in recent years, generally have been giving fewer comments to S-1s than before 2010.

An S-1 allows a reasonable and flexible amount of response time (unlike a Form 10 filing, which, as will be discussed later, comes with a ticking 60-day clock); however, a response to the SEC is mandatory. If they do not receive a response, the SEC will eventually decide, after a warning first, that the registration has been withdrawn and abandoned.

SEC comments tend to be divided between financial and non-financial topics and, therefore, must be reviewed with auditors as well as company officials. The team then responds to the comments. In some cases, agreeing with a comment is no problem (such as when it suggests that a risk factor is too generic and must be removed). In some cases, responding to a comment requires a project, such as making changes to the financial statements or altering a business description.

In other cases, the company simply disagrees with a comment and wishes to express its view. For example, occasionally the examiner misunderstands a disclosure of some kind or the SEC is requesting disclosure that is not required and that the company prefers not to make.

After reviewing the comments and, occasionally, discussing them with the SEC staff, an amendment is filed, along with responses to the comments, and then the SEC enters another round of review and provides another comment letter, ideally with fewer comments than the previous letter. This continues, essentially, until they are out of comments. The number of rounds of filings this takes is a function of the company's willingness to play ball with every SEC comment, the capability of the SEC examiner, and, frankly, the SEC's apparent comfort level with the filing or transaction in question.

Once the SEC has completed its comments, it declares the registration statement effective and it can be used to resell the securities that were registered through that process. Typically, effectiveness is accelerated by a formal request asking for a certain effective date.

FINRA can be more difficult, and some filings cannot go ahead without its approval. There is simply no way to predict how long a FINRA review will take. Comments in the third round of communications can be brand-new and of the type that should have been raised in the first round. It can take 45 or 60 days to get one round of comments.

Establishing a Trading Market

Once the S-1 is effective, the company is public—no IPO, no reverse merger with a shell with the lingering evergreen problem and seasoning issues. Financing has been obtained either before or right after the filing becomes effective, or carefully while it is pending under the 2007 interpretation.

There are now enough shares in the public float to qualify for, say, the OTCQB or OTCQX. FINRA and these platforms unofficially require at least 35 to 40 nonaffiliate shareholders with at least 100 tradable shares apiece. This requirement is not on any official list of rules, but as a practical matter the regulators will bury your application to trade if you do not meet this criterion.

All that is missing is a quotation or listing on an exchange or market, without which the shares may not be traded through brokers. Most companies going through a self-filing do not yet qualify for the higher exchanges, so broker-dealers serving as market makers will be needed to get trading going since that is required in the over-the-counter markets. I generally recommend that a company encourage market makers to start the application process while the S-1 or other filing is pending, so as not to waste time. The process of obtaining approval can take a few months, so the sooner the process starts the better.

In general, the over-the-counter platform will begin reviewing an application for a company that is not yet public as long as the company has initiated the process. Running these two processes in parallel gives the company the best chance of having a listing by the time the SEC clears the registration so that the shares can begin trading.

Self-Filing Through Form 10 Registration

When is it preferable to use Form 10 instead of Form S-1 to take a private operating business public? Because a Form 10 filing does not contemplate an offering, a company can use it and at the same time raise money privately without needing to comply with the 2007 SEC interpretation that permits raising money while an S-1 is pending. Under that interpretation, the company can only do so after confirming that investors did not learn of the company or the offering from the company's S-1, and that the company did not solicit investors with the S-1. For some, taking this risk may not be desirable.

In addition, if the company has a number of shareholders who have held securities long enough to be able to sell publicly under Rule 144, filing an S-1 resale registration may not even be necessary. If a PIPE investor wishes to have securities registered, an S-1 can be filed after the Form 10.

Form 10 versus Form S-1 (Exchange Act versus Securities Act)

Form 10 is remarkably similar to the S-1, except it does not describe a securities offering. The company description and other sections are basically the same as those on an S-1 or any public offering document.

S-1 is a form created under the Securities Act of 1933 (as is Form 1-A for a Reg A+ offering), and Form 10 is a form under the Securities Exchange Act of 1934. Following the great stock market crash of 1929, Congress sought to regulate the ailing securities markets. The '33 Act, as it is often called, or the Securities Act, as we will call it here, established guidelines for companies conducting public offerings, requiring them to register any such offering with the SEC.

The '34 Act, also referred to as the Exchange Act, officially established the SEC and set up the integrated disclosure system and series of periodic and current reports required of reporting companies, among other things. If a company is subject to the reporting requirements of the Exchange Act, it may be able to list its securities on the OTCQB or OTCQX or any national exchange. Non-reporting companies' stock may only trade on the OTC Pink. As we have noted, the QB and QX recently amended their rules also to permit Reg A+ issuers to have their stock quoted there, with certain limitations, even if they are in the light reporting system.

When a company goes public through a public offering by it or its shareholders, for example, on Form S-1, it is automatically subject to the reporting requirements through the end of its first fiscal year after the offering. (This is pursuant to Section 15 of the Exchange Act.) After that, continuing to be a reporting company is by choice (pursuant to Section 12 of the Exchange Act). Some companies simply cease reporting after this one year and their stock trades on the OTC Pink.

Most companies completing a public offering immediately become reporting companies through a very simple filing known as Form 8-A. If this is filed within the first full fiscal year after the offering, a company automatically becomes permanently subject to the reporting requirements. As discussed, Reg A+ issuers must file their Form 8-A much closer to the time of completion of the offering.

After this time, or if a company has not yet conducted a public offering, if it wishes to become a permanent reporting company, it must file a more complex form, known as Form 10, in order to have a class of its securities, typically its common stock, registered with the SEC, rather than individual shares. No offering is involved and no shares become tradable by virtue of this filing unless an exemption from registration, like Rule 144, applies.

Form 10 typically is used in two situations. One is when a company has conducted a public offering, its stock is trading, and it is beyond its Section 15 mandatory filing period. Now it seeks to become a reporting company either to complete a merger or move up to a higher exchange.

In another case, a company goes public through a Form 10 filing. This is how the form is used within the context of a self-filing. A private company wants voluntarily to subject itself to the SEC's reporting requirements. Trading can commence, even if no shares individually are registered, in one of two ways. Either enough shareholders have held their shares long enough under Rule 144 to allow them to become tradable without being registered once the company is reporting and has a ticker symbol, or the company intends to file an S-1 resale registration to release some shares from restriction immediately following the day when the Form 10 filing is completed and effective.

The question then becomes, why file an S-1 after a Form 10 rather than just going public through an S-1? The answer, as mentioned earlier, is restrictions on financing. If a company needs to complete private placements and raise money while waiting to become public, it may be concerned it cannot satisfy the SEC's requirement to ensure that an investor was not solicited with the S-1 nor did the investor learn about the company or the offering through the Form S-1. Using the Form 10 eliminates this concern.

If it seems a little tedious to deal with two different filings, consider that the second filing, taking place right after the first, is likely to get much less SEC scrutiny (assuming the SEC has carefully reviewed the Form 10 before its effectiveness, which is likely). In this way, a company is able to finance itself while waiting to go public without concerns about the 2007 interpretation, can close a PIPE when the Form 10 is effective, and can then file the S-1 resale registration with its money already in the bank and likely a speedy SEC review.

Filing Form 10 and Automatic Effectiveness

The process of preparing the Form 10 and getting it filed basically is the same as that for an S-l. The difference comes into play after the filing is made. Under SEC rules, Form 10 is *automatically effective* 60 days after it is filed. In other words, if the SEC chooses not to comment, the form is effective after the 60 days have elapsed and the company is thereafter public and subject to the Exchange Act reporting requirements.

If the SEC does comment, the form still becomes effective 60 days after its original filing date, provided the amendments have been filed and all comments have been cleared before 60 days pass. Miss this deadline and the SEC will either allow the form to go effective and treat future responses to the comments as a so-called post-effective amendment, or insist that the form be withdrawn and refiled, starting another 60-day period.

Developing a Market After Filing a Form 10

As mentioned earlier, the process of obtaining a ticker symbol and getting trading started is a little more complex with a Form 10 approach. Hopefully, the company has at least 35 to 40 nonaffiliated shareholders with more than 100 shares each that have been held a sufficient time to be tradable under Rule 144. If so, trading on the over-the-counter markets can commence immediately upon the form's being declared effective. If not, an S-l needs to be filed and brought to effectiveness before trading on the OTC markets can begin. In the meantime, if there are some shareholders with tradable shares, a ticker can be obtained and trading can commence on the OTC Pink.

And so . . .

If we ever publish a second edition to this book, I am willing to predict that we will be talking about more successful self-filings than we are able to currently. There has been a trend of companies staying private longer, especially since legal changes in the JOBS Act now permit the ability to bring in more shareholders before being required to be a full reporting company.

As a result, companies are growing quite large and flush with (mostly private equity) cash while staying private. According to www.techcrunch.com, there are over 250 "unicorns," private companies with estimated market values in excess of $1 billion. As of this writing in fall 2017, the list includes behemoths like Uber, Airbnb, WeWork, Pinterest, and Dropbox.

Many of these companies, as with Spotify, have raised billions of dollars from the largest institutional investors. Yet many would appreciate the benefits of a public trading stock either to develop a path to liquidity, make growth through acquisition a little easier, or provide their executives with incentives through valuable stock options.

Many smaller companies are in a similar boat, having raised cash, and simply do not need the further dilution from an IPO. It will be interesting to see how the interest in self-filings develops in the next few years.

CHAPTER 13

Other IPO Alternatives

The securities laws permit a number of other methods for going public. Currently, however, none of these is in wide use, and a number of states prohibit some of the techniques discussed ahead.

Going public through Rule 504, an intrastate offering, or through Regulation S is technically legal. As discussed ahead, despite a recent encouraging change, Rule 504 is prohibited in most states, it can be difficult to properly use an intrastate exemption even with some recent rule amendments, and the wild days of Regulation S have been tamed by regulatory reform. Nevertheless, a full account of these techniques is provided in order to understand the context in which they exist alongside Regulation A+, reverse mergers, special purpose acquisition companies (SPACs), and self-filings.

Interestingly, in my reverse merger books, old Regulation A was included with this group as an alternative that was not much used. It turns out I may have been a bit prescient in my 2009 second edition when I said, "I have been hearing for a number of years that a potential overhaul of Regulation A is in the works, but no change seems imminent. There was talk, for example, about increasing the amount allowed to be raised." It was about a year later that I took that idea and presented it to the 2010 Conference.

In my prior book, I also described some of the challenges in making old Reg A successful, noting,

> In part because of its reduced disclosure, both at the time of the going-public event and afterward, Regulation A has been used by some unscrupulous players to use these public entities to manipulate trading and give the public virtually no information about the company. Others have used Reg A to go public and then voluntarily provide some reporting or other information. Most securities lawyers cannot remember the last time someone they know has used Regulation A, but it is out there as an option.

The other big challenge I mentioned was blue sky:

> Although I don't have specific experience, I assume the individual states where such offerings are taking place are not too thrilled with Regulation A either, and one of the reasons for its limited popularity may be the inability to "clear" blue sky review and let an offering be completed.

Bingo!

How things have changed. Reg A goes from a brief reference noting its lack of utility to half of this book covering this exciting new technique. Here are a few others still out there, several of which have been the subject of recent SEC rulemakings intended to enhance their attractiveness.

Intrastate Exemption

The SEC and federal agencies are only able, generally speaking, to regulate interstate commerce. This means that a transaction occurring wholly in only one state may be outside their jurisdiction. In fact, the federal securities laws contain an express exemption from registration (in Section 3(a)(11)) for an offering that takes place wholly within one state.

Some have gone to a state where regulation of securities is light (these are becoming fewer and fewer) and completed an offering solely within that state to avoid the necessity of SEC registration. The company also previously was required to be physically located and incorporated in that state. The key is being in a state whose regulation would somehow allow for an easier time than SEC registration. The prior rules also required all offerees to be residents of the single state.

Most states provide that an offering that would otherwise be public for SEC purposes requires the preparation and approval by state regulators of a full disclosure document. It is not clear whether shares are restricted after being offered in an intrastate transaction. If they are restricted, although the offering itself is exempt, the shares still must be held for the requisite Rule 144 period before trading can commence.

In 2016, the SEC adopted new Rule 147A, intended to make meeting the intrastate exemption a bit easier. First, they no longer require that your company be incorporated in the state in question. Second, they no longer focus on offerees, but rather purchasers, who must be state residents. This allows offering information to be available on the Internet, for example. It also facilitates complying with some of the intrastate crowdfunding statutes that have been passed. Again, those crowdfunding rules do not lead to trading and so are not a focus of this book.

Interestingly, the SEC had to sidestep Section 3(a)(11) of the Securities Act, which as noted provides for the intrastate exemption, to adopt Rule 147A. They felt that there was no way to implement the changes above within the confines of 3(a)(11) and therefore took it upon themselves, under their "general exemptive authority," to adopt the new rule. While this seems a little "inside baseball," it is important because it shows how the Commission felt it needed to prioritize making this change to enhance instate fundraising.

The important effect of this change is that intrastate offerings now can be conducted with advertising and general solicitation, including over the Internet. Of course it is very important, when conducting a one-state offering, to ensure that the offering is exempt from state registration as well.

Rule 504

An SEC exemption from registration under Rule 504 of Regulation D, previously considered a rather dangerous transaction to get involved with, may increase in interest following recent SEC changes. Here is how it works: Rule 504 allows an exemption from registration if a company raises a limited amount. The original intent was to let small issuers raise smaller amounts, subject primarily to state blue sky regulation and federal antifraud rules.

In 2016, the SEC amended Rule 504 to increase the amount that can be raised in a 12-month period from $1 million to $5 million. This change was effective in January 2017. To my knowledge, there were no requests for this change; the SEC acted on its own. Some feel it was a gift to the states following the harsh treatment they received with the Reg A+ rules preempting state merit review. This change may indeed increase the attractiveness of this previously maligned technique.

Other Regulation D offerings require significant disclosure to any nonaccredited investors and limit the number of nonaccredited investors participating in a deal to 35. In a Rule 504 transaction, a company can complete an offering to any number of accredited and nonaccredited investors.

There are two ways to complete a 504 offering. If the company does not desire for the stock to trade, it can complete the offering much like any other private placement, file Form D with the SEC, and inform investors that they must hold their stock for at least a year under Rule 144 unless it is registered. With this option you can go to an unlimited number of accredited or nonaccredited investors. Advertising and general solicitation, however, are not permitted with this option. There are also no specific information delivery requirements with this approach. This, then, creates the opportunity to conduct a private placement of up to $5 million to any number of investors, whether or not accredited, and do it all with a simple subscription agreement and no other information provided.

The major attraction of 504 had been, however, a separate option to conduct a small public offering, issue unrestricted securities, and allow trading of the stock. With this approach, you can do advertising and general solicitation to seek investors. Because the company will not be reporting after the offering, the only trading option would be on OTC Pink.

To utilize this option to get to trading you must choose one of three approaches. First, you can offer and sell only in states that require formal state registration, public filing, and delivery of disclosure information to investors. Some practitioners try to choose "friendly" states where review tends to be minimal and quick. Others are willing to go through full state review and feel it is still better than dealing with the SEC.

The second option to get to trading is that you pick at least one state that requires registration, go through that process, and then you can sell in states that do not require registration as long as you deliver offering materials to all investors in all states. The third way to conduct a 504 and start trading is to go to any state, even those that do not require registration, as long as they permit general solicitation, but then you must limit the offering to accredited investors.

Think about that last one. Now you can raise up to $5 million from accredited investors, not register in any state, and start trading your stock. When 504 was limited to $1 million there was not that much attraction to using it, and many states effectively prohibited it as noted earlier. It will be interesting to see if that begins to change as dealmakers and investment banks see a new way to crowdfund a private or otherwise non-reporting company. Blank checks cannot use Rule 504, nor can SEC reporting companies or investment companies.

As historical reference, during the 1980s and 1990s in particular, Rule 504 caught on as a way to take companies public. Unfortunately, many players in this field were unsavory types and many SEC investigations and actions resulted from Rule 504 offerings gone bad. That is why prior to this SEC change only a small handful of states permitted 504. It is not clear whether that will change with the increase to $5 million. I know of a number of players starting to inquire about the process of completing a 504 offering given the recent increase.

One hopeful change the SEC made when they increased the amount that may be raised in 504 offerings was to ban bad actors from being involved. Previously no such restriction existed. In general one is a bad actor if he or she has had a securities-related legal problem in the recent past. The SEC bans bad actors from involvement in basically all Reg D offerings (and Reg A+ for that matter as has been discussed).

Regulation S

In 1990, the SEC passed the now-infamous Regulation S, or Reg S. After several court cases, the SEC had to admit it had no jurisdiction over events outside the United States. Then it came up with a way to regulate foreign companies and offerings as long as some U.S. connection existed. Regulation S originally exempted from registration securities offerings by U.S. companies if the investment came completely or partially from foreigners, or where a foreign company raised money from foreign sources but some directed selling efforts took place in the United States.

The major advantages were, first, that no information delivery or accredited investor status mattered, and second, that the original rule seemed to suggest that shares issued in a Regulation S exempt offering could be resold publicly without restriction 41 days after being issued. So one could offer shares to any number of offshore investors, whether or not accredited, without any information and without requiring SEC registration by a U.S. company. There were some who argued the SEC had no right to regulate this kind of offshore offering in any event, but because the regulation focused on U.S. companies, the SEC won the argument.

Resell after 41 days? Doesn't Rule 144 require a six-month waiting period? And doesn't everyone else have to be registered if they want to sell before that? The SEC says they meant the shares could be sold publicly *outside the United States* in 41 days. But the rule neglected to make that distinction. So savvy promoters, with extremely well-paid lawyers in tow, went forward, doing these deals with solid legal opinions as to the shares' ability to be resold in the United States in 41 days.

So what happened? I will give you the end of the story and then we can go back to talk about how Regulation S involved the birth of PIPEs. In 1998, the SEC finally got its act together and, rather than admit the mistake, it simply amended the rule to say you can resell publicly after one year—in other words, the same basic time period as was then the case in Rule 144. (As mentioned earlier, that period is now six months in most cases.) This effectively mooted the question of whether it meant "sale in the United States." That was pretty much the end of the use of Regulation S in the manner I am about to describe.

So what happened when Regulation S came along? Offshore hedge funds and investors had a field day. Company after company went public through a Regulation S offering where the offshore investors resold their shares in the United States just 41 days after what was basically a private offering permitted under Regulation S. Investors loved that they could invest privately and then have a public market almost immediately. Sound familiar? Yes, these deals were the predecessors to modern PIPEs, and indeed many PIPE players got their start doing Regulation S deals in the early and mid-1990s.

Some unscrupulous actors clearly took advantage. They made no disclosure, got foreign investors in, and then got them out in 41 days. The company got its money, the original investor made a tidy profit, and shares traded after that based on essentially no information. Good guys made disclosure prior to the investment. Some became reporting companies voluntarily. Some took the conservative approach and only allowed resale outside the United States.

Since 2002, life has been much different in the PIPEs world. The PIPE market mostly took a pause after the 2008 crash and following some well-publicized SEC investigations and class action suits against some PIPE funds relating to how they calculated the value of their illiquid securities, among other things. PIPEs and PIPE funds have resurfaced along with the current bull market and PIPE investors truly are more like investors now, betting on the longer-term upside potential of a company's stock. The Rule 144 amendments in 2008, which shortened the holding periods, included some conforming amendments to Regulation S that basically mirror the holding periods in amended Rule 144.

These days, about the only real benefit Regulation S has is for a foreign company seeking to raise money from foreign investors, but possibly through a U.S. investment bank. The 41-day exemption still applies in that circumstance. But for some, it was quite a ride there for a while.

Reg S often is utilized to handle a foreign piece of a traditional Reg D private placement. We do not get into too much detail of that since the focus of this book is on methods to become a company whose stock is publicly traded. Companies and investment banks appreciate the flexibility of allowing non-accredited foreign investors into a deal.

Reg D can be used for foreign offerings but the same limitations on accredited versus nonaccredited investors apply. Of course it is also important to remember, if you are conducting an offering in a foreign country, that you comply with any applicable securities regulations in that country.

And so . . .

As should be clear at this point, I strongly favor Reg A+, and in some cases reverse mergers and self-filings as the most regulator-friendly, efficient, and currently popular techniques for going public without a traditional IPO.

The excitement, performance, and promise of Reg A+ cannot be understated. Heck, it motivated me enough to write a book about it! More and more small-cap players are building comfort with the rules and are understanding the benefits of this streamlined and cost-effective process.

A reverse merger with a clean non-trading shell is probably preferable in most circumstances to a merger with a trading shell. Taking over a trading entity that has minimal operations, if it avoids footnote 32 features, could be attractive to avoid seasoning restrictions. Reverse mergers seem most effective when speed is essential, since it can be the fastest way to get to trading.

Self-filings provide a way to avoid the dilution of merging with a shell and the cost of shell acquisition, and (one hopes) still raise money, but the process takes longer and developing a trading market may be more challenging. The self-filing process also requires the steady hand of a Wall Street veteran and has the significant benefit of avoiding the reverse merger seasoning limitations.

Although the guidance provided here should be useful in determining the circumstances in which each of these transaction structures make sense, each company and financial advisor must look at the unique situation in which a company finds itself and analyze which approach is the most logical one, given all the facts specific to the individual company.

Enough from me; now let us see what the *real* experts think about all this.

CHAPTER 14

The Experts Speak—A Look Ahead

This final chapter includes commentary from experts in the field about where we may be headed with Regulation A+ and other alternative techniques to initial public offerings (IPOs). It is quite different from the same chapter we included in the first and second editions of the reverse merger book, because so many things have changed in the eight years since publishing the second edition.

Indeed, any attempt at pinning down current trends in the area of alternatives to IPOs is like taking a picture of a fast-moving train as it speeds past you. What was true a year or two ago, or even six months ago, is not true today. Some of what appears in this edition may not even be applicable by the time the book is published because of changes in the financial marketplace, regulatory amendments, and other developments. The only thing we can rely on is that I can repeat this paragraph in every book on the subject that I write (and I have!).

Even though it is difficult, the intent of this chapter is to predict the future. What is an important trend now? What trend is up and coming? What will be an important trend one year from now? For this, we turn to the experts.

The cast, in alphabetical order, includes:

- Teri Buhl, investigative journalist and Reg A+ specialist at the popular industry newsletter *Growth Capitalist*
- David Bukzin, senior partner with national CPA firm Marcum LLP, who has audited a number of Reg A+ issuers
- Cromwell Coulson, president & CEO of OTC Markets Group Inc., the operator of the OTCQB, OTCQX, and OTC Pink trading platforms
- Mark Elenowitz, CEO of BANQ, a division of TriPoint Global Equities LLC, and selling agent for Myomo Inc., the first Reg A+ deal to trade on a national exchange
- Dan McClory, head of Equity Capital Markets and managing director of Boustead Securities LLC, the lead underwriter for Adomani Inc., the first Reg A+ IPO to trade on Nasdaq

I wish to thank each of these contributors for taking the time to offer their thoughts on where they believe things are headed as the alternatives for private companies considering their options for capital formation continue to increase and improve. Here is the usual disclaimer: *These are the views of the contributors, not necessarily those of their companies or of me or my law firm.* Beware: If we publish a new edition in a few years, get ready for the postmortem on whether these predictions were right.

The topics we covered include Reg A+, reverse mergers, SPACs, and self-filings, along with other hoped-for regulatory improvements under President Trump and SEC Chair Clayton, but first a brief review of the political and economic situation.

Current Political and Economic Environment

At the time of this writing in late fall 2017, there is tremendous political uncertainty in the United States. President Donald Trump came to office in January with a promise to reduce burdensome regulations, in particular on small business. His new chair of the SEC, Jay Clayton, has expressed similar sentiments, including specific comments about deregulation leading to a stronger IPO market. There is not yet much concrete evidence of implementing any changes, but the market believes they will come.

The fear some have, however, is that Mr. Trump's presidency may end up sabotaged, either by fallout from the current investigations into his campaign's alleged ties to Russian hackers, or his own apparent efforts to interfere with that investigation. One would think, in the worst case, that this would presumably lead to a President Mike Pence or President Paul Ryan, both of whom also likely would pursue traditional Republican deregulation strategies. The concern, however, is that the country will be mired in a multiyear scandal that could stall all efforts at implementing Trump's agenda.

Through most of 2017 the U.S. economy continued its very long, sluggish recovery that has buoyed corporate profits, and hence the stock market, but has not led to significant job or wage growth, other than lower-paying and even part-time jobs. This has contributed to the weak growth as middle-class workers do not have increased disposable income and in most cases have no or limited investments in the stock market to help them feel richer.

That said, things are dramatically better than the time of the last book in 2009. Then I said, "The economy remains in a recession that began in early 2008, and there are only a few signs that this condition will change any time soon, although some economists predict that things will begin to turn in the economy in late 2009 or early 2010." The stock market hit bottom in March 2009 and has enjoyed a steady bull march since then to its current record highs. The economy is indeed in recovery and there is positive growth in GDP.

Where is it headed? A wise man once asked me where I think the economy is going. I may have said something about it appearing to be ready to turn around fairly soon. His response, "Yes, but how do you *know*?" I realized that anyone who *knows* when and how the economy or stock market will change should be the richest person on the planet. One can easily say the same about where things are headed in U.S. politics as well (nod to the late, great Ted Ellenoff).

Therefore, the impact of all of this is so speculative that we will not delve further into it, and instead we focus with the experts on the long-term trends they see in our smaller but in some ways equally speculative world of IPO alternatives.

Current Developments

As of this writing, these are the more interesting trends in Reg A+, reverse mergers, SPACs, self-filings, and the IPO alternative business. Here they are, in no particular order, with some thoughts from the experts:

Reg A+ Could Bring Back the Small-Cap IPO

Our experts generally appear very optimistic that, as noted by accountant David Bukzin, Reg A+ could "reignite access to capital for small companies." Journalist Teri Buhl thinks, however, that it may still be too early to answer this question. "It really depends on if the offers that have listed on national exchanges can show growth and the ability to trade above the IPO price," she notes.

OTC Markets chief Cromwell Coulson votes very positively. He states,

> We are strong advocates of Reg A+ and its potential to increase public capital raising options for small companies. It is part of the larger JOBS Act story, which increased opportunities for transparent and online capital raising so that small-cap companies could use the power of technology and the Internet to improve access to capital.

Banker Dan McClory notes the benefit of smaller companies being more willing to consider going public than in the past: "The vast majority of companies pursuing Reg A+ filings and offerings have no intention whatsoever of culminating with a senior exchange listing. Most are for aspirational companies attempting to up their game and raise semi-public capital for the first time." He does feel, however, that "Reg A+ will definitely be a stimulant for the return of the small-cap IPO." He believes that the Reg A+ market will be limited to around 100 deals per year, since "many are still daunted by the costs and disclosures of even the Reg A+ Form 1-A Offering Statement."

Fellow banker Elenowitz perhaps is the strongest believer in the group, saying, "I firmly believe that Reg A+ is going to bring back small-cap IPOs. It's an innovative way to market an opportunity to non-accredited investors, across all 50 states, using general solicitation, including the Internet and social media."

Talking further about the unique benefits of expanded testing the waters in Reg A+, he says,

> The traditional IPO has a significant amount of regulation that limits what information can be communicated to potential investors and when. Reg A+ allows the use of testing the waters, which allows communication about the offering before filing, during the filing process, and after qualification. This is a huge change that allows issuers to now be able to gauge interest not only from the Wall Street community, but also from the crowd.

While he is excited, Elenowitz acknowledges it may take time for Reg A+ to take hold, noting, "I still think we have three to five years before it is mainstream and we have hundreds of deals completed annually."

When asked what types of companies they believe will be best suited for Reg A+, the experts provided an interesting variety of responses, indicating that there may indeed be attractiveness to this approach for a number of different types of businesses. Dan McClory believes the best candidates are those that "have the ability and resources to go the route of an 'industrial strength' S-1 registration statement, and we can then shrink them down into the 1-A context." He is also focusing on companies that can qualify for listing on a national exchange. Last, he feels it is important that the companies themselves arrange to raise the minimum offering amount to provide "skin in the game."

Mark Elenowitz is focusing more on "companies with large consumer awareness, customer bases, and affinity groups" to take advantage of building interest at least in part through crowdfunding. His ideal Reg A+ clients "are iconic brands or have celebrity endorsement. They have revenue and have been funded previously with private equity, venture, and friends and family," and, very importantly, "investors have 30 seconds to understand the company." He is not optimistic that biotech companies will easily benefit from Reg A+, because he feels impatient investors "will move on their search before the story is properly explained."

CPA Dave Bukzin is feeling less focused on industry or online following and thinking more traditionally that "the key to success will be management experience and successful marketing of an investment, allowing many types of companies to take advantage of Reg A+."

OTC Markets head Coulson is excited about early-stage companies taking advantage of Reg A+, but issues a warning:

> Reg A+ is designed for small companies, startups, entrepreneurial innovators, and those seeking to alleviate the cost, time, and complexity associated with the traditional IPO process. It is ideal for any company with a strong business plan, a good base of operations, and a community that would support the capital raise. However, just because you can efficiently and transparently offer securities online, does not guarantee that investors will buy them.

He suggests companies utilize the testing-the-waters opportunity to be sure there is real interest out there for their offering. Cogently, he adds, "The most successful offerings will provide financially attractive terms that bring together a passionate community of investors who want to buy and hold their shares over the long term."

Teri Buhl reminds us of the e-REITS and others but also agrees with Mark Elenowitz:

> Real estate–backed investment companies showed they could raise money fast as early adopters to Reg A+ offerings. But as broker-dealers have started to embrace selling Reg A+ offers as public offerings, I see companies that can show revenue growth with a product that Main Street can visualize or touch as the best suited.

Reg A+ Is Encountering Early Growing Pains

When asked what fears the experts have about the rollout of Reg A+, Dave Bukzin says bluntly, "I have concerns about potential fraud." He worries that, "The biggest challenges for established players is the early-stage nature of the business and its management team." Thankfully, in the first 2+ years under the Reg A+ rules we have not yet seen a penchant for serious problems regarding potential fraud.

Mark Elenowitz's biggest fear is much different, namely "unlicensed service providers filling the CEO with outlandish valuation dreams," which he says has been a "huge issue."

He believes that "transactions should be structured based upon defensible projections, assumptions, and peers' valuations. Those CEOs who recognize this are the ones that will have successful offerings."

Cromwell Coulson simply warns players to stay away from the dark side:

The JOBS Act was a monumental piece of legislation created to shine a light on an exclusive, opaque capital raising process by allowing transparent securities offerings to leverage the Internet and address many of the problems facing small-cap companies. It has gone a long way toward democratizing the capital raising process and improving access to capital for small companies, and it works best when both companies and investors act responsibly.

That is great advice.

Another concern in enhancing adoption of Reg A+, according to banker Dan McClory, is getting away from a perception that Reg A+ is somehow "IPO Lite" or a "mini-IPO." He says, "Getting the investing public and institutions and funds to understand that there is no second-string connotation or qualitative drop-off in companies listing through a Reg A+ IPO versus a traditional S-1 will be key."

Journalist Teri Buhl is concerned about the SEC's limited review of Reg A+ filings. "The SEC is rubberstamping some of these offers, especially the Tier 1 offers, without a detailed review. This sets up a recipe for unethical players to file offerings that are not transparent." She is also concerned about misleading statements being made by some and not carefully checked by regulators.

My next question was simply, "What mistakes have you seen Reg A+ promoters making?" Mark Elenowitz answers, "Backing too early of a company." He believes a Reg A+ issuer needs to understand the costs and burdens of going public, including ongoing compliance expenses and the need to be "acting in the best interest of all shareholders." He recommends that CEOs "look in the mirror" and make sure they are comfortable, ready, and able and can benefit from being public.

Crowell Coulson agrees, saying,

Advisors are often deal-driven and short-term in trying to get any transaction done quickly, without considering the long-term sustainability of the structure. Management and directors need to be focused on building long-term value for each share held by investors. We see banks and advisors looking to target fast money or sell private shares at a discount with dilutive terms to more sophisticated short-term investors.

Those same advisors are often fast-tracking early-stage companies, to access the public markets by listing a company's stock on a national exchange before the company is truly ready, just to let their investors quickly flip the stock. This can create unnecessary regulatory complexities as well as a constraint upon the management teams' resources, saddling them with millions of dollars of ongoing compliance costs.

Dave Bukzin worries about planning for contingencies. He says the biggest mistake is "not having a backup plan for raising capital . . . spending too much of their initial funding chasing a Reg A+ capital raise."

Dan McClory repeated the concern about marketing pitches noted earlier. "Some outlandish claims and marketing pitches are being made in mainstream media by issuers and promoters of Reg A+ offerings, on TV, radio, and print. These are borderline noncompliant and will attract a regulatory backlash, as they should." He also worries that relying on an online following could be unsuccessful since many who show "indications of interest" do not ultimately invest.

Reg A+ Can Be Improved

I also asked the pros what changes they would like to see to Reg A+. Some of them, as we have previously discussed, included allowing at-the-market (ATM) offerings, allowing foreign companies and reporting companies to use Reg A+, clarifying the testing-the-waters requirements, and allowing resale offerings without having to conduct a contemporaneous IPO. Says Dave Bukzin of these, "All those are good suggestions."

BANQ impresario Elenowitz agrees with allowing reporting companies access and resale registration. He separately would like to see the SEC raise the maximum Reg A+ limit to $100 million, and allow these companies to utilize short form S-3 registration six months after the IPO rather than the one year current wait.

Somewhat different views come from Dan McClory. He is for allowing foreign and reporting companies to use Reg A+. However, he believes that "ATMs don't have a place in Reg A+." Dan suggests that companies become full reporting and exchange listed and then have the opportunity to complete an ATM thereafter. He feels the same about standalone resale registrations without an IPO, which he believes should not be permitted.

With of course a slightly different perspective, Cromwell Coulson, consistent with his SEC petition on the subject, believes that SEC reporting companies should be permitted to use Reg A+ and that ATMs also should be permitted. He feels this would be possible "as long as they come with sufficient dilution and discount protections." Teri Buhl also agrees that reporting companies should be permitted to use Reg A+.

Reg A+'s Attractive Features Are Working

Now that dozens of deals have closed, hundreds of millions raised, and a growing handful completed with an exchange listing, it was time to ask the experts, "What do you see as the most attractive features of Regulation A+ for companies you have been working with?"

Some of the most valuable benefits of Reg A+ are accessible only if a company trades in the over-the-counter markets run by Coulson's OTC Markets Inc. He says,

> We let companies choose whether to be fully SEC-reporting or use their lighter Reg A+ disclosure, which does not require Sarbanes-Oxley reporting or certain other burdensome disclosures. We have created lighter-touch corporate governance standards that are customized to meet the needs of early stage companies and are tailor-made for companies completing a Reg A+ offering.

The benefit of preempting blue sky review of a Reg A+ IPO onto the OTC markets also remains a huge advantage.

The three most attractive features of a Reg A+ offering and IPO to Dan McClory are "faster approval times, lower costs as a result, and greatly enhanced marketing flexibility." Dave Bukzin is a fan of testing the waters, general solicitation, and the ability to list directly onto a national exchange.

Testing the waters with any investor is the clear major benefit to BANQ's Mark Elenowitz.

You can now be loud and proud versus a quiet period. Issuers can now spend time developing investor interest and more importantly can do so using the Internet and general solicitation across all 50 states to nonaccredited investors using social media, text, email, and modern communication.

Reverse Mergers, SPACs, and Self-Filings Will Continue as Viable Alternatives

Our experts offered at times differing views on the role that these additional alternatives will play in the years ahead, but the majority view was that all will and should have their place.

Reverse Mergers

Mark Elenowitz believes that the *RTO* (reverse takeover, another term for a reverse merger) is "a tool that is effective and useful for certain transactions. I don't expect in the near term any major decline as certain investors and issuers still find them beneficial."

Teri Buhl, however, believes that Reg A+ should kill reverse mergers. "We don't need them with this new path to access capital," she states. Dave Bukzin agrees with Elenowitz that "higher end reverse mergers (larger companies/better funding) will still be a component of the new product landscape for the capital markets."

Dan McClory also is a bit skeptical of the future of reverse mergers, stating that his firm in recent years "has deemphasized reverse mergers in favor of prototypical IPOs onto Nasdaq and NYSE. Frankly, traditional IPOs, even for pre-revenue, early-stage, high-growth companies, are cheaper, faster, and certainly better." Dan likens reverse mergers to off-Broadway versus an IPO's on-Broadway debut.

A bit stronger defender of reverse mergers, with a caveat, was Cromwell Coulson. He notes,

A reverse merger transaction, if done correctly, can be a cost-effective, simple, and fast way for a small company that lacks a base of seasoned shareholders to go public. This is one of several IPO alternatives that can offer a faster, lower cost, and less burdensome path to a public listing.

In our view, the biggest challenge to traditional reverse mergers will be that companies successfully using online crowdfunding platforms will already have a base of outside investors and won't need a reverse merger to create a trading float.

He indicates these companies may consider a self-filing.

SPACs

Mark Elenowitz admits he has "never been a SPAC fan. To me they are overpriced shells. I don't believe they will remain at their current pace." Strong disagreement comes from Dave Bukzin, who states, "I think SPACs are going to become more prevalent. They take a lot of risk out of the IPO process." To be fair, Dave is really the only expert in our group who has been active in the SPAC market.

Dan McClory believes the SPACs tied to a "name-brand investor or established operator that invests significant capital into his or her SPAC personally" will continue to succeed.

He believes, however, that "I don't see the speculative or purely opportunistic SPACs as having much appeal or longevity." He believes the viability of SPACs can be hurt when investors focus more on getting their money back than supporting a transaction.

Self-Filings

We have seen several other monikers to label a company simply listing its shares for trading without raising new money. Direct listing is one. Cromwell Coulson has a new one, the "SlowPO." As noted, he believes this will become more popular with companies that have a strong following already, with a large shareholder base, and do not need to raise much money currently but see the benefit of a publicly trading stock. He states, "The SlowPO is a well-established and popular method for companies with an established shareholder base to start public trading on our OTC markets."

Mark Elenowitz also is a fan of the self-filing. "If you do not need funds, but want to expand your reach and provide the fans to become shareholders, this is a great way to do it. This is exactly the methodology we utilize for Reg A+."

Very much in agreement is Dan McClory:

> I do see the advent of an "introduction" onto a senior exchange such as NYSE or Nasdaq, for strong issuers with investor interest and momentum, as a viable listing design. Allowing the now-listed issuer to see how the aftermarket reacts to the share price and drives it up or down will be telling, and dictate if and when those "introduced" companies may seek additional capital.

More Regulatory Changes from the SEC or Congress Would Be Welcome

A key question was posed to the experts: What regulatory changes, outside of Reg A+, affecting small public companies would you like to see under new SEC Chair Clayton and the Trump Administration? Mark Elenowitz, as noted, would like to see companies have the ability to use short registration Form S-3 in as little as six months.

Dave Bukzin sounded a small alarm, noting,

> I am concerned that reduction in certain regulations would increase fraud/poor reporting, and so on. No company ever went bust because they had an extra 10-Q to do. If a company qualifies for Sarbanes-Oxley reporting, then their market cap is high enough that they should do an outside auditor's attestation of the adequacy of their financial controls under Sarbanes Section 404(b). Rules that make it easier to access the markets and encourage investors and liquidity of the markets is the way to encourage companies to go public.

Boustead's McClory also would like to see Form S-3 available to all reporting companies and to reduce the Rule 144 holding period to three months. He agrees with Dave Bukzin about reporting. "Quarterly reporting is essential, if only to allow smaller companies to be comparable to large caps that would most certainly continue to file every three months." He also believes all smaller reporting companies should be eligible to be emerging growth companies under the JOBS Act.

In his typically methodical fashion, Cromwell Coulson lays out this series of changes he would like to see, stating as follows:

> To lay the foundation for growing companies to benefit from more efficient capital formation and go public, we need our public markets to be a competitive source of capital.

- One easy solution is to let public companies sell their shares in the same way they can now buy them back: through brokers directly into their established public markets. Removing the outdated restrictions on selling shares publicly will significantly lower the cost of capital and attract more growth companies to our public markets.
- Existing shelf registration rules, which are intended to allow companies to issue securities rapidly to take advantage of market conditions, are only available to larger issuers. These rules need to be streamlined and broadened to cover all SEC-reporting companies traded on an established public market.
- Public companies should not be required to file a "supplemental registration statement" to cover issuances of already authorized shares into the market. The safe harbor rule that allows a company to purchase shares in the public markets should be expanded to include sales of legally authorized shares.
- Lastly, a broker executing an order must be able to sell shares without being subjected to onerous underwriter obligations. Higher-quality public company reporting has eliminated the need for extensive underwriter liability. The broker, as with any retailer or distributor, should play the role of intermediary and sales agent. The public company, as issuer of the shares, should be responsible for appropriate disclosure and be solely liable for any false statements.

And so . . .

An old friend from high school is a true "intuitive." She can look at a picture of anyone and tell you in great detail their entire true personality and "soul." She also is a legitimate psychic and knows what people have done and are doing. And yes, she is becoming a more accomplished medium and communicates with those in the hereafter.

What is the relevance of my high school friend to Reg A+? I wish we had that crystal ball to know where things are headed in this truly exciting new world (I asked her; she would not tell me). What I do know is that the uphill battle we fought in the 2000s to legitimize the previously maligned and shady reverse merger was fairly epic. We were constantly on the defensive, warning bad actors to steal somewhere else. Only recently have the SEC and Department of Justice taken meaningful action against criminals in the reverse merger world.

We are, thankfully, not facing this type of battle here. There is some concern about fraud, but so far it has not reared its ugly head in any noticeable way. With an SEC excited about its now-toddler set of Reg A+ regulations, it is a pleasure to deal with the staff as we machete our way through the implementation of this very new regime.

Our battle now is one of education and experience. One hopes with meetings, appearances, deals completing, and now this book that the veil is being lifted and players can understand the process and how to bring in the right professionals to implement any of the various IPO alternatives explored in these pages.

To quote the wonderful song, "The Book Report," in the sweet Broadway show, *You're a Good Man, Charlie Brown*:

> "The very, very, very end."
> To which I add: for now!

About the Author

Often referred to as the "Godfather" of Regulation A+, David Feldman is a prominent corporate and securities attorney, entrepreneur, and partner in the global law firm Duane Morris LLP. Having literally coined the term *Regulation A+*, Feldman is a strong advocate and practitioner of this exciting and emerging streamlined process of completing a smaller public offering. Feldman is a thought leader and frequent public speaker on all things small business and the small-cap markets. He received his BS from the Wharton School of Business at the University of Pennsylvania and is the former Chair of Wharton's worldwide alumni association board. He earned his JD at the University of Pennsylvania Law School. Feldman's blog, visited by thousands each month, can be found at www.davidfeldmanblog.com.

Index